On the Wing

A Lifetime Afield with Shotgun and Dogs

Copyright © E. Donnall Thomas Jr.
All rights reserved.

This book, or parts thereof, may not be reproduced in any form without permission of the author.

Thomas Jr., E. Donnall
On the Wing

1. Wing-shooting
2. Sporting dogs
3. Wildlife
4. Habitat
5. Travel

ISBN: 979-8-218-36429-8

Cover and interior design by: integrativeink.com
Photography by Don and Lori Thomas

Printed in the United States of America

1 3 5 7 9 1

Also by E. Donnall Thomas Jr.

Longbows in the Far North
Whitefish Can't Jump
Fool Hen Blues
Longbow Country
Dream Fish and Road Trips
To All Things a Season
The Double Helix
Outside Adventure: Fly-Fishing
By Dawn's Early Light
The Life of a Lab
Labs Afield
Hunting Labs
My Kingdom for a Lab
Redfish, Bluefish, Ladyfish, Snook
How Sportsmen Saved the World
Language of Wings
Have Bow, Will Travel
Traditional Bows and Wild Places

On the Wing

A Lifetime Afield with Shotgun and Dogs

By
E. Donnall Thomas Jr.

Foreword by
Steve and Jake Smith

*To my wife Lori, without whom none of
this would have been possible.*

Acknowledgements

I have been fortunate to find a number of editors who allowed me to defy stereotypes of the "hook and bullet" genre. I can't thank them enough. To avoid an unintentional omission, I won't name names. They know who they are.

Table of Contents

Preface xiii
Introduction xv

I. UPLAND BIRDS 1

Pheasants 5
    1. One-Rooster Days 7
    2. The Devil's Birds 15
    3. Beginning, Middle, and End 23
    4. Cattails 31
    5. Company Afield 37
    6. Fifty Years of Opening Days 43
    7. The First of November 49

Grouse 57
    8. Prairie Natives 59
    9. The Once and Future Sage Grouse 67
    10. Pearls from the Sky 75
    11. Singing the Blues 85
    12. Sentimental Journey 91

Partridge and Quail 101
    13. Dinner for Two 103
    14. Little Fools 109
    15. The Best Little Partridge on the Prairie 117
    16. A Quail for All Seasons 125
    17. The Bird that Lives Straight Up 131

    18. Quail Hat Trick 137
Odd Birds 145
    19. Lone Star Doodles 147
    20. Snipe Hunt 155
    21. On the Wings of a Dove 163

II. WATERFOWL 173
Ducks 177
    22. Fowl Weather 179
    23. Redheads and Oyster Beds 187
    24. Big Water 195
    25. The Fog of War 203
    26. The Heron Rookery 209
    27. Prairie Waterfowl 215
    28. Who's the Fairest? 223
Geese 231
    29. Big Birds 233
    30. Snowstorm 241
    31. Accidental Geese and The Big Show 249
    32. The Captains' Geese 255

III. DOGS 265
    33. One Hundred Straight 269
    34. Pointers on the Prairie 277
    35. All About the Dogs 283

IV. THE WIDE WORLD OF WING-SHOOTING 293
    36. Wings Over the Kalahari 297
    37. No Barnyard Guineas 305
    38. Ducks of Paradise 311
    39. Doves, Ducks, and Beyond 317
    40. Probably Not 321

About the Author 327
About the Photographer 329

Preface

Despite the many factors pointing me toward a medical career since early childhood, I always knew I would wind up being a writer. I made this choice—if there ever really was a choice—for the simplest reason of all: I enjoy writing.

The transition still proved challenging. When I made it, I decided to follow an old adage and chose a topic I both knew and cared about: the outdoors. The results form the body of what follows, much of which has previously appeared in magazines including *Gray's Sporting Journal, Shooting Sportsman, Retriever Journal, Pheasants Forever, Strung, Montana Outdoors, Big Sky Journal, Sports Afield,* and others. All have been reworked for inclusion in this book.

Friend and fellow writer John Barsness once divided hunters into two broad categories, specialists and generalists. The former become true experts in one particular activity, while the latter become competent at best in many. I am a generalist, simply because I find so many exciting and gratifying activities in the outdoors that I don't want to limit myself. This book might seem to contradict that principle since I've focused upon wing-shooting, with no mention of fly rods, longbows, or any of the other subjects I've covered previously. However, the world of wing-shooting is a wide one.

I avoid "how-to" writing for two reasons: I find most of it boring and unhelpful, and I don't want to pretend expertise that I lack. However, experience is a powerful teacher, and some advice has crept into this text, even if by accident. I hope it doesn't suffer from the two faults just mentioned.

Lastly, I cannot say enough about my wonderful wife Lori, who accompanied me on so many of these adventures, offered encouragement when I needed it most, and contributed her skill to the photographs that accompany the text.

Don Thomas
Lewistown, MT

Introduction

I remember it like it was this morning. I'd just hired on and was starting my training as a magazine editor, working for and with my dad, Steve Smith. During one of our long conversations, he told me:

"I'll tell you something that's going to happen to you because it happened to me. In the twenty-plus years I've been starting and editing magazines, and of the dozens, maybe hundreds of folks who've written for me, I've found there are a few for whom that I'm their biggest fan. Gene Hill, George Bird Evans, Mike McIntosh to name a few I'm sure you've read.

"Well," Dad continued, "there are a couple who write for me – us – who fit into that mold. One of them is the only guy who writes for all three of our magazines: Don Thomas. His stuff is clean, non-repetitive, original, and Lori's photos are first rate. When his stuff comes in, I go get a cup of fresh coffee, shut my office door, prop my feet up, and read it. I don't feel like his editor; I feel like his publisher. You'll get to feel the same way about him as you take over."

That was more than 20 years ago, and my now-retired dad was right. And this book is proof of everything he said. I've sipped a lot of coffee while reading Don's submissions.

I still remember the first article of Don's I ever read, published in one of those magazines Dad started, *Game & Gun*. We ask a lot of our dogs, day in and day out; but the article, "Asking a Friend," conveyed the stark struggle faced when staring down a situation when we must ask a little more, to give above and beyond, and the painful debate over whether it's worth it. And realizing that it is *all* worth it.

A teenager at the time I didn't have my own dog, but I was well on my way to learning just how precious that hunter-dog bond truly is, and how my future hunting memories would revolve, sometimes exclusively, around the performance and enthusiasm of the dog. All these years later, after countless times I've had to ask my canine friends to go out there on their own and do what they were born to do—in a situation either risky or benign—that struggle remains as real and stark. And it speaks to the truth Don shared so many years ago.

In everything he's experienced throughout the world of wingshooting, Don speaks – and writes – from a place of truth. And the truth in his writing comes from the fact that in what he shares, he brings you with him. He makes you feel like you are alongside to see the sights, sense the adrenaline, feel the warm, soft Labrador fur under your hands and the jolt of the recoil on your shoulder.

I've already read these stories; many I've published in our magazines. I'm a bit envious of those of you who are about to experience them for the first time. I know you'll enjoy the journey.

Jake Smith
Editor, *The Pointing Dog Journal, The Retriever Journal, Just Labs*
Traverse City, MI

I.
Upland Birds

When you have shot one bird flying you have shot all birds flying. They are all different and they fly in different ways, but the sensation is the same and the last one is as good as the first.

– Ernest Hemingway, *Shooting Flying*

For many of us, the terms *upland* and *wing-shooting* are synonymous, as if there were no other way to enjoy the outdoors with shotgun and dog. I'll attempt to refute this impression in the section on waterfowl. However, I certainly appreciate the classical aspects of hunting gallinaceous gamebirds: autumn foliage, crisp air, and the magic of pointing dogs doing what they do even though it defies explanation.

There are other uniquely appealing elements of the upland experience. The startling nature of an abrupt covey rise. The crazy shot angles that can challenge even the most experienced guns. The rewarding sense of vigor attained during a long day on foot in rugged terrain. The culinary rewards almost all these species provide.

The poet William Cowper wrote that variety is the spice of life, and those who agree will find plenty to savor in the section that follows. Hunting quail and pheasants differs in ways that hunting teal and mallards does not. I'll examine hunting nearly a dozen North American upland species in the pages ahead while exploring their behavior and habitat. If this section seems weighted toward hunting the West, that's because that is where I have lived my adult life and accumulated the most outdoor experience. Finding myself living in places that offer good bird hunting was not an accident.

Pheasants

1.

One-Rooster Days

Ernest Hemingway once wrote that all bad writers are in love with the epic. (In fact, many bad writers are in love with Ernest Hemingway, but that's another matter.) I confess my own guilt. It's easy to write about a day when the cover is spewing birds, shotguns are barking without a miss, and all the dogs are behaving like champions. We all enjoy those outings and remember them as the pinnacles of our seasons.

Or do we? What could be more boring than driving for an hour, getting out of the truck, and shooting a limit of pheasants in ten minutes? That happened to me a few seasons back, and during the drive home I couldn't help feeling disappointed. I hadn't had a chance to set my legs against the coulee's pitch, and the older I get the more I need that kind of exercise. I hadn't missed any birds, but the shooting was kid stuff. The dog hadn't done anything I couldn't reproduce with a training dummy in my yard. Yawn.

In contrast, I often find that pheasants satisfy the most when I have to earn them—because the terrain is rugged, the cover is thick, the weather is nasty, the birds are educated, or all of the above. That often means coming home without a lot of birds, or even empty-handed. Consider the course of events during another solo hunt I made later in the season just described.

UPLAND BIRDS

The weather was too brutal for any reasonable person to be hunting pheasants. The thermometer registered just below zero—not bad for the high plains in December—but a brisk northwest wind was creating knee-high ground blizzards from the previous night's newly fallen snow. Often during the first hour after I left the truck, I could scarcely see my own feet, and a frozen dog whistle made it difficult to communicate with my flushing Labrador retriever. So, what was I doing out there? Lori, who almost always accompanies me on pheasant hunts, asked me the same question before I left, and I'll give you the same answer I gave her: Beats me.

I knew the cover on that ranch well and was frankly surprised when I tromped down the creek bottom for a mile without flushing a bird. I knew they were there somewhere and they were. The problem was what a biologist would term non-random distribution, as the next patch of snow-encrusted buffaloberry proved. I was still 50 yards away with Rocky, my male yellow Lab, padding along obediently at heel when the pheasant bomb detonated ahead of us. Dozens of birds including enough roosters for multiple limits were suddenly rocketing away on the wind, not one within shotgun range. Rocky patiently worked the frozen, tangled cover for fifteen minutes in search of a straggler, but I'd known from the start that we wouldn't find one and I was right. Time for Plan B.

That involved hunting up two steep, brushy coulees that ended at a stubble field high above the creek bottom. They almost always hold some roosters, and the birds usually race uphill until they run out of cover at the edge of the grain. Hunting with a partner, one of us would circle wide and block at the apex of each draw. I can't imagine how many pheasants Lori, my friends, and I have killed that way over the years.

But the only partner I had that day was my Lab. After anchoring Rocky with a whistle blast at the bottom of the first draw, I scrambled ahead and then called for him to work toward me while I circled to the top. I'd no sooner reached the edge of the field where I expected to intercept the birds when a pair of roosters flushed below me out of range. I had outsmarted myself, defying the logic of staying with the dog. Enough of that.

In the next draw, I stuck with Rocky. Halfway to the top, he started acting birdy and moments later I heard roosters cackling as they flushed up at the edge of the field. They weren't just out of range; they were out of sight.

By this time I was starting to feel the cold, but I was also starting to feel motivated. I make a point of never letting myself feel angry toward any of the game I hunt, but those birds were testing my patience to the limits. I didn't have a lot of hunting left in me, but in an attempt to salvage some dignity before heading home I decided to work a little strip of willows that I often ignore because I have a three-bird limit of roosters in my game vest by the time I get there on my way back to the truck.

We didn't find anything epic in the willows. But Rocky worked them diligently, and at the end of the strip a lone rooster squirted out across the field in front of me. I'm not sure what I would have done had I missed the passing shot, but in the event the issue never arose.

The long walk back to the vehicle with the freshening wind in my face proved to be a character-building experience. Not that I needed it; the single rooster I carried had already built enough character to last me through the end of the season.

Smart roosters and tough hunting conditions are always a good bet to make those one-rooster days register in the memory. However, nothing can turn a single pheasant into an unforgettable experience like a memorable performance from a favorite dog.

Years ago, my father dropped in one October (funny how that was always his favorite time to visit), and we spent a long day hiking coulees that failed to produce a bird. Finally, Sky, my first great Lab and barely more than a puppy then, nosed up a rooster at marginal range. My father sent it tumbling into the brush with a broken wing and not much else. The bird soon emerged in the open running like an Olympic sprinter and quickly disappeared up the hill and out of sight. Lost bird, I mused to myself. I felt particularly disappointed since my father hates unrecovered game just as much as I do.

I had reckoned without young Sky's tenacity. Moments later, he erupted from the brush hot on the trail of the wounded pheasant. (This episode illustrates why I don't make my retrievers steady to wing and shot in pheasant cover.) Since the bird had a long head start and a huge tangle of thick cover lay over the rise, I still felt pessimistic. There was nothing to do but sit down in the grass and wait.

Twenty minutes later the dog appeared on the horizon carrying the bird, which was still kicking. Sky had some spur marks on his muzzle, but the bird lay unruffled in the dog's soft mouth. The performance felt especially gratifying since my dad, a dedicated pointing dog enthusiast, had openly questioned my decision to hunt upland game with Labs. Now he understood.

That pheasant was the only bird we took back to the house. When we got home I had to pluck a couple of sharptails I'd left hanging in the barn the previous day to come up with a gamebird dinner for the family. But that day, one pheasant was enough.

I relived that memorable day many seasons later thanks to Maggie, at the time the latest addition to our crowded kennel. I had become interested in German wirehairs the previous winter after hunting quail in Arizona with a friend who owned a superb young dog out of the dam that became Maggie's mother. By six months of age, Maggie had graduated with honors from basic obedience school, loved to hunt, and showed real aptitude as a retriever. She just needed to throw the little switch in her brain that told her to point.

That milestone passed at the tail end of an extended late October hunt on northern Montana's Hi-Line. Along with a group of old friends from Texas who readers will meet again, I'd spent the week hitting the pheasant cover hard with the Labs. At the end of each run through the brush I released Maggie from the dog box for a quick romp. As usual, she obeyed commands and ranged beautifully, but even though she ran past a few pheasants she just didn't seem ready to point. Were I a professional trainer, I would have addressed the issue with planted birds back at home. However, I'm not a professional trainer and I didn't have any live birds to plant.

On the last afternoon of that long hunt, we switched gears and headed for some open grasslands in search of Huns, and did we find them. By late afternoon we'd broken up so many coveys we couldn't keep track of which birds we were hunting, although high, gusting winds had led to some embarrassing whiffs by some of the best wing-shots I knew. That's when I decided to put the Labs away and give Maggie a crack at the scattered partridge.

For some reason we couldn't find the Huns again, but Lori had killed a pair of sharptails by the time we finally decided to call it a day. Plenty tired myself after chasing birds for hours, I admit that I wasn't paying much attention as we walked back down the last hill to the truck. That's when I noticed that Maggie was missing.

"Look up there!" Lori suddenly shouted, pointing back toward the top of the hill we'd just descended. There was Maggie on solid point, 200 yards up the draw behind us.

Did I really want to let an unproven puppy's nose drag me all the way up that hill at the end of the long day? It didn't matter what I wanted; I *had* to go. Maggie held the point while I double-timed toward her on aching legs, but just as I neared shotgun range a lone cock pheasant flushed in front of the dog. There was nothing I could do but watch it sail away toward the next county on the howling wind.

When I was growing up my father always stressed the importance of killing the bird on a young dog's first few points as a means of reinforcement that can be reproduced in no other way. Now I'd just blown a perfect opportunity to do so through simple inattention. That failure haunted me all the way home despite the cooler full of birds in the back of the truck.

Work kept me out of town the following week. By the time we returned home again it was early November, and I spent the next several days with my longbow trying unsuccessfully to will the whitetail rut to start before the deer were ready. But I couldn't stop thinking about the way I'd neglected Maggie's first point. I finally loaded her into the truck to try to make amends.

I decided to explore some new bird cover. The ranch owners were old friends and I'd hunted part of their place for sharptails and Huns before. They also farmed a chunk of ground some distance from their house that included promising creek-bottom pheasant habitat although I'd never hunted it. After reconfirming my standing invitation to hunt the place, Maggie and I set off into the unknown.

There's a huge difference between hunting cover you know well and hunting cover you've never seen before. We spent an hour sweeping through some grass adjacent to a stubble field that looked as if it might hold Huns, but didn't find a bird. I deliberately started there because I think Huns make an ideal quarry for a young pointing dog. They're certainly less likely to play dirty tricks than pheasants that have already been hunted for a month. When we couldn't find any, I turned my attention to the creek bottom.

The meandering creek contained a maze of beaver ponds that made dry-footed crossing impossible. An hour later I was soaked to my knees and we still hadn't seen a bird. All I wanted was a single for the dog to point, but as I reluctantly began to swing back toward the vehicle I began to despair of finding one.

Suddenly, Maggie was on point. She'd been false pointing as young dogs will, and I'd already watched her hesitate before an assortment of field mice and meadowlarks, a list that fortunately didn't include any skunks or porcupines. However, her body language established that this was the real thing. "Steady!" I whispered as I moved in. "Steady!" And then the pheasant erupted directly into the sun.

I was so anxious to kill a bird over the dog that I had my gun halfway to my shoulder before the internal safety in my brain made me hesitate. As the bird turned downwind, a glimpse of the hen's dull, tawny plumage confirmed the wisdom of that decision. All I could offer poor Maggie was a subdued "Good girl!"

There wasn't much cover left to work, but as someone once noted, it ain't over 'til it's over. Five minutes later, Maggie was on point again. As I moved in behind her, I realized that I'd never wanted to hear a rooster's cackle more. Then I heard it. Do *not* miss this bird, I told myself as my shotgun came up. I didn't. Then Maggie finished her day's work with a creditable (if less than polished) retrieve. I declared victory and headed for the truck.

I was only carrying a single pheasant, but it might as well have been a big whitetail taken with my bow for all the satisfaction I felt. I could have stayed and hunted a little longer, but I couldn't imagine how another bird or two would have improved the day.

Maggie at the end of a one rooster day.

I'm not going to try to con anyone into believing I don't enjoy those magical outings when birds are abundant and cooperative, the action fast and furious. Of course I do, but that doesn't happen every day. There are several possible approaches to the rest of the time, and since the rest of the time is most of the time, we'd better learn to exercise them.

One option is simply to hunt harder, working the cover relentlessly until your game vest is full or the sun goes down, and I've done my share of that. But as I grow older I've also learned to look for the little gems of experience hidden in days afield that don't add up to much according to conventional standards of success. The more I look, the more such gems I find, and the more I find, the more I appreciate them.

Someone is sure to point out that this principle should also apply to days when you don't shoot anything at all. Of course they're right, and perhaps we'll get to that. But somehow the difference between one bird and no birds is bigger than the difference between three birds and one, even though the math says otherwise. One bird in the vest represents a retrieve or a point for the dog, a shot for you, and a pheasant dinner, even if it's only for two. Perhaps we should all learn to let that be enough for any day.

2.

The Devil's Birds

Here on the high plains the last week of October often marks an abrupt transition from Indian summer to winter, but the snow hadn't arrived yet that year and the landscape in the foothills looked as lovely as I'd ever seen it. I've never engaged in formal botanical study of the draws that mark those hillsides like scars from a raptor's strike. The autumn colors register better without analysis. On a good year, that medley of gold, orange, maroon, and scarlet justifies the drive from home to the field all on its own, and the cover those lines of tangled brush provide our local ringnecks almost seems incidental.

But not for long that day, as an explosion of canine enthusiasm reminded me as soon as I unlatched the dog box in the back of the truck. Both yellow male Labs, Rocky was a wise veteran that year, Kenai a powerful and determined youngster. Over the previous weeks they had provided an ideal blend of innocence and experience in the field. The combination of Rocky's aging legs and Kenai's naïve brain could have been a disaster, but they'd treated us to the best of seasoned wisdom and youthful athleticism instead, and the local ringnecks had already paid a heavy price.

But the birds were quickly growing wiser as they do every fall, a development that seems to occur independently of hunting pressure, a hard phenomenon to explain. Perhaps natural selection during all those pheasant seasons leaves survivors programmed to escape danger by running instead of flying by late October. I didn't expect an easy limit from the cover ahead even though I hadn't hunted it yet that year and doubted anyone else had either. But if I'd been interested in anything easy, I wouldn't have been there in the first place. Those coulees were just too steep and demanding.

That western colloquialism describing the steep gouges in our hillsides derives from the French verb *couler*, to flow. Since the coulees are usually dry by hunting season that reference might seem obscure, but if you stand back and imagine sudden spring runoff coursing down the flanks of those hills you can visualize the abrupt violence that created them. Over the ages more water created more erosion, which concentrated more water still until the coulees claimed most of the scarce local moisture for their own. That allowed brush to grow where it could not otherwise survive, providing pheasants with the final entry in Aldo Leopold's quartet of wildlife necessities: food, water, space, and security cover. The ecology seemed logical enough. Now all the dogs and I had to do was find some pheasants.

I've climbed plenty of hills in search of big game with my bow, but deer and elk can be physically less demanding than pheasants, at least until I kill one. When I'm bowhunting hills and mountains I usually climb for elevation and then sit and glass if I'm hunting smart. Not so when pheasants are the quarry. An upland bird hunter who stops moving has stopped hunting.

Twenty minutes after leaving the vehicle, I was climbing along the rim of a tight little coulee with Rocky at my side while Kenai did our dirty work down in the brush. Without the dogs, this would have been an exercise in futility. The chance of a wild pheasant flushing spontaneously from the brush within shotgun range invites comparisons to snowballs in hell. As he aged, Rocky, a terrific waterfowl dog, had become a reliable no-slip retriever in tough pheasant cover. He liked to pretend that he now stayed glued to my side because he's read the training books even though I know the truth: just like me, he wasn't as tough as he used to be. No matter—with Kenai hitting the brambles as if they'd insulted his mother, I was happy to have the old master beside me where he could mark falling birds. No upland species I know demands the services of an experienced retriever like pheasants. Our kennel's one-two canine punch had allowed us to hunt hard for the first two weeks of the season without losing a rooster.

In Midwestern pheasant habitat hunting can be a highly social affair. Out here, the terrain is too complex for large parties to hunt without a whole lot more committee work and debate than I like. Furthermore, solitude brings out the best in the landscape like an essential herb in a good pot of soup. While I enjoy hunting pheasants with Lori and a few other companions experienced enough to get to the right place at the right time without discussion, I'm also happy to hit the cover alone except for the dogs.

Nonetheless, the absence of hunting partners makes a hard game harder. As we continued on up the draw Kenai's body language told me we had birds running ahead. The pheasants could run uphill faster than I could. A hundred yards above us the coulee split into three small fingers and ended. With nothing but rock and sparse grass beyond, I expected the running birds to flush there when they ran out of cover. Leaving Kenai to work the brush, I cut across the hypotenuse of the triangle to station myself at the head of the nearest finger of buffaloberry.

The once pleasant pace of the climb deteriorated into a lung-searing sprint. When I arrived at the tip of the coulee's nearest terminal branch, I spotted Kenai working diligently toward me deep in the thicket below. Then the sound of wings erupted. Our determination and teamwork had delivered the goods… except that the bird was a hen.

So was the next one and the one after that. Rocky had dropped down into the brush to join the cause by rooting out yet another hen by the time a rooster's cackle finally shattered the still morning air. However, the cock bird had chosen the far branch of the coulee as his escape route, and he was 60 yards away by the time I saw his brilliant plumage flashing in the sun. I may enjoy an edgy relationship with pheasants, but I respect them too much to risk wounding one by shooting at irresponsible distances.

By the time both dogs rejoined me, we'd seen what the first coulee had to offer. I had to feel sorry for Kenai, whose only reward for his effort was new scratch marks from thorns. Sadly, Labrador retrievers do not appreciate the difference between cocks and hens and the legal basis for the restraint the latter demand. After working that hard a young dog deserves a retrieve, and I regretted my inability to provide him one. At least that failure hadn't arisen because of poor shooting.

As I caught my breath, I studied the landscape around us. A dozen more coulees beckoned. The dogs were still willing, the day was young, and pheasant season wasn't over yet.

No upland game rivals the devil's birds wiliness and tenacity.

The ringneck pheasant (abbreviated to "pheasant" herein even though American hunters have attempted to establish populations of several other pheasant species) makes no appearance in John James Audubon's iconic *Birds of America*. Neither do gray partridge or chukar, for the same reason. All three popular western gamebirds are Old World imports that had yet to see our shores when Audubon was busy hunting, sketching, and painting.

The pheasant's arrival in America came about through a combination of political happenstance and old-fashioned Yankee ingenuity. An avid sportsman, Owen Denny served as a political gadabout in the Far East for several American administrations. As Consul to Shanghai, he acquired a taste for oriental game birds. In 1881, he shipped a crate of pheasants across the Pacific to his brother's farm in Oregon's Willamette Valley. While most such hastily conceived transplant efforts fail miserably, the pheasants thrived. Ten years after their introduction, Oregon held its first pheasant season. Records indicate hunters killed thousands of birds on opening day. The rest, as they say, is history.

Hunting Midwestern cornfields with lots of company and guns can produce plenty of shooting and pheasant dinners, but the ambience of that hunting style differs so much from western pheasant hunting that it's sometimes hard to recognize the quarry in each case as the same bird. No offense intended; this opinion reflects decades of personal experience rather than Wild West chauvinism. Nonetheless, all those seasons have convinced me that solitude and effort constitute important elements of the pheasant hunting experience.

I spent my early childhood hunting ruffed grouse and woodcock over German shorthairs in upstate New York, a backstory we'll revisit frequently throughout this text. Good pointers embody style in the best sense of the term, but I didn't own one for years after I moved to western pheasant country. I needed dogs that would break rules as well as follow them and settled on Labs that would attack tangled, thorny cover like maniacs and follow running cripples tenaciously. The choice was a practical matter. Asked to pick between canine elegance and gamebird dinner, I decided upon Grilled Pheasant Breasts in Basil Pesto Sauce.

Whether the quarry is moose or mallards, nowadays I'm usually more interested in observing and learning than killing. Pheasants are an exception, and not just because I find them delicious. There's something audacious and conniving about pheasants that makes me enjoy slapping the trigger and watching them fold. After years spent facing dangerous game around the world armed with nothing but a longbow, I admit that it seems strange to feel such aggression toward a mere bird. Understanding why I do is essential to my appreciation of wild pheasants and their pursuit.

While deferring detailed debate about avian intelligence—how to define it, whether it even exists—to a later chapter, I will ignore spoiler alert signals here and declare the pheasant the smartest gamebird in America, including the wild turkey. As usual, I look to scientific theory for explanations of the natural phenomena I observe in the field. Except for two exploratory bowhunting trips to Siberia decades ago I've never hunted in Asia, but I have hunted free ranging big game of Asiatic origin (chital and rusa deer, for example) in the Pacific and Latin America. Those experiences left me with the impression that game of Old-World origin is inherently warier than similar species that evolved here. Our native grouse and quail never faced human predation until the first Eurasian immigrants crossed the Bering Sea land bridge some 15,000 years ago (a figure admittedly subject to considerable debate). By then, pheasant ancestors had been evading human hunters for millennia in their native home. Their dumb genes got roasted over open fires; the smart ones came across the Pacific courtesy of Owen Denny.

Pheasants aren't just smart; compared to other upland game, they're diabolical. At the risk of over-the-top anthropomorphism, I'll venture that wild roosters *enjoy* humiliating experienced hunters and talented dogs. Intellectually I know that can't be true, but as Will Rogers would have put it, it might as well be. I can hear contempt in every rooster's cackle when the bird has doubled back to flush safely out of range or waited until I've broken my gun to cross a fence before erupting beneath my feet. Affection helps define my relationship with other game birds. While granting pheasants respect and admiration, I'll reserve the sentiment for grouse and quail.

Hitchcock made a mistake when he cast seagulls as the eyeball-pluckers in *The Birds*. He should have used ringneck pheasants. I sense they would have enjoyed the experience.

It's all different now, in the third week of December. Brilliant autumn colors have yielded to whitened ground and lead grey skies overhead. The casual hunters have retreated to an indoor world of fireplaces and televised football games. The naïve birds are out of the gene pool for good while those that remain know more about pheasant hunting than I do. This is the season of survivors.

Late season pheasant hunting makes October look like a driven shoot on a European estate, complete with tea and crumpets. Never mind the chill and the labor of slogging through snow for miles. By now, the birds have refined the art of humiliation. Wilder and cagier than ever, they seem to understand the effective range of my double as if they'd patterned the gun themselves. I know this cover well. With snow to concentrate the birds in the willows and cattails, I fully expect to fly several dozen roosters along the creek bottom before the morning is done. Of those, I'll be happy to take home one pheasant dinner.

As the season progresses, educated birds require ever-increasing levels of hunting strategy, so I have an experienced friend from town hunting with me today. His gun and Lori's make three. With ten weeks of pheasants behind them, the dogs are sharper than ever. Even so, as we spread out to converge upon an isolated creek bottom oxbow, I feel the odds stacked against us.

With Lori blocking at the apex of the oxbow, my friend and I set off through the cattails with the dogs. In no time at all we've got birds flushing wild, exiting the cover between Lori and me, my friend and me, and Lori and my friend as if a geometry teacher had asked them to bisect each leg of the triangle as precisely as possible. All pass out of range of everyone, and the cold air remains silent except for cackles from the escaping roosters.

This kind of bird hunting boils down to creating as many opportunities as possible for a pheasant to make a mistake. As the noose tightens today, one finally does. In the flat light I must stare briefly at the bird to be sure of its gender and the delay almost costs me the shot. But as tricky as pheasants can be on the ground, they're one of the West's less challenging game birds on the wing. This one allows me sufficient time to catch up and make him fold cleanly at the shotgun's report. Despite the density of the cover, Rocky makes the retrieve look routine. The next three roosters that flush squirt out between us unscathed, but their escape hardly compromises our shared sense of satisfaction.

Satisfaction… for an easy shot on a common game bird by an experienced hunter? You bet, and therein lies the *sine qua non* of pheasant hunting's appeal, at least as it's practiced here in the West. Somewhere between the rise and the retrieve grouse and partridge lose their individual identity, and their pursuit becomes a matter of process and ambience rather than a one-on-one dynamic between hunter and quarry. Not so with pheasants. Even at the end of a long season I can close my eyes and remember details of encounters with one individual bird after another, including many that just plain outwitted us. Cock ringnecks may be the most beautiful game birds on the continent as well as premium upland table fare, but it's their character that draws us to them in the end.

Four hundred years ago John Milton's *Paradise Lost* reminded us by accident that it's fun to be the devil. For the same reasons, it's fun to hunt the devil's birds.

3.
Beginning, Middle, and End

Everyone knows that pheasant season takes place in the fall, but the reality proves more complicated than the generalization. Even the casual scientists among us know that fall lies between the autumn equinox and winter solstice, a slab of time discordant with pheasant season by a week or two on either end here in my home state of Montana. Furthermore, the nature of the hunting varies so profoundly between early October and late December that it can be hard to remember one is hunting the same species in the same terrain.

Years ago, it occurred to me that pheasant season logically breaks down into thirds. You won't find these divisions on the calendar or in the regulations. They depend on the subjective interpretation of natural phenomena for their definition, but as with good art you'll know them when you see them. There are sound, practical reasons to appreciate the differences in the way the birds behave during each of these phases. If the goal is a limit of pheasants, I approach the problem one way in October and in another way entirely by December. But esthetic differences in the hunting experience may be even more dramatic. Credit the ring-neck for providing more variations on the *feel* of upland hunting than any other game bird in America.

Indian Summer. The unusual combination of warm sun and crisp air defines early autumn here in ringneck country. It's the kind of weather that makes wild pheasants live where they do. Opening day's position on the calendar depends on the workings of numerous game commissions, but in most major pheasant states, reading the tea leaves produces the same conclusion give or take a week or two. Pheasant season begins between the time the leaves start to acquire their autumn colors and the first serious snow of the year.

Fickle mistress that she is, Nature can always defy simplistic definitions. This year in Montana, for example, pheasant season began on a wet, blustery day memorable for horizontal rain and impassable back roads, and during seasons past I've endured a blizzard or two at the same time of year. Fortunately, such events represent the exception rather than the rule.

Far more often, the first few weeks of the season offer a delicious feast for the senses: foliage awash in crimson and gold, still air and invigorating daytime temperatures that practically beg hunters to keep hiking and explore the next coulee. During the course of the long season ahead, there will never be a more inviting time to be outdoors.

This is prime time for hunters interested in killing pheasants as well as smelling the proverbial roses. Cooperative young roosters routinely flush within shotgun range and thick ground cover encourages birds to hold rather than run. Wild roosters seldom remain naïve for long, so enjoy it while you can. This is a great time of year to trade the 12-gauge for the 20, work the younger dogs, and carry the camera along on every hunt.

Around our place this is the social phase of pheasant season. Pleasant weather, gorgeous scenery, and abundant birds make an irresistible invitation. My popularity during the first few weeks of October seldom ceases to amaze me. My parents always visited then. Several groups of out-of-state friends usually find their way to our door as well, providing opportunities to meet new dogs, catch up on family matters, and otherwise enjoy the rich traditions that bind outdoor enthusiasts together. After hours, the kitchen becomes the equivalent of a Paris salon for a week or two, albeit with more time spent discussing birds and dogs than politics and art while pheasants complete the transition from gamebirds to dinner.

There are disadvantages to every phase of the season, even this one. Warm weather can compromise scenting conditions and even veteran bird dogs can misbehave on opening day. There will never be more hunters in the field. Sometimes the hunting can almost be too easy, as described in an earlier chapter. I might feel guilty then if I didn't know what lies ahead.

November Moon. While natural transitions often represent a gradual process, there's seldom anything subtle about the arrival of pheasant season's second phase here on the high plains. One morning you wake up to find the colors gone, all that gorgeous autumn foliage lying scattered on the ground, and barren branches pointing toward gray skies that were clear and blue the last time you looked. The outdoor world suddenly seems to be shot in black and white.

Subtler signs also mark this passage. Contracting daylight hours make it impossible to sneak out for a quick hunt after work. The cries of migrating geese rise above the sigh of the breeze at night while blackbirds gather in great, noisy flocks in preparation for their own journey south. The promise of enduring snow feels present in the air even if it isn't already on the ground.

Where to place these events on the "official" calendar, the one that hangs on the wall as opposed to the version waiting every time you slip on hunting boots and step outside? The answer varies by location and from season to season. In my part of the world this transition can take place any time between the third week of October and mid-November. If you still find yourself heading out the door without a wool hat and gloves, it hasn't happened yet.

The pheasants waiting for you out in the cover will have changed as profoundly as the weather, the scenery, and the day-night cycle. By now, the naïve birds of the year that provided easy limits a few weeks earlier are either educated or dead. Pheasants learn survival skills quicker than any other upland game bird, and they know all about flushing dogs by now. No longer content to burrow into the cover and rely on their camouflage, they'll begin to take evasive action at the sound of a truck door closing. There's nothing more discouraging than the sight of distant cover belching birds before you've even had a chance to load your shotgun.

As we've seen earlier, each phase of the season offers balances to the drawbacks entered in its ledger. Out-of-state hunters who timed their visits to coincide with the most pleasant and productive weeks of the season will be gone, while locals are devoting their time outdoors to deer and elk. That means solitude in the bird cover, for which I'll trade easy shooting and creature comfort any day. The birds may be smarter, but they're also easier to find. As ground cover yields to frost and cattle, pheasants naturally congregate in the thickest of what's left. Run some determined hunters and hard-charging dogs through a dense patch of cattails or a tangle of buffaloberry and you may see some of the most spectacular rises of the year, with multiple roosters exploding from the cover at once. They may or may not flush in range, but that's your problem.

The offense should have learned right along with the defense during the halcyon days of the early season. While opening day rustiness can provide even good shots with an excuse for a miss or two, shortcomings in established shooting form should be worked out by now. A few weeks of practical experience in the field can do wonders for a dog after a long, boring summer. By the time the leaves have fallen from the trees my Labs are usually hunting like the pros they were supposed to be a few weeks earlier.

These considerations mark a change in my own attitude that exceeds the sum of its parts. As much as I miss the camaraderie and spectacle of the early season, November is when I become a serious pheasant hunter.

The final month of pheasant season offers special challenges and rewards.

The Edge of Winter. Thanksgiving has always been a big deal around our place. Kids come home from college and beyond. The whitetail bucks rutting in the coulees around the house demand attention from my longbow. Friends who love to cook and eat gather in the kitchen to engage in friendly culinary competition involving heavy doses of fish and game. Sometime thereabouts, Nature inevitably rolls the dice again and ushers in the final phase of pheasant season.

Here in Montana we get lots of opportunities to mix it up with ringnecks then, since our season extends all the way through December. Then the character of the hunting changes dramatically from all that came before. Weather turns the trick when the first serious Arctic high—an Alberta Clipper in local parlance—arrives, affecting a transition that can be shockingly abrupt. When I awake for the first time to a sparkling landscape of pristine snow, my pheasant season has entered the homestretch. I can only hope I'm capable of keeping up with it until the end.

At our latitude and elevation, these can be challenging times outdoors. Contracted daylight hours leave little time in the field. Temperatures range from brisk to ridiculously cold. Anything above zero represents luxury and I've tackled December roosters below that artificial (at least in degrees Fahrenheit) mark on the thermometer. Engines balk, chains may be necessary to reach the field, and cold gun barrels can bite exposed fingertips. The quarry has been culled and educated into a population of survivors that will make dogs and hunters work for every bird. This is no time for the faint of heart, but I wouldn't trade the last month of pheasant season for all that came before.

While crisp December days can be visually stunning in their own way, it's usually the acoustics that demand my attention first. Cold air is dense air, and all those molecules packed tightly together can amplify ordinary sounds of the hunt into auditory delights: the *chink* of brass on steel as you drop a shell into an open chamber, the trill of a dog whistle fading into the distance across a frozen slough. You've never heard a rooster flush until your ears have absorbed those raucous cackles on a calm, sub-zero day.

Tracking snow doesn't lie. On some late season pheasant hunts I'm so busy studying the data underfoot that I can scarcely keep track of the dogs. Fresh pheasant tracks always quicken my pulse, while the delicate brushstrokes left by a flushing rooster's wings remind me of fine calligraphy. This winter exercise always involves more than the species I've come to hunt. From hoofed game to other predators, all wildlife leaves an honest record in the snow. I can only thank the ringnecks for providing an excuse to sharpen my eye prior to mountain lion season.

Weather will have contracted the birds' options for food and shelter by this time of year. With bugs and berries long gone, pheasants are often visible against a background of snow as they forage for grain in stubble fields. They can also be practically impossible to approach on open ground. Snow covered cattails provide ideal security habitat and I love to hunt them wherever I find them next to grain.

Birds won't flush readily from that kind of cover unless forced into the air by an aggressive dog. By December my Labs have reached the peak of their game and I hardly need to talk to them once they've left the warmth of the kennel. Three short months can turn a novice into a veteran. This is the time of year when I enjoy seeing what progress my younger dogs have made against the toughest upland birds they'll ever be called upon to hunt. When one of my old-timers outwits a running rooster deep in the brush or makes a spectacular retrieve on a tenacious cripple, the sense of satisfaction cannot be measured by the weight of the bird in my game vest.

However much I enjoy the challenge and solitude of winter pheasant hunting, my keen appreciation of the season's final phase ultimately derives from the bittersweet realization that it's all about to end. From kisses to glasses of fine wine, life's pleasures always seem more appealing when we recognize that they do not come in an infinite supply. In October, one can engage in the willing suspension of disbelief and hunt as if there were no tomorrow. By Christmas that's become impossible as the season's close stares back from the calendar every day. All the more reason to bundle up and push on while the opening day warriors curl up in front of the television to watch the game. There's always time for one more rise, one more *thump* of stock against shoulder, and one more retrieve by the dog, especially when it could be the last.

Until next year.

4.
Cattails

Cold but bright, the winter sun made the hoarfrost sparkle as Lori and I set off down the first draw with the dogs. The native grasses, wild roses, and snowberry had been beaten down, first by drought, then by cattle, and finally by snow and ice. The terrain offered easy walking and let us keep a close eye on the dogs, but I didn't feel optimistic about the cover. A fresh dusting of powder snow overnight confirmed my suspicions when I didn't see a single pheasant track all the way down the coulee. I had suspected it might come to this, and now it was time to tackle the real late season pheasant cover.

A short hike across a stubble field brought us to a dense patch of cattails covering two acres along a spring-fed creek. I immediately encountered abundant fresh pheasant tracks along the edge of the grain. There were always birds somewhere in the thicket, and now the sign suggested there were even more than usual. No wonder. With the surrounding area devoid of good security cover the birds had gone right where I would have gone if I were an educated late season rooster.

Knowing they were in there was one thing but shooting any of them would be another. I gave Kiska, our young female yellow Lab, the recall command, which quickly had her sitting at attention beside my right leg. The time had come for Max, our aggressive male

German wirehair, to do the heavy lifting. When I cast him back, he immediately disappeared in the tangle. The sound of breaking ice intermittently punctuated the rhythm of his locator collar, reminding me why I was still standing up on the bank. Previous forays into the same cattails under similar conditions had left my legs coated up to my knees in frigid water and black mud.

Then Max's steadily beeping collar indicated a point. Having trained the dog to steadiness, I didn't want him flushing the bird. I didn't want to do it either, since swinging a shotgun while standing in a bed of tall, frozen reeds can be next to impossible. I knew we'd have a better chance of clear shots from our position on the bank. Kiska's time had come.

I didn't know if she had learned to zero in on the sound of a collar announcing a point, but she acted as if she did. Late season pheasants are not distributed randomly, especially when good security cover is limited. Find one and you'll likely find more, often a lot more. As the sound of Kiska crashing through the cattails converged on Max's collar, a rooster rose cackling loudly. When it made the mistake of flying over Lori's head, she provided Kiska an easy retrieve by dropping it dead in the stubble.

The sound of her shotgun broke the spell. Suddenly the air was full of pheasants, giving us a lot to do and a short time in which to do it. I had worked out an approach to these situations many seasons prior. *Ignore the long shots and wait for shorter ones to come. Don't break the gun to reload one barrel too soon. Try to mark fallen birds and keep track of the dogs. Regroup once the shooting is done.* I was sure four more birds had fallen but made no effort to determine which of us had shot what. Three lay dead in the stubble, but the other two were down in the tangle. Max soon emerged from the cattails with a rooster in his mouth and delivered it to hand. Just as I whistled him off the easy birds he'd spotted in the open field, Kiska appeared at my side after completing the second tough retrieve. Fortunately, all the birds had fallen dead, saving the dogs from a tough run through the cattails.

From that point on, mopping up was easy. Let the dogs have fun picking up the easy birds in the grain, get them in our game vests, check our shotguns and the dogs' collars, examine their feet for cuts from broken ice, pick some burrs from Max's muzzle. Then it was time to set off again along the edge of the reeds in search of one last bird to complete my limit.

It took determined dog work to flush this rooster from a bed of cattails.

Tough, hardy birds, pheasants don't need much to thrive, but they do need a reliable food source and good cover in which to hide. Farmland stubble fields offer lots to eat but little security habitat, which is why good cover nearby concentrates birds. That habitat can take many forms: thick native grass; hawthorn, buffaloberry or other brush; hedgerows or CRP. None provides pheasants better security than cattails.

This is especially true wherever environmental conditions or agricultural operations compromise the quality of the alternatives. We have already seen an example of that during the late season, when freezing temperatures, snow loads, ice, and grazing have compromised a lot of early season habitat, circumstances that make cattails especially inviting. However, reed beds can also be productive early in the season, especially during drought conditions. If there is moisture located anywhere in dry, rolling terrain, cattails will find it. So will the pheasants.

Hunting cattails differs from hunting most other kinds of cover. They are almost always thick and difficult to walk through. Footing often consists of mud or shallow standing water fed by underground springs. When temperatures drop and ponds begin to freeze, ice in cattails often reaches a maddening thickness that is too thin to support a hunter's weight but too thick to slog through. After years of hunting cattails I can't count the number of times I've slipped, tripped, or broken through ice that felt solid, only to wind up drenched. No matter how tough you think you are, frigid water can end a hunt long before you planned to leave the field.

There are a number of ways to address these challenges, the most important of which can be summarized in one word: dogs! Without at least one good dog (and the more the merrier, provided they are trained), hunting pheasants hiding in cattails is a fool's errand. Different breeds can do the job, but I fare best with a pointing dog ahead and a Lab at heel. A versatile pointing dog with sound retrieving abilities, like our wirehairs, makes another good choice. Cattails are also a great venue for a well-trained flushing retriever.

No matter what the dog's pedigree, certain canine traits are especially important in this kind of cover: tenacity, obedience, enthusiasm, and retrieving ability. Pushing through reeds is hard work for dogs as well as people. A dog that won't stop on command will likely lead to birds flushing beyond shotgun range. Trying to recover a wounded pheasant from a cattail tangle without a capable dog is almost impossible.

A basic rule of pheasant hunting holds that the larger and more poorly defined any cover, the greater the difficulty of getting a rooster airborne within range. Finally, some good news about hunting reedbeds. Because of their need for water, they often lie in long but narrow strips along creek beds or coulee bottoms wherever moisture accumulated during the summer. Many of these are less than shotgun range wide, allowing a relatively straightforward plan of attack with a hunter on each side and dogs between them in the middle. A third member of the party, if there is one, can post at the end of the strip to intercept birds running out ahead of the dogs.

Larger reedbeds present larger problems, since they often grow around the edges of ponds and marshes that make them impossible to cover completely. It may be tempting to wade into the tangle and take your chances, and I do that several times every season. However, getting clear shots is difficult and trying to swing a shotgun through stiff, head-high reeds can be frustrating. I usually do better by standing on a bank in the clear and letting the dogs do their job.

The descriptions of wet, muddy footing I've offered here lead to a final suggestion: hip boots. While I wouldn't plan on walking in them all day, having them available in the vehicle will allow you to put them on before you tackle cattails. Knee-high footwear doesn't do it for me, as they usually lead to nothing but boots full of ice water.

There's my take on cattails—day savers at the start of dry seasons, last refuge for educated roosters at the end.

5.

Company Afield

Despite an ominous weather forecast dawn broke still and clear, promising a fine day during a not so fine bird year. The season was still young, but I'd already confirmed my worst suspicions about our local spring hatch. Poorly timed rains during the critical nesting period had led to pheasant concentrations that official reports euphemistically described as "spotty." A week of hunting in every direction from home had convinced me that the "spots" were a lot smaller than the blanks surrounding them. While the rain had left the cover in great shape I'd seldom seen it produce so few rises.

However, our guests had traveled far to hunt birds with us, and Lori and I weren't going to disappoint them. I'd hung plenty of crepe at our dinner table the night before, but our visitors still buzzed with enthusiasm as we loaded the rigs to head afield. Two old adages came to mind as I kenneled Rocky and Kenai in their crates and closed the tailgate behind them. The first began "When the going gets tough…" while the second started with "The worst day of hunting beats…"

Our visitors hailed from Texas. My own family roots extend deep into the heart of the Lone Star State, and I enjoyed hearing the soft, comforting drawl that still flavored my parents' speech even after decades of exile. Our guests were old friends whom I knew to be experienced hunters and excellent shots, although they had not spent much time hunting wild ringnecks. Unfortunately, I knew they couldn't have picked a less promising year to enjoy western pheasant hunting at its best.

After we pulled into the ranch I planned to hunt and unloaded guns and dogs we huddled and studied the terrain. The only reason there weren't more theories about how to attack the heavy cover was that Lori and I tactfully withdrew from the discussion. Finally our friend Dick, a seasoned outdoorsman from San Antonio, brought the meeting to order, split the party in two, and sent one group to each end of a long slough running between two cut fields. The logistics may have been complex, but the logic appeared sound. Absent escape routes to either side, the birds should have had no place to run from one group of guns and dogs except into the other. Even so, it took a lot of work to get everyone pointed in the right direction.

Experienced hands know how readily wary ringnecks can divorce expectation from reality. Events began according to script when one of the dogs at the opposite end of the slough nosed a bird from the cattails and sent it directly over our heads. Of course, the bird was a hen. When the first rooster of the morning rose from the grass in a burst of noise and color, it split the defense like an experienced wide receiver, managing against all odds to sail over the next hill without passing within shotgun range of anyone. As did the second and third.

But as our two groups converged, patience and determination began to earn their reward. As Marshall's Lab began making game and plowed into a clump of brambles, the cock bird that exploded from the other end gave him the kind of shot he doesn't miss, and he didn't. Then Monty's Brittany went on point. The bird ran out on Monty and his hard-working dog but fell to Chris's gun after it flushed. By the time we'd finished working the cover in the middle of the slough, four birds rested in our game vests. Each felt like a triumph given my limited expectations for the day.

With that, we regrouped to discuss our approach to the next piece of cover, and the fact that the planning took almost as long as the execution scarcely seemed to matter.

As a kid hunting grouse and woodcock in upstate New York, tight cover and the reclusive nature of the quarry limited the scope of its pursuit. Most of my childhood expeditions through grouse coverts involved no company other than my father and the dog. When we moved West everything seemed to come a few sizes larger, including the bird hunting. More room for birds meant more room for the people who hunt them, creating a natural venue for larger hunting parties. No game bird illustrates this principle better than the ringneck pheasant.

Even in the wide-open spaces beneath Montana's Big Sky, I enjoy hunting alone or with company limited to Lori, one of the kids, or a single experienced hunting partner. Then our house becomes a popular place in October, when pheasant season opens, autumn foliage reaches its fullest expression, and distant friends and family suddenly realize just how badly they've missed us. With archery elk and antelope season over and the whitetail rut yet to come, I'm happy to treat mid-October as our social season, and the process has taught me plenty about hunting birds with lots of company.

It's important to acknowledge the real advantages of having more than one or two guns in the field when hunting pheasants. No upland bird evades determined pursuit quite like the wild ringneck, especially several weeks into the season. Even willing legs and determined dogs can't eliminate all the escape routes when hunting solo. Thinking of the cover as a chessboard and strategically placing blockers and drivers can result in more birds than any attempt to cover the same ground on your own.

Getting everyone where they need to be requires planning, especially when those involved aren't familiar with the cover and the game. When I'm out with one of my regular local hunting partners, two of us can work complex terrain for hours while rarely exchanging a word, with the right person winding up in the right place at the right time practically by instinct. Even highly competent visitors who haven't had a lot of experience with pheasants need a bit of direction.

The trick is to take enough time to be sure they get it without sounding like a drill sergeant.

Choosing the right cover helps. When I'm hunting by myself, I'm happy to wade into the guts of the thick stuff and rely on my dogs to do the rest. But with larger parties, maintaining visual contact can mean the difference between order and chaos. Hunting open ground helps, and I like to establish a designated meeting area at the end of each push so that everyone knows where to regroup.

The larger the party, the more likely it will contain hunters of varying ages and physical capacities. All should be able to participate enjoyably with a little foresight and common sense. Timing the pace to the group's slower members represents sound hunting strategy as well as courtesy. (Ever wonder how many birds you walk past when you push through cover in a hurry? You probably don't want to know.) I try to position older hunters in strategic blocking positions they can reach by walking on level ground while taking the dogs into the nasty stuff myself. My own willingness to perform these chores reflects enlightened self-interest as well as the good manners my parents taught me, since I hope my own kids will be doing the same for me some day.

Hosting family and friends is an important pheasant season tradition.

Hunting dogs deserve their own chapter in the book of pheasant hunting etiquette. Everyone will want to take their own dog along, and who can blame them? Experienced trainers recognize the combination of big cover, multiple guns, and lots of dogs as a prescription for canine confusion, especially among young dogs. I seldom take my own youngsters along in such circumstances. If visitors are really interested in working their own dogs, I'll leave mine behind in the truck. My dogs will have plenty of time to fetch birds after our guests have headed home. To minimize confusion, one should avoid unnecessary whistles and commands and, of course, not give orders to other people's dogs. Should you be the honored guest, if your dog is difficult to control by virtue of youth, inexperience, or insufficient training, do your hunting partners a favor and leave it behind… or at least make the offer. Everyone understands occasional canine lapses, but hunts with large parties aren't the place for basic training. Heedless dogs can test even the best friendships to their limits.

While I've left safety considerations for last, they really should come first. Most of my hunting takes place with folks I've known and hunted with for years. My trust in their judgment derives from experience. Conversely, I always feel a little edgy whenever I head into the field with someone with whom I've not shared time afield before. Although I've never experienced a frightening safety lapse, I still exercise extra diligence when hunting in large groups. I never assume I know where someone is just because they're supposed to be there. Hunter orange isn't mandatory when hunting upland game in Montana, but I wear it anyway and make sure everyone else does too. Low flying birds can always be left for another day. No one enjoys being reminded of these obvious principles, but as a rural physician in hunting country I know the price of ignoring them. I've seen more than enough.

The secret to successful, enjoyable hunting in parties comes down to simple consideration for others, as useful a definition of good manners as any. Much as I appreciate the excitement and satisfaction of good dog work and fast shooting, I've enjoyed my share of both.

Good friendships are even more difficult to come by than good hunting. I've never regretted the decision to make time for them.

Any essay of this nature should probably conclude with a conventional description of more rises, shooting, and retrieves, but I have something different in mind. As hunters (and writers) we'd all be better off if we spent more time celebrating eating what we shoot, and nothing heightens an appreciation of wild game on the table like good company. No wonder our kitchen becomes such a busy place during hunting season.

The day had provided another fine outing during that same less than fine bird year. The roosters came in hard-earned singles and pairs rather than mad flurries, but they came. Despite the tired legs resting around the table, complaint was conspicuously absent. Appropriately enough for, to paraphrase Tom Hanks in *A League of Their Own,* there's no crying in bird season.

If I seemed a little livelier than our company, it was only because Lori and I had left the field early to return to kitchen duty. No microwave fast food that night, not at Chez Thomas. Pots had been bubbling all afternoon and even a bird dog's nose would have had trouble analyzing the bouquet of herbs and spices hanging over the stove. The ambitious surf-and-turf menu reflects the geographic background of the meal's participants: teal and snipe from Texas, seafood from our own second home in coastal Alaska. Pheasants? They're hanging in the barn, enjoying the cool weather prior to an appearance later in the week.

I never appreciate a day like that one until I've distilled the experience through the multiple retellings of events only good company can provide. The arrival of food at the table barely interrupts the narrative flow: shots made and missed; dog work critiqued and praised; unanimous appreciation for the wild and beautiful places pheasants call home. When the last drive is done, the ability to relive the day through the eyes and ears of others may be the greatest benefit hunting in the company of others can provide.

6.

Fifty Years of Opening Days

That year, my high-mileage body had yet to recover from the two weeks I'd just spent guiding bear hunters on the Alaska Peninsula. Two days of rain had left the fields slick and muddy. I could have headed to our local spring creek with my fly rod, but I spent October's second Saturday right where I'd known I'd spend it all along. I really didn't have a choice. It was the opening day of pheasant season.

A dozen roosters eyed us suspiciously as Lori and I drove through our friends' barnyard. They always have birds around their house, and as a simple courtesy we leave them alone. It still felt good to see some pheasants. During the critical week in early June when eggs were starting to hatch, the little creek that runs through their ranch had spilled beyond its banks and flooded a wide swath of prime nesting habitat.

Pheasants, however, are survivors. Given good cover they can endure almost anything. The cover on that ranch is excellent, thanks to grazing practices that keep the cows out of most of the wildlife habitat. Those barnyard roosters confirmed some success from the late hatch. Since I'd left home with modest expectations—a few birds for our traditional opening day dinner; a point or two from Maggie; an opportunity for Kenai to make what might be his final retrieve—we wouldn't need many birds to meet our needs.

But we would have to hunt for them. Because of the mud, I parked the rig at the first gate to avoid tearing up the field. The dogs came boiling out of the back of the truck as if they'd been waiting all year for this moment which they probably had, given my absence during so much of the early sharptail season. Then Lori and I loaded our shotguns and set off slipping and sliding around the edge of the alfalfa toward the cover.

As Maggie disappeared into the brush ahead, a sobering thought occurred to me. I'd been heading into the field on the opening day of pheasant season for half a century.

There wasn't a lot to my first pheasant opener. Thirteen years old and living in upstate New York at the time I'd already enjoyed some wing-shooting experience, all of which involved ruffed grouse, woodcock, and waterfowl. I had never seen a ring-necked pheasant.

Then my father learned of an area where the Department of Conservation had released some pheasants and set an open season. (Don't hold me to the details; it's been a long time.) We arrived on the appointed day, and before long Bits was on point. The noise and color of the rise that followed left a lasting impression, even though I wasn't the one who shot the bird. Woodcock didn't cackle, and grouse didn't glow in the sun like neon signs. The hook had been set.

Even so, when we finally left to spend the afternoon in nearby grouse cover, I felt as if something had been missing. Despite the dramatic rise, that first pheasant somehow felt like a minor league version of the upland game I'd hunted before. Although I couldn't identify it at the time, the missing ingredient was wildness. The roosters my dad shot that day had begun life in pens. Only later did I recognize that planted birds represent an admission of defeat. Provide the right habitat and they become unnecessary. That realization required an introduction to wild pheasants.

That came when my family moved to the Pacific Northwest while I was in high school. The night before the pheasant opener in our new home state, my father and I drove from our new home in suburban Seattle and across the Cascades. Going "east of the mountains" eventually became shorthand for going bird hunting because of the superior habitat there as compared to the wet forest closer to home. Early the next morning we set off along a creek bottom that bordered a stubble field on one side and a sagebrush flat on the other. I can still remember the excitement I felt.

Bits was starting to show his age, but he still possessed an exceptional nose not to mention years of upland experience. Shortly after we set out on foot, the bronze bell on his collar fell silent somewhere down in the brush. (This hunt took place long before electronic locator collars arrived.) Before we could reach the dog, his bell was tinkling again. "He's following a running pheasant!" my father called out. This was a new experience for me, since neither grouse nor woodcock ever ran ahead of the dog.

The bird led us all on a merry chase through the brush before it finally erupted across the creek from me. My father sent it tumbling, and Bits ran the cripple down after a long chase unlike anything I'd ever seen. The initial impression those docile planted birds had left back in New York evaporated. My instincts told me I'd just met a quarry capable of providing a lifetime's worth of challenge.

I still had a lot to learn. A decade later I wound up as a medical officer on a remote Montana Indian reservation located in some of the best upland game habitat I've ever found. My legs were young and posted signs were as rare as art museums. By the time I left two years later I could call myself a real pheasant hunter at last.

I had a secret weapon then: Skykomish, my first great Lab. The initial opening day in my new home ended quickly. As soon as I left my truck, loaded up, and sent Sky into the buffaloberry, the brush started to belch roosters, offering easy shots for me and routine retrieves for the dog. I had expected the excitement of opening day to last longer. I addressed the matter by packing up and heading for the nearest duck marsh.

Eight years later, I missed the opening day of pheasant season. I had a good excuse, since the nearest roosters were over a thousand miles away. That summer, I'd pulled up stakes and moved to Alaska. Years of outdoor excitement followed but there weren't any pheasants. Their absence probably influenced my eventual decision to move back to Montana more than Alaska's dark, punishing winters.

Back on the edge of the prairie, opening days became a family affair. Son Nick and daughter Gen accompanied me frequently, and my parents' annual visit always took place at the beginning of pheasant season. When the kids grew up and age finally began to limit my folks' ability to get around in the field, I faced a few openers with no company other than the dogs, but not for long.

By the time of our marriage, Lori had realized that if she wanted to see much of her husband, she was going to have to acquire some outdoor skills. She accepted the challenge of the fly rod and the longbow quickly and successfully, but the shotgun took a bit longer. When she finally started shooting her 20-gauge birthday present, she proved a quick learner. We've spent opening days of pheasant season together ever since. I keep waiting for an invitation from Dr. Phil to explain this pathway to marital bliss on television. Its failure to arrive must be another sign of our politically correct times.

After years of nothing but Labs in the kennel, I rediscovered my pointing dog roots by acquiring a female wirehair puppy. Maggie— introduced to readers earlier— grew up to look like a shorthair, and she bore a remarkable resemblance to old Bits both in appearance and hunting ability. Following her through the cover added a whole new dimension to pheasant season.

Decades' worth of opening days passed with disconcerting speed. A few provided quick limits, others produced little more than long miles and pleasant memories, and most fell in between. I spent some of those days hunting in shirtsleeves and others bundled up against the first indication of winter's impending approach. Labs were always around, as Sky led to Sonny, Sonny to Rocky, Rocky to Kenai, and Kenai to Rosy, with a few forgettable washouts in between. One factor remained constant. On each of those opening days I learned something—about wildlife, shooting, dogs, habitat, or sometimes simply about myself.

None of that would have been possible without the pheasants and the people who provided them with Aldo Leopold's quartet of simple factors all wildlife needs to thrive: clean air, clean water, ample food, and a place to live. Earlier, I used different words to paraphrase that observation, but the core meaning remains unchanged.

Maggie at the end of a successful opening day.

Meanwhile, back at the ranch...

Technical progress always comes at a cost. Whenever I heard Maggie's collar beeping to announce a point down in the brush, I felt nostalgic for the gentle sound of the bell Bits used to wear and the excitement I experienced when it fell silent. But there's only so much room for sentiment today, for we've covered a mile of tough cover without firing a shot by the time Maggie locates the first bird. As I direct Lori into the most favorable position, I make three simple wishes: I want the bird to be a rooster, I want my wife to kill it, and I want old Kenai to make a good retrieve. When Lori shakes her blond head in dismay after the rise and the shot I realize that I'm going to have to settle for one out of three, but I've settled for less before.

And that summarizes the action, for when we finally return to the rig our game vests aren't holding any pheasants at the end of opening day for the first time in years. But as I load the dogs for the drive home and we try to decide what we're going to substitute for pheasant in the kitchen that night, I come face to face with the most important lesson of all from the last 50 years.

There's no such thing as a bad opening day.

7.

The First of November

Every narrative has a backstory. For a simple hunting tale this one is longer than usual. I cannot precisely date the beginning because it has to do with weather, one of our planets' great mysteries. Perhaps a butterfly flapped its wings too hard in Australia, perhaps it was global warming—this is not the place for that discussion. Whatever the cause, drought had held Montana in its grip for several years, to the determent of farmers, ranchers, fire-prone forests, and upland bird cover. Grass and brush stunted by lack of moisture were just one aspect of the problem. As hay prices climbed, stockmen had to run their cattle for longer periods of time in places rarely grazed before. Gamebirds had less to eat and fewer places to hide than in any season I could remember.

Of our regional prairie Trifecta, no species suffered more from this development than pheasants. Birds of open plains, sharptails and Huns evolved to survive in short grass habitat with no agricultural food sources. They're accustomed to dry years and sparse cover. Roosters crave dense security cover of just the sort the drought had cost them. Although I knew what was coming, the meager first weeks of the season proved even more challenging than expected. Lori, the dogs, and I covered long miles on ranches that ordinarily produced lots of pheasants—shotgun aerobics, as I call such days. We enjoyed scenery and fall foliage largely uninterrupted by the distraction of flushing birds, and the dogs seemed happy just to be running free. We did scratch out a few roosters from coulees that collected enough scarce moisture to support patches of cattails and buffaloberry, picking up some Huns and sharptails as we went. By the end of October I had yet to shoot a daily limit of pheasants.

I've always felt a stubborn refusal to give up and I didn't, aided by enthusiasm from my wife and dogs. I finally called an old friend whose ranch had been an ace-in-the-hole for years. If we couldn't find birds there, it would be time to start campaigning local whitetails with my bow. His bird report was pessimistic, but it's logically impossible to prove a negative. Furthermore, surveying bird numbers from the seat of a tractor isn't the same as evaluating them behind enthusiastic dogs working the thick cover.

We felt disappointed when we found the rancher and his wife away from home when we arrived. Old friends whose families I'd known for years, I always enjoy visiting with Will and Nan (as I'll call them here out of respect for their privacy), who remind me of the rural Montana I knew 50 years earlier. After a recent total knee replacement Will had gone to town for physical therapy earlier that morning, delaying my offer of an unofficial house call. We left a note on their door promising to swing by again on our way out and then headed for some of my favorite pheasant cover.

When we pulled off the county road, I received one of the few pleasant surprises of the season. The terrain on that ranch ranges from mountain foothills occupied by sharptails and Huns to brushy creek bottoms that concentrate ringnecks. The best pheasant cover runs along a winding, steep-banked prairie creek, and the ground cover there looked better than any I'd seen all season. That pasture hadn't been grazed all summer—a specific favor to me, as I later learned. I tried to justify that courtesy by remembering the years I had spent providing medical care to our friends' families, but I couldn't make it add up. As I said, the Montana of 50 years ago…

The dogs were the first order of business, as I wanted them to burn off some of their excitement before we hit the bird cover. My approach to pheasant dogs may be a bit unconventional. I have no doubt that Labrador retrievers have contributed to more successful pheasant hunts than any other breed in the country, and I'd killed plenty with mine. However, after several winters in southern Arizona quail habitat, I had rediscovered my pointing dog roots. While I had hunted pheasants with flushing Labs ever since I arrived in Montana decades earlier, I no longer hit upland cover without a pointing dog. While Max, our male German wirehair, was a highly capable (if somewhat unpolished) retriever, I couldn't leave the Labs at home all the time. Hunting one of them from heel so they didn't interfere with Maggie or Max, I used them to assist on tough retrieves and flush birds holding tight for a dog on point in thick cover. Kiska, our young yellow female Lab, accompanied us that November day.

With photo light too gorgeous to ignore, Lori left her 20-gauge behind in favor of her camera. Despite the quality of the cover, I began to feel discouraged when we hadn't flushed a bird after working the brush for nearly an hour. To further complicate matters, I had mixed up my e-collars before leaving home and Max's had no locator function. It was nearly impossible to keep track of him in the high grass along the creek bed.

Then we broke out on top of a bank and spotted him on point beside a little stock pond. Kiska stayed at heel until we made our way within shotgun range. The chest-high brush exploded in wingbeats when I sent her in ahead of Max. Facing the sun, I needed more time than usual to separate hens from roosters. By the time my first barrel sent one down in a cloud of feathers, the second bird I could identify as a cock had reached the edge of shotgun range. It dropped a leg when I fired, only to sail back into the tangle a hundred yards ahead of us.

This rooster completed my limit after the strangest retrieve of the season.

After regrouping, reloading, and accepting the first bird from Max, we continued in that direction. Absent distinctive landmarks, I could do no better than head to the general area where the bird had gone down. Then Max hit the brakes, frozen in the kind of point that announces a bird right under his nose. Assuming he had located the cripple, I sent Kiska in to find it, dead or alive. To my surprise the bird flushed vigorously, looking healthy save for a dangling leg. I shouldered my shotgun only to find its selective safety jammed, a mishap I experience occasionally despite conscious efforts to keep it properly positioned to the side. By the time I had that problem sorted the bird was nearly out of range. Once again I hit it, but not hard enough to crumple it. I wouldn't have taken that shot if the bird hadn't already been wounded.

The rooster flew another hundred yards to the county road, landed—not dropped—at the edge of the gravel, and disappeared.

Max had broken, and since I didn't want him on the road my first obligation was to get him back at my side. He is obedient though, and he returned promptly at the sound of my whistle. It was hard for me not to imagine him wondering how many times I was going to shoot this bird before he got to retrieve it.

Now we faced a dilemma. The bird had gone down right in front of my friends' nearest neighbor's house, which lies next to a shelterbelt that is full of pheasants every time I drive by. I had never met him, but he's the kind of guy who points to one of the several No Hunting signs around his yard every time he sees me. My friends don't get along with him even though they get along with almost everyone. While I felt certain the wounded bird was holed up in the shelterbelt, I also felt certain that asking for permission to recover it would be a fool's errand that could lead to conflict I didn't need. As much as I despise failing to recover downed birds, I decided that there was nothing more to be done about that one.

With the dogs at my side, we reluctantly began to work our way back along the other side of the creek. Its course wanders and its steep, chest-high banks make it more like a trench than a creek bed—terrain that is usually good for wet feet and several hard falls. This year it was dry except for a few pools adequate for dog water, and we survived the inevitable tumbles without damage to bodies, shotgun, or camera.

On our return trip we had the prevailing west wind in our faces, and the dogs took full advantage of the improved scenting conditions. Max quickly went on point, only to have Kiska flush a hen 20 yards ahead of him. We repeated that frustrating scenario three more times in the next 200 yards. I have never learned how pheasant cover can produce such consecutive runs of hens, especially when I'm eager to reward a dog with a dead rooster.

The fourth point finally produced one and I downed it with an easy shot. The bird hit the ground running across an open section of grass and quickly disappeared over a rise. Anxious to avoid the disappointment of a second lost pheasant, I sent both dogs in pursuit. When Max returned with the bird held gently but securely in his mouth, it was hard for me not to read an element of pride in his body language. I know that's romantic nonsense on my part, but still.

The next mile of hiking proved unproductive. By the time we drew even with our truck, I was still one rooster shy of Montana's three-bird limit. I don't know why that should have mattered. I've already discussed the ways in which leaving the field with just a bird or two can prove gratifying. I'm not one to keep score in the field, whether it's inches of elk antler or the number of birds dropped without a miss. Nonetheless, shooting limits can lead to a sense of accomplishment, whether justified or not. I hadn't done it all year, and that day felt oddly incomplete without a third bird in my game vest. After hiking three miles across uneven terrain, wading through high grass, and doing more broad jumping than I had since high school, I felt pleasantly tired and knew the dogs did too. I wasn't worried about Lori, who is younger than I am and doesn't know how to say "quit."

While we were working the last bit of cover, which produced nothing but two more solid points on hens, we watched our friends' truck go by on the county road. I made the executive decision that it was time to stop worrying about a third pheasant and turn polite and sociable. After watering the dogs, snapping a few photos, and wiping the dirt off my shotgun, we drove to the ranch house. After we checked Will's knee and found nothing but normal postoperative swelling, Nan made a pot of coffee while we reminisced about our late parents (they'd known mine as well as I'd known theirs) and talked about cattle prices.

Finally, we headed down the road in the direction of their neighbor's house. As we drew closer, Lori spotted a dark object at the edge of the road where we'd last seen the lost rooster. "It couldn't be!" she cried, but it was. We came to a stop, stepped out, and picked up the pheasant—dead, still warm, one leg broken, and obviously the same bird I'd hit earlier.

THE FIRST OF NOVEMBER

It's easy to write about days when elk are charging in to calls and the sky is raining ducks. However, I sometimes prefer to narrow the scope and examine the little aspects of a hunt that can make an ordinary day afield a great one. What's not to like about good dog work (in which the pointer out-retrieves the retriever, no less), great photo light, a workout for our legs, an hour with old friends, a limit of roosters, and one of the longest, goofiest retrieves ever?

I can't think of anything.

Grouse

8.

Prairie Natives

As usual when heading afield with shotgun and bird dogs, the terrain defines the promise of the day ahead. On this early September morning, a cloudless azure sky stretching horizon to horizon reminds me why the words Big Sky appear on Montana license plates. A panorama of undulating hills suggests slow-rolling waves at sea. Each rounded ridge lies separated from its neighbor by a coulee steep enough but not quite deep enough to qualify as a canyon. The green chokecherry and buffaloberry along their flanks contrast sharply with the sea of gold and brown surrounding them, suggesting that they enjoyed moisture denied to the rest of the surrounding prairie.

Yet to be grazed by livestock, the native grasses on the open ground stand nearly to my knee, high enough to hold gamebirds feeding on berries and grasshoppers. There's just so much of it though, and even with two eager German wirehairs ranging ahead of us we'll likely cover lots of ground before our first contact with game. The alternative is to hunt the landscape's only concentrating features, the brushy coulees, although I don't expect to find sharptails there until rising temperatures send them in search of shade. After some thought, a plan emerges. We'll hunt the open, grassy ridgetop a mile uphill toward the head of the first coulee. If we don't find birds, we'll descend and work the brush and steep sidehills back to the truck.

Inevitably, this carefully devised stratagem earns a comment from Lori. "You always come up with a plan," she observes as she breaks her 20-gauge open and drops a shell into each chamber. "I just wish more of them worked."

So do I.

Montana's open grassland habitat offers wing-shooters a choice of three prized gamebirds. (As discussed in the following chapter I do not include sage grouse for several reasons, including lack of challenge on the wing, marginal table quality, and concern about the species' future.) Of the three, ring-necked pheasants are the largest, noisiest, and smartest. Huns (properly, gray partridge) offer fast, tricky shooting and wonderful opportunities for pointing dogs. Theoretically, we might encounter one or both in the inviting habitat ahead, but today I'm focused on the third and in many ways my favorite my favorite: sharp-tailed grouse.

Tympanuchus phasianellus enjoys a wider geographic distribution than its two open country cohorts, ranging north all the way from Montana to the Yukon Valley. I never got around to hunting them when I lived in Alaska, but friends enjoyed the challenge of a unique Far North grouse trifecta: spruce, ruffed, and sharptails all on the same day. Having shot my share of sharptails back in Montana I preferred to hunt ptarmigan, which were still new and exciting as discussed shortly.

Fowl-like in size and contour, sharptails are often called "chickens" by locals, although true prairie chickens do not occur as far west as Montana. Dressed in mottled gray, a sharptail may seem drab compared to a pheasant. A closer look reveals a subtly beautiful bird sporting complex patterns of white spots on the wings and delicate, arrowhead-shaped markings on the breast. Nature seldom does pretty without a practical reason, and in this case a sharptail's plumage provides superb camouflage when the bird is evading predators on the ground.

Gregarious by nature, sharptails are seldom found alone. During September, they commonly occur in family groups of six to ten birds. By the time snow starts to accumulate in November, they have often coalesced into large, loosely formed flocks. It's hard to know just what to call those early season groups. Their numbers resemble coveys, but they do not demonstrate true covey behavior such as flushing simultaneously like quail or Huns. I unscientifically refer to them as "bunches."

One of my reasons for admiring sharptails above all other prairie gamebirds derives from their status as true natives. Pheasants and Huns originated in Eurasia and arrived here as the result of deliberate introductions, in the late 1800s in the pheasants' case and the early 1900s in the Huns'. In contrast, sharptails were abundant here at the time of first European contact, which took place on September 12, 1804 in what is now South Dakota, when Captain William Clark observed large numbers of fowl-like birds on the prairie. In a typical example of their astute wildlife observations, Meriwether Lewis, Clark's co-leader on the Voyage of Discovery, wrote that these "Sharpe-tailed Grows" (his spelling, not mine) had pointed tails with "the feathers in its center much longer than those on the sides," thereby distinguishing them from the true prairie chickens they had encountered earlier.

As our iconic native upland quarry, sharptails, in my opinion, would have made a wonderful choice for Montana's state bird. Precedence for honoring gamebirds this way has already been established for others, including the California quail (California), ring-necked pheasant (South Dakota), and ruffed grouse (Pennsylvania). When Alaska school children were tasked with selecting a bird to represent the nation's newest state, they chose the willow ptarmigan—a close biological relative of the sharptail. I can't avoid feeling regret about my home state's choice of the meadowlark despite its melodious voice, since it rudely abandons us every winter as soon as the going gets tough.

Hunters aren't the only parties enthusiastic about sharptails, one of those fortunate species that appeals to a variety of stakeholders with opposition from none (in contrast to large predators like wolves and grizzlies). Part of the species' popularity among bird watchers, photographers, and casual wildlife observers arises from their spectacular spring mating behavior, properly known as lekking.

At first light sometime in March or April, sharptails of both sexes begin to fly in to lekking sites from all directions. Once enough participants have arrived at the party, males begin to display for the seemingly indifferent hens, cooing and bowing with wings extended while shuffling and stomping in an elaborate sequence of dance steps. Everyone interested in wildlife deserves to watch this remarkable spectacle at least once.

Because leks often remain in the same place, local knowledge may be all you need to find, visit, and observe. Absent such a tip, drive backroads (lots of prime sharptail habitat lies on public land) early in the morning, watch carefully for grouse on the ground or in the air, and locate a lek to return to the following morning. Otherwise, hike open ground looking for signs of lekking activity such as droppings, shed fathers, and trampled grass. Perhaps the easiest option is to contact the local biologist and ask.

Newcomers to the experience should follow certain guidelines to avoid disrupting the process and negatively impacting the local grouse population. Arrive early, since birds are spookier in daylight. A lightweight portable blind will allow close observation and photographic opportunities. Minimize movement and don't approach an active lek on foot. A parked vehicle will bother birds less than moving people, if you can locate one near a county road or authorized backroad travel route. If the birds appear to be noticing you, back off.

Above all, enjoy the show.

A versatile German wirehair pointer, Max both pointed and retrieved this sharptail.

For the upland hunter, September and early October are prime time for sharptails. Weather is usually pleasant, although hunters will have to carry adequate water for dogs and watch for snakes. Thicker ground cover at that time of year encourages birds to hold for pointing dogs. With pheasant season yet to open, hunting pressure is often light. However, with seasons in most districts running through the end of the year, one should not ignore opportunities to hunt late season sharptails, a different, more challenging experience.

Large late season flocks always seem to have sentries posted and approaching them can be difficult. Years ago in northeastern Montana, I decided to make a quick solo hunt shortly after Christmas. Pheasants were my primary quarry, but when I drove past a stubble field and noticed large numbers of sharptails silhouetted against the snow, I couldn't resist. After parking several hundred yards away, I stepped out of the truck and started around to the dog box. Before I could get there sharptails began to flush, filling the air with the sound of wings and the birds' characteristic reedy alarm calls. Counting birds accurately proved impossible, although they certainly numbered over a hundred. The spectacle lasted several minutes as grouse took off and poured over the horizon in their typical flap-and-glide wingbeat pattern. I worked the perimeter of the field for stragglers but never fired a shot.

On another December morning in central Montana, I set off in the wake of a heavy overnight snowfall to set up for mallards on a spring-fed slough. Plan A worked like a charm, and an hour later I was carrying a limit of greenheads as my Lab and I headed back to the truck along a line of snow-laden buffaloberry. I wasn't paying much attention when the dog veered off course and vanished into the brush, which soon erupted in wingbeats and explosions of powdery snow. A large flock of grouse had taken shelter from the storm, but I doubt I ever would have noticed them save for the dog's nose. I had unloaded my shotgun by then, but as I fumbled for shells I asked myself if I wanted to take advantage of the birds' vulnerability and decided that I did not. That decision did not represent pure altruism. While young early season sharptails are delicious, their meat becomes darker and tougher as the season progresses. The sight and sound of all those flushing birds still provided a memorable experience. The walk back down the brush line to the truck could have served as a sporting clays course although I remained unloaded all the way.

Back on the prairie that September day, Lori and I felt pleasantly tired as we reached the apex of the ridge without flushing a bird. As we started down into the adjacent coulee, I called a halt beside a stand of chokecherry to allow the dogs a rest in the shade and offer them water. I was enjoying the break myself when I glanced down the draw and spotted Maggie on point beside a dense cluster of buffaloberry. The time to start hunting again had arrived.

By the time we reached Maggie, Max had moved in to honor the point. Locating birds in such dense, thorny cover is one thing, but getting them airborne is another. As much as I enjoyed the sight of the two dogs on point, I began to regret my decision to leave our flushing Labs back in the kennel. After shouting and shaking branches failed to produce a rise, our only option was for one of us to wade in. Ever the gentleman, I suggested to Lori that she post up in the open on the far side of the brush, since I knew I would never get a shot off from the middle of the thicket.

After confirming Lori's position, I unloaded my shotgun, left it behind on the ground, and fought through a dozen yards of thorns before wingbeats erupted in front of me. As suspected, I couldn't even see the birds, but I did hear Lori shoot twice. "Need a dog?" I asked.

"I need *both* dogs!" she shouted back.

"Fetch!" I called over my shoulder, releasing both wirehairs from their obligation to stay put.

I surmised, correctly, that Lori had killed two young birds of the year, which would be delightful on the table. After praising the dogs and reloading, we started back down the sidehill, savoring the satisfaction of having begun another Montana upland season in style.

9.

The Once and Future Sage Grouse

The Big Sky: A. B. Guthrie got it right. More interesting than most visitors first assume, our West's sagebrush steppe teems with unique wildlife ranging in size from the misnamed mountain plover to sharp-tailed grouse and pronghorns. On a daylong hike, the deceptive terrain can challenge even the best-conditioned legs. But it's always the sky that dominates—overreaching, soaring horizon to horizon, reminding us what puny specs of matter we really are.

One September afternoon some years back, Lori and I had seen about all the Big Sky we needed for one day. We'd set out looking for Huns along a vast series of stubble fields and found enough to keep us going but not enough to make us stop. We were down to our last water bottle, and Kenai was panting. When I noted an earthen dam at the bottom of a sagebrush-lined coulee, I suggested that we drop downhill and see if it held any water.

Kenai began to look excited as we approached, but not because of the puddle behind the dam. Sage grouse don't need much surface water, but they will take it when they can get it. We had blundered right into a flock in the dense sage above the waterline. Ponderous wingbeats filled the air as Kenai put his nose to work. I'd killed plenty of sage-grouse before, but Lori was still new to the shotgun then. "Take that one," I encouraged her, deliberately pointing out a young bird of the year, and she did. I'd sawed my way through plenty of old sage grouse on the table and I didn't need to do it again.

Save for the wild turkey, the sage grouse is the country's largest upland game bird. When the dog delivered Lori's, I stood back and let her savor the moment. Over twenty years had passed since I'd shot my last sage grouse, and a lot had happened to the birds during that time. Little did I know how much lay ahead.

Echoing the history of the sharptail, western science received its first description of the sage grouse courtesy of Meriwether Lewis, writing near the mouth of the Marias River on June 10, 1805. While many of Lewis's wildlife observations were remarkably detailed and accurate he didn't have much to say about the bird, which he referred to as the "Prairie Cock" or the "Cock of the Plains."

The sea of sagebrush habitat Lewis and Clark travelled through may have seemed inexhaustible then, but time proved otherwise. Sage grouse lack the muscular crop found in other gallinaceous birds, so they cannot digest hard seeds. They are almost entirely dependent on sagebrush leaves for food, especially in winter. Their natural range closely corresponds with the distribution of the big sagebrush (*Artemisia tridentata*). As goes the big sage, so goes the big bird.

Sagebrush habitat had begun to disappear by the early 1900s for a variety of reasons including drought, fire (to which big sage is particularly vulnerable), agriculture, over-grazing, conifer encroachment, and the arrival of invasive weeds such as cheatgrass (*Bromus tectorum*). Sage-grouse populations reflected this trend, dropping from historic population highs in the millions to somewhere between 200 and 500 thousand today. They have disappeared completely from their native range in British Columbia, New Mexico, and Nebraska. Although most studies have shown that hunting has little if any effect on their numbers, hunting seasons have been reduced or eliminated in the eleven states in which they remain (at the time of this writing, Oregon, Washington, California, Nevada, Idaho, Wyoming, Montana, Colorado, Utah, and the Dakotas). All except Washington and North Dakota had limited sage grouse hunting seasons when Lori killed her first one, although their duration had been reduced substantially since I arrived on the plains.

The United States Fish and Wildlife Service (FWS) received its first petition to list the sage-grouse as endangered under the terms of the Endangered Species Act (ESA) in 1999. This petition only addressed the isolated Columbia Basin population in Washington State. The Service determined that these birds represented a Distinct Population Segment (DPS), and that listing was "warranted but precluded." The latter term, which appears frequently in FWS rulings now, means that biologic data make the species a candidate for listing, but the Service has higher priorities.

Seven more petitions directed at all or part of the sage grouse population had been filed by 2003, and various environmental groups challenged the conclusions of all but the first in court. The first range-wide ruling, issued in 2005, determined that listing was not warranted, but that if habitat conditions did not improve the Department of the Interior would revisit the issue. Following court challenge, that decision was remanded back to the FWS on the grounds that the initial findings may have been politically influenced. In 2010, the Service issued a warranted but precluded ruling for sage grouse across their range, leading to more litigation. A Multi-District Litigation Settlement in 2011 required a final decision by the FWS by September 30, 2015.

An odd alliance of private stakeholders including farmers, ranchers, hunters, local residents, and development interests recognized that addressing sage grouse populations and habitat concerns voluntarily was preferable to having the species listed. This understanding led to the Sage Grouse Initiative (SGI), a combination of government and private conservation efforts begun in 2010 with funding from the Department of Agriculture's Natural Resources Conservation Services. The goal was to improve habitat and stabilize or increase sage-grouse numbers while avoiding the impact of an endangered species listing.

Over the next five years, the Initiative worked successfully to improve 4.4 million acres of habitat on over 1,100 voluntarily participating private ranches in sage grouse country. These efforts included conservation easements, improved grazing practices, replacing or flagging fences prone to sage grouse collisions, reversing conifer encroachment, and improved control of rangeland fires, which have a major negative impact of sagebrush ecosystems.

"The initiative has certainly had a positive effect on our ranch," one local rancher and old friend said when I spoke to him about the program. "We've put in pipelines and water tanks, and initiated a rest-rotation grazing program that keeps livestock off twenty percent of the pasture for periods of a year and a half. The impact for us has been huge. I never thought we'd see this increase in production. Now we have more pasture and more wildlife."

Everyone recognized the importance of direct state involvement. In 2013, Montana Governor Steve Bullock announced the creation and funding of a sage grouse management plan in Montana, which still allows the most liberal hunting season in the country. Similar state-led programs emerged elsewhere around the West, and Wyoming's plan became a model for others.

Private sector support was equally crucial, especially in Montana where sixty percent of the sage grouse population lives on private land. Favorable response from private landowners was hardly unanimous, and some claimed that state plan provisions were "worse than a listing." This shortsighted opinion ignored the fact that restrictions imposed by a formal ESA listing become mandatory on all private (as well as public) lands in the recovery area. The terms of the state plans were voluntary and well received. Two months before the final listing determination, Department of the Interior Deputy Assistant Secretary Jim Lyons called the Sage Grouse Initiative "the most extraordinary private land conservation effort I've ever seen."

Meanwhile, petitions directed at two specific sage-grouse populations offered a preview of the pending range-wide ruling. In 1995, biologists proposed that the isolated sage-grouse population along the Colorado-Utah border constituted a separate species, an opinion formalized by the American Ornithological Union in 2000. These birds became the Gunnison sage-grouse (*Centrocercus minimus*) as distinct from the more numerous and widely distributed greater sage grouse, *C. urophasianus*. At the time, fewer than 5,000 Gunnison sage grouse remained in fragmented habitat.

The FWS received a petition to list the bird before it had even been named. In 2010, the Service issued a "warranted but precluded" determination. Following more litigation, the Gunnison sage grouse was listed as "threatened," disappointing stakeholders on both sides of the debate. Farmers, ranchers, hunters, and various state and local groups who had worked to improve Gunnison sage-grouse habitat felt that their efforts had been ignored, while environmental groups involved in litigation hoped for a more restrictive "endangered" designation. The FWS defines an endangered species as one that faces an immediate threat of extinction throughout all or a significant portion of its range. A "threatened" species is one likely to become endangered in the foreseeable future. An endangered designation allows stricter federal control over management decisions.

In April 2015 the FWS ruled on a petition directed at the distinct "Bi-State" sage-grouse population along the California-Nevada border. In this case the FWS found listing not warranted, largely as the result of voluntary conservation efforts. Would similar reasoning apply to the more far-reaching decision due five months later? Stakeholders on both sides of the issue awaited a ruling all but certain to leave some of them unhappy.

Predictably—and a bit desperately—some parties began to attack the basic assumption that the grouse was in trouble at all. Citing unpublished, non-peer-reviewed reports, a consortium of western counties and industry-backed groups filed suit in March 2015, claiming that the preponderance of biologic evidence establishing the grouse's decline was flawed. In response, biologists Ed Arnett, working with the Theodore Roosevelt Conservation Partnership, and Terry Riley, of the North American Grouse Partnership, wrote: "Without exception, all field studies on sage-grouse include assumptions and limitations, and some even have flaws, but the *weight of evidence* regarding threats to sage-grouse and sagebrush ecosystems cannot be denied." They concluded with an unsettling prediction: "…one thing is certain: the courts will decide the fate of sage grouse, regardless of what the USFWS decides."

In September 2015, the FWS ruled that the greater sage grouse would not be listed, largely due to the success of voluntary efforts through the Sage Grouse Initiative. On the occasion, Secretary of the Interior Sally Jewell noted:

> "This is a truly historic effort. It demonstrates that the Endangered Species Act is an effective and flexible tool and a critical catalyst for conservation… This epic conservation effort will benefit westerners and hundreds of species that call this iconic landscape home, while giving states, businesses, and communities the certainty they need to plan for sustainable economic development."

This decision allowed state plans developed as part of the SGI to go forward without further federal intervention, with a review scheduled in five years to ensure compliance. While oil and gas leasing was allowed to proceed in areas of limited concern, that would not be the case in critical habitat areas. That definition varied from state to state—within four miles of a known sage grouse lek in Wyoming, for example, and within 0.6 miles of a lek in Montana. Development limitations were also designed to connect key areas in order to provide the birds with the large, contiguous areas of healthy sagebrush habitat they require.

This story has implications that extend beyond the sage-grouse, or even the sagebrush steppe regions it occupies. The introduction to the Endangers Species Act reads: "The purposes of this Act are to provide means whereby the ecosystems upon which endangered species and threatened species depend may be conserved..." in other words, not to list, but to *avoid* listing proactively. Perhaps the Sage Grouse Initiative will serve as a model for a new paradigm in which parties with opposing views on wildlife management work cooperatively to solve problems instead of hiring lawyers to litigate them.

Unfortunately, litigation remains likely. Meanwhile, upland hunters are free to pursue one of our country's truly special game birds in accordance with state regulations.

Male sage grouse on full display during spring lekking activity.

This chapter may seem an anomaly in a book that is mostly devoted to the process of the wing-shooting experience. Much of it may already be outdated. I still feel it warrants inclusion for several reasons. No discussion of North American wing-shooting would be complete without mention of our largest upland gamebird. The conservation status of our most imperiled wing-shooting quarry should be of interest and concern to all who care about wildlife whether we enjoy them with shotguns and bird dogs or cameras and binoculars. The sage grouse's spring lekking displays are just as spectacular as those of the sharptail. The sagebrush steppe these birds inhabit may be one of the country's least appreciated habitats. I have always considered it important to draw attention to the role hunter-conservationists have played in the preservation of wildlife, as we did through the Sage Grouse Initiative.

My personal attitude toward hunting sage grouse is less stuffy than I may have made it sound. I have hunted them in remote corners of the prairie and am glad I had the opportunity to do so. As with some other outdoor activities I enjoyed at the time—catching billfish on flies, for example—I no longer feel an urge to repeat it. I would argue that anyone involved in wing-shooting deeply enough to be reading this book should be able to hunt these remarkable gamebirds at least once. I have enjoyed helping visiting friends do so.

Hopefully, the big birds will thrive sufficiently for such opportunities to remain.

10.

Pearls from the Sky

Southwestern Alaska's barren tundra makes me imagine the Eastern Montana prairie with more rain. Both largely treeless landscapes invite attention from binoculars whether glassing for pronghorns or moose. The vistas look vast, and once you start walking across them they seem even more so. In both places inviting mountains loom in the distance but are too far away to be anything more than scenery. Not that I need more of that now, for the time is late August and the complex tundra ground cover is already assuming its striking autumn color scheme of red, maroon, and gold.

Ptarmigan hunting can be a utilitarian affair with no purpose other than fresh meat in moose camp, but the company of pointing dogs can elevate it to a pinnacle upland hunting experience. Yesterday, I sat Maggie on the back seat of the Super Cub, flew through Lake Clark pass, and landed on a "sand blow" somewhere south of King Salmon. Although a friend accompanied me in a second airplane, the sense of isolation in an enormous universe felt pleasantly overwhelming around last night's camp dinner. The opportunity to experience it is one reason I love hunting ptarmigan.

Our quarry today is the willow ptarmigan—Alaska's state bird and a subspecies of Scotland's famous red grouse (yeah, the one on the scotch label). Distinguishing among Alaska's three ptarmigan is of limited interest to anyone except biologists and collectors. Save for differences in habitat preferences and distribution, there isn't much to tell them apart. Alaska hunting regulations treat them all the same, which is fortunate since they can be hard to identify by species on the wing, especially in winter plumage. The name of today's quarry contains an important clue about where to look for them, for I usually encounter them near the stunted willows dotting the tundra.

Hiking here is easier on the low ridges where the caribou moss (actually a lichen) grows, so that's where we head as we leave camp. Even a small elevation gain affords a sweeping view of the terrain, and I pause reflexively to scan for bears. That's just force of habit since I feel confident that at this time of year they're all miles away on the nearest salmon stream. With a clear coast ahead, I release Maggie from heel and direct her toward the nearest strip of willows.

Just shy of the foliage, the dog hits the brakes and skids to a stop as if she has hit an invisible wall. One of the pleasures of hunting early season ptarmigan over pointers is the birds' willingness to hold tight for a dog, a habit rarely enjoyed later in the season. After approaching at a leisurely pace, we're well within shotgun range when I hear the first alarm call from a flushing bird. The rich, reedy chuckle reminds me of sharptails, to which ptarmigan are closely related.

The rise that follows is leisurely and staggered. The birds are in transition plumage, their superb natural camouflage now compromised in flight by their flashing white wings. There's not a lot of challenge to the shooting at this time of the year, although that will be a different story a few months later as we shall see. Ptarmigan are not fast fliers, and this bunch (like sharptails, they aren't true covey birds) is rising at close range in twos and threes. I even have time to break my gun and reload midway through the rise, but my hunting partner and I have each doubled (admittedly no demonstration of great shooting skill). Four birds from one bunch feels like plenty.

Like their sharptail relatives downed ptarmigan generally aren't hard to recover, but with one cripple waddling back into the willow tangle I'm still glad my bird dog comes from a versatile breed. The other three birds are down in plain sight, but to give Maggie an opportunity to do what she loves I choose to leave them until she returns from the willows with the cripple in her mouth. As I accept the final bird from her I notice a jaeger overhead, not a true raptor species but an avid hunter just as its German name suggests. Spending most of their time offshore, they are seldom seen inland except on open tundra during their summer nesting season. Spotting one always reminds me of my presence in a special place.

By the time we've completed the two-mile loop back to our improvised landing strip we're carrying all the birds we want in our game vests. While I haven't come prepared for big game, the sight of a lone caribou bull silhouetted atop a nearby ridge offers a compelling invitation to spend another night in the wild. However, our last weather forecast described an ominous low-pressure system moving in from the Gulf and neither of us feels like a white-knuckle flight home. The time has come to get while the getting is good, no matter how reluctantly.

A long way to travel for a dozen small gamebirds and tired legs? Sure, but I never decline an excuse to visit my favorite habitats.

Lori Thomas and the late Lori Egge hunting willow ptarmigan on Kodiak Island.

Most Alaskans know that ptarmigan hunting isn't all bird dogs and double-barreled 20-gauges, as illustrated by a trip I made to the same area several seasons prior.

Three friends and I were taking our annual float trip down the Mulchatna River, which rises from the western flanks of the Alaska Range and flows through a hundred miles of wilderness on its way to the Nushagak and on to Bristol Bay. The Mulchatna doesn't host the massive red salmon runs that attract the huge lake-anadromous rainbows that make the Bristol Bay region an internationally famous angling destination. However, there were always plenty of smaller rainbows, char, and grayling to catch as we floated, and we usually had the river to ourselves.

Fish weren't our primary objective anyway. Back then the local caribou were abundant enough to earn their own name: the Mulchatna herd. (Their population subsequently crashed for reasons that still befuddle biologists.) For several years, the four of us had enjoyed remarkable success on big bulls even though we all limited ourselves to traditional archery equipment—longbows, recurves, wooden arrows, the whole deal. That herd was migratory, and on any given day we were likely to see either none or hundreds. The long float provided an effective means of addressing that crapshoot. If the caribou weren't where we camped on any given night, we just continued downstream until we found them.

As always, weight was a consideration on the long flight in even though our rafts and other gear meant flying in an aircraft that could haul a heavy load, usually a de Havilland Beaver. While it's seldom wise to skimp on food, there were always fish (although we didn't kill rainbows) and one of us had usually taken a caribou in a matter of days. Not on this particular trip, however.

Midway through the float, our provisions were down to noodles and rice, which we supplemented regularly with char. Although they are one of my favorite freshwater food fish, five days of them was plenty. Fortunately, I had planned for this contingency by bringing along a dozen extra arrows, not that I thought I'd need them for caribou. I've always prided myself on one-shot bow kills and had never needed a second arow for big game on these trips. On our sixth morning in the field, I set off less interested in antlers than dinner.

After crossing the brushy river bottom, climbing a low tundra ridge, and locating several long strips of willow, I started hiking. I hadn't gone a hundred yards before I heard a soft cluck from the open tundra ahead. In contrast to the loud chatter flushing ptarmigan make, this subtle call suggests curiosity rather than panic. As I stopped and nocked an arrow, heads began to appear above the ground cover, most of them already within bow range.

When the first arrow flew true and pinned the bird to the ground, I had to wonder how a bowhunter capable of hitting a target that size could miss an elk from the same range (regrettably, a question that arose from personal experience). By this time a dozen more birds were walking slowly away, and the rising tempo of their clucks suggested that this golden opportunity wasn't going to last for long. Before they finally began to flush, I had managed three more shots with only one miss. I had deliberately tipped these shafts with clever heads called Judo points, whose protruding wire prongs kept arrows from disappearing forever into the soft carpet of moss and lichens behind the birds. After collecting the three birds and four arrows I'd shot, I set off for the next line of willows.

Several hours later I arrived back in camp with two more birds in my daypack. My hunting partners had begun to stagger in after covering a lot of ground without seeing many caribou. Nobody had killed a bull—although one unnamed party had to confess a miss—and everyone was starving. It was time for me to reprise my frequent role as camp cook. Classical upland wing-shooting? Of course not, but gratifying in its own way even without a shotgun and bird dog.

Winter can be a challenging time in Alaska. Rise in the dark, go to sleep in the dark, and accept that there won't be much sunlight in between. Alaskans recognized Cabin Fever long before the phenomenon acquired its proper modern name: Seasonal Affective Disorder. Acknowledged or not, almost everyone gets it, and case to case differences are only a matter of degree. Distraction becomes a desperate goal. Christmas celebrations commonly drag on for weeks. Airports fill with Alaskans heading to tropical locations, more for the sunlight than warm temperatures. Divorce rates skyrocket and some people simply drink too much.

During periods of stress I have always sought relief in the outdoors, but at that latitude options are limited on either side of the Winter Solstice. Ice fishing is one angling activity for which I have never acquired a taste. Caribou season remains open in many areas, but my first winter caribou hunt was my last, as recounted shortly. I did some cross-country skiing and shot a lot of snowshoe hares with my bow, but ptarmigan were the real cure for my SAD.

Nothing in nature is as white as a winter ptarmigan. All three species turn the color of snow around the time it starts to fly. Seasons stay open for the entire winter in most areas, and the birds are widely distributed. This does not mean that hunting them is easy, a qualification that is largely self-imposed. I learned early on that hunting or fishing from Alaska's limited road system can be crowded, although I seldom saw anyone else hunting ptarmigan in January no matter where I was. However, getting into the Bush had already become an integral part of all my Alaska outdoor experiences, and I didn't want to give that up just because the temperature was below zero.

The first year I was eligible for a resident Alaska hunting license, I drew a tag for the Resurrection caribou herd near my Kenai Peninsula home. Despite its relative proximity to civilization the hunt promised to be challenging, as there were no roads or places to land an airplane anywhere near where the caribou lived. While reaching them would be possible with an ambitious hike, making the return trip carrying a caribou would be another matter. However, there was a reason why I'd trailered my horses all the way up the Alcan Highway and this was it.

The caribou hunt was interesting but tangential to the current discussion, so I'll cut to the chase. Another horse-owning friend and I packed in later in the season than we should have. I shot a large bull at the onset of a blizzard. After hunkering down for a few days, we headed out in snow so deep the horses' bellies were dragging. At the top of a pass five miles from the road, we ran into flock after flock of rock ptarmigan, intelligence that immediately went into my hard drive.

Early the following October, another friend and I made the hike. I realized that the concentration of birds I'd seen previously could have been a one-off and didn't know if we'd find any at all. I needn't have worried. Tracking pure white birds against a background of snow made for interesting shooting, but we kept Sky busy for hours. As in most areas away from population centers a generous limit was in effect, and we reached it. We did some slipping and sliding beneath full packs on the way back downhill but carrying 20 ptarmigan is a lot easier than carrying half a caribou. While this was certainly no catered lodge shooting expedition, it sure helped me get through a few more months of Alaska winter.

By then the sun was on its way back north. A stable high-pressure system had brought calm winds and sunlight sparkling from a fresh dusting of snow—ideal conditions for another version of winter ptarmigan hunting.

This technique begins with the unlikely observation that it's possible to spot ptarmigan tracks on fresh snow from the air. Unfortunately, that means flying low and slow while scanning the ground, which every pilot knows as a recipe for trouble. Friends and I learned how to solve that problem with two Super Cubs. The first flew over likely looking patches of willow paying attention to nothing but flying the airplane while the second trailed at higher altitude. Whenever the lead Cub flushed a flock of ptarmigan, they were easy for the second to spot, at which point it became time to look for a place to land.

That day, I was flying in the trailing position with Sky on the rear seat when a huge flock of ptarmigan erupted beneath the lead airplane. Fortunately, a frozen lake lay nearby. Landing on bare ice in an aircraft equipped with skis can turn you into a hockey puck, with no brakes and the end of the lake approaching at alarming speed. There wasn't much snow on this lake, but there was enough to slow us down with room to spare. Then it became time to let Sky bound down from his seat, have our usual debate about whether or not we needed snowshoes, grab our guns, and go look for the birds.

Earlier, I alluded to the differences between summer and winter ptarmigan hunting, which the next hour's events illustrate nicely. At that time of year, the birds will no longer be in naïve family groups. Like their sharptail relatives, once the snow starts to fly they often congregate in huge flocks like the one I spotted from the air, and they always seem to have a sentry or two posted to watch for trouble. I felt certain those birds had never heard a shotgun bark, but they had faced a steady onslaught of predators since they hatched the previous summer—raptors, lynx, foxes—all highly efficient and adept at keeping themselves fed. The easy birds were long gone.

I knew we were facing a challenge when I spotted a pair of birds perched high in a line of barren brush, an unusual hangout for ptarmigan unless they are alert to trouble. There was no point in strategizing an elaborate stalk. Some birds would either hold or they wouldn't. They didn't. When we were still well out of shotgun range, brush began to belch ptarmigan—a dozen, two dozen, a hundred—until making even rough estimates of their numbers became impossible. The hunt was over, but we were still left enjoying a remarkable sight—pure white birds scattering as if someone had spilled a box of pearls from the sky.

Sometimes a large flock like this will leave a few cooperative stragglers behind, but not that day. Pursuing the main body of birds was obviously futile, since they were last seen heading west toward the crest of the Alaska Range. With the equinox over a month away daylight was still limited, so it was time to head for home. While our trip may have come a cropper as a bird hunt, at least I got to see the sun again after spending months feeling like it was gone forever.

By this point it should be clear that there is no such thing as a typical ptarmigan hunt. Early season willow ptarmigan on the tundra with pointing dogs are clearly the cream of the crop, and there is always the allure of the wilderness. I can only imagine what it would be like to meet *Lagopus lagopus* in the Scottish Highlands: beaters, loaders, hides, tweeds, and vintage wines waiting upon return from the field. That would be shooting rather than hunting, but I'd still like to see it someday.

I guess.

11.

Singing the Blues

Aldo Leopold once observed that game is a phenomenon of edges. As usual Leopold was right, especially in the case of early season blue grouse. The edge I chose to hunt that September morning ran along an open sub-alpine park covered with native grasses and teeming with snowberry, rose hips, and grasshoppers, all favored grouse foods. A steep mountainside covered with lodgepole pine lay behind it, and the two habitats met on a well-defined ridgeline. The meandering edge between them practically defined blue grouse habitat.

I was there early that morning because I knew it was going to be scorching hot down on the prairie where we had opened the upland season a few days previously. We'd shot some sharptails, but they'd been scarce and Huns had been scarcer. I didn't want to subject the dogs to another day of hot weather hunting with so little game available. At least the mountains would provide cooler temperatures and a change of scenery.

With Lori running errands out of town and Max enjoying a well-earned day off back in the kennel, Maggie and I made a bare bones team as we set off into a light and variable mountain breeze. Several hundred yards from the truck I heard a bird flush wild down in the trees, but it didn't sound as if it flew very far. When I set off downhill to investigate, the bird exploded from a lodgepole high overhead, and

I snapped off a shot through the branches that produced nothing but pine needles. Blue grouse hunting can be like that.

Ten minutes later, Maggie went on point near a copse of stunted pines. This time the birds cooperated, and a pair of blues thundered into the air as I walked in behind the dog. A blue grouse's wingbeat has the speed of a ruff's coupled with the deep bass undertones of a wild turkey's and can be unnerving no matter how many times you've heard it. The first shot again required me to deal with some obstructing branches, although I had the distinct impression that the bird had gone down along with the pine needles. The second shot was longer but open, and I would have felt embarrassed had I missed. Maggie made short work of the two routine retrieves.

We had to cover a lot of rocky ground and cross our share of contour lines before we found the next group of birds. By the time we had circled back to the truck my game vest was dragging at my shoulders, delightfully laden with some of the best eating that upland hunting has to offer. As Maggie lapped down a bowl of water, I gazed off the ridge and across the prairie below, where silver buffaloberry was already shimmering in the heat. For once, one of my unconventional decisions had worked out according to plan.

That doesn't happen every day.

Pausing with the dogs to appreciate the scenery from blue grouse habitat.

For readers east of the Mississippi there is only one grouse. Fair enough—the ruffed grouse is a noble game bird with a storied role in the history of American wing-shooting that deserves its near monopoly on wing-shooters' attention in New England and the upper Midwest. Options among the grouse family expand considerably in mountain, prairie, and tundra habitat, where in addition to ruffs hunters can pursue sharptails, sage grouse, spruce grouse, three species of ptarmigan, and the focus of this piece—blue grouse.

Alert readers will note that I have presented a biological inaccuracy. In 2006, the splitters won the battle with the lumpers, and the American Ornithological Union divided what we'd always known as blue grouse into two separate species. The newly created sooty grouse occupies coastal forest habitat from northern California to Alaska, where I have hunted them in the state's southeastern panhandle. That's a strange business though, which often involves locating males in dense rainforest habitat during the spring mating season by blowing into an empty beer bottle to imitate their calls. I've done it as a means of providing fresh camp meat during wilderness expeditions for bears and steelhead. However, spring "hooter" hunts are more like hunting turkeys than grouse and are not to be confused with real wing-shooting.

The second new species, the dusky grouse, inhabits mountainous interior terrain from northern Canada to our own Southwest. Few bird hunters target them, but I consider them one of our premier upland gamebirds. Having referred to both new species as blue grouse for over 50 years I'll continue to do so here, as does almost everyone else I know who hunts them. Old habits die hard.

Blues of both species are big, weighing nearly twice as much as ruffs. Among North American upland game birds, only sage grouse are larger. This is good news given their exceptional table quality. I enjoy eating blue grouse as much as any other bird I hunt, an important source of motivation when climbing the hills to reach them.

During the early part of the season the dusky grouse's diet consists mainly of seeds, berries, and insects. At that time of year birds are most likely found at elevations from four to six thousand feet in open areas along the edges of coniferous forest. As snow begins to fall sometime between September and November, their diet changes to needles from various evergreens. Then they move upslope and "go to the trees," making them one of the few mountain wildlife species that heads to higher elevations as winter approaches.

This phenomenon makes them harder to hunt, not just because it requires more effort to reach them. On sparse forest floor, the birds become spookier and less likely to hold for a pointing dog. When they flush beyond shotgun range—an event more often heard than seen—they are likely to wind up high in a pine tree where dogs are unable to locate them. While I don't shoot sitting birds from trees no matter how good they taste (at least not with a firearm), I'm not above taking a High House Station One skeet shot as one departs—if the dog and I can locate it in the first place. Furthermore, as blues begin to act like spruce grouse they also begin to taste more like them. Blues for the table are best targeted before they go to the trees. I'll add some brief notes on spruce grouse shortly.

This late season behavior stands in contrast to what a hunter with dogs can expect from dusky grouse earlier in the season. While there's always the possibility of a wild flush then, given adequate ground cover in grassy edge habitat blues are likely to hold for dogs and offer good shooting in semi-open terrain. Rises are noisy and the birds are fast, offering plenty of challenge even for experienced guns. While blues are solitary for much of the year and are not true covey birds like Huns and quail, they are often still organized in family groups in early autumn much like sharptails. The sight of a half-dozen big blues exploding in front of a pointing dog and thundering away against a background of autumn scenery can be as exciting as upland wing-shooting gets. They like to flush downhill, a point to remember when walking in ahead of a dog.

Now, all you must do is find one—and hit it.

The time was early November, the place high in one of central Montana's isolated "island" mountain ranges. Snow had fallen several times since the upland opener, but it had yet to accumulate for more than a day. The natural phenomena by which I mark the end of fall—the sight of whitetail bucks chasing does and the sound of migrating geese overhead—had yet to greet my eyes and ears. After two months of sharptails and Huns and one month of pheasants, I woke up that morning in the mood for something different.

That's why Lori, Max, Maggie, and I headed for the hills. I'd hoped to find blues in another series of high meadows where we'd found them earlier. However, the two wirehairs swept energetically across the cover for over an hour without a hint of interest in game. I deduced that the blues had gone to the trees. Now we were going too.

The contour lines grew closer together as we headed uphill, but we finally reached a timbered ridge that offered reasonable walking. I ranged the dogs downhill onto the steep, shady, north-facing side of the mountain. On top of the world, or at least that part of it, we could look down upon a yawning abyss that stretched for miles toward the prairie below and all the way to the distant Missouri River. I reminded myself that climbers did this just for fun even when they weren't carrying shotguns.

We soon lost visual contact with the dogs as they vanished into dense stands of pine. Then I heard the steady beep of Max's collar indicating a point below us. As Lori and I started to slip and slide downhill through the pine duff, the low throb of beating wings filled the air. We then caught a glimpse of a blue grouse setting its wings and gliding off into the middle of nowhere. We weren't going after that bird.

After collecting the dogs, we continued along the ridge. The next collar to sound off belonged to Maggie, and it didn't take long to reach her. She was holding still with her eyes darting through the pines overhead like a hound that has treed a cougar without being able to pinpoint the tree holding the cat. After reaching her side, I studied the limbs above me for several minutes before identifying a plump, dark form sitting near the top of a lodgepole.

Spruce grouse—the true fool hens—don't do that. When a spruce grouse flushes into a tree it seldom lands much above eye level, making it an ideal target for a bow (I've fed plenty of moose camps that way) or even a rock, if you're hungry and have a good pitching arm. Late season blues are more likely to head high as this one did, leaving me scratching my head about what to do next. Sixty years earlier, my father had taught me that one simply doesn't shoot sitting grouse with a shotgun. No matter how badly I wanted the dogs to sniff some feathers, it wasn't going to happen that way.

Fortunately, the bird resolved the problem by going airborne and hurtling away through the tops of the pines. Despite its humble beginnings the shot turned into a pleasant challenge, although a lot of pine needles came down with the bird. At my command, Maggie tore off downhill through the scree and retrieved the grouse while Max stood by with a bewildered look on his face.

By the time we set off downhill toward the truck, we'd hiked for miles in rugged terrain and enjoyed a total of three blue grouse encounters that produced one shot and no solid points, all on the same mountain where I'd enjoyed fast shooting and good dog work two months prior.

If it were easy, everyone would be doing it. Everyone wasn't, and solitude during the middle of a busy upland season may have provided the day's greatest reward—except for the roasted blue grouse on the table that night.

12.

Sentimental Journey

As I step out onto the deck with a cup of steaming coffee in my hand, all my senses concur. Autumn—the brief window of time between Indian summer and winter here in the Mountain West—has arrived. The air feels crisp against my face, but the absence of breeze eliminates its potential sting. A flock of mallards newly arrived from Alberta sends a chorus of feeding chuckles up the hill as the birds circle the creek in the valley below. The new morning sunlight has left the coulee behind our rural home awash in gold, for my standard description of our local terrain as "high plains" comes with an asterisk. While the prairie to the east offers all the benefits of savannah habitat, the valley where we live lies nestled in a ring of isolated mountain ranges. The one rising right behind our house contain long fingers of deciduous trees that turn gold for several weeks before the snow flies. There are few places like it elsewhere around Montana. During our brief autumns I can almost imagine myself back in upstate New York where my wing-shooting career began more years ago than I care to remember.

That theme defines my plans for the morning even though they have to compete with a number of options. Brown trout are running up the creek below the house. Although the whitetail rut still lies several weeks away, I feel confident I could fill a doe tag with my longbow today if I cared to. All those northern mallards will be feeding somewhere nearby. But this feels like a perfect day to address the mission that's been floating around my head during six weeks of sharptails, pheasants, and Huns even though it involves nothing more dramatic than a short hike down the coulee and a longer walk down memory lane.

Today I plan to re-explore my neglected relationship with the game bird that started it all: *Bonasa umbellus,* the ruffed grouse.

One October day circa 1959, I set off eagerly beside my father toward a favorite piece of grouse cover we called the Hole. By then I'd trudged along behind my dad through lots of classical grouse habitat such as abandoned apple orchards and beech-studded ridgelines. This cover was different. A nasty bog overgrown with tangled alders, the Hole could have contained grizzlies as well as grouse for all I knew. Although it probably didn't cover more than 50 acres it looked like vast wilderness to my young eyes. Once or twice each season we'd find it stuffed with migrating woodcock, but grouse provided its main attraction. There were always birds there, at least for those willing to hunt hard enough to find them.

Because of the difficulty of the terrain and the thickness of the cover, the Hole offered a legitimate wing-shooting challenge no matter what the level of ability behind the gun. During the seasons prior to my family's move to the Northwest, I knocked a lot of leaves to the ground for every bird I slipped into my game vest there. That morning, I was carrying my own shotgun into the field for the first time in my life.

Full disclosure, now that the passage of decades has exceeded the statute of limitations: I didn't have a hunting license. The state of New York didn't think I was old enough for one but I was, and not just because I'd been holding my own on Sunday mornings with the senior members of the local skeet club for several years. My father had been drumming the principles of woodsmanship, hunting ethics, and firearm safety into me since I'd been old enough to read *Winnie the Pooh* on my own. For several seasons I'd followed diligently behind him and the dog, observing, asking questions, and scanning the treetops for grey squirrels so I could ask for his shotgun and enjoy an opportunity to add to our bag. I was ready. My father knew it, and his was the only opinion that mattered.

I already recognized that hunting the Hole would be an exercise in futility without the services of a good dog. Fortunately we had one: Bits, who is worth a story by himself. After an unfortunate experience with an English pointer that proved good field trial dogs don't necessarily make good grouse dogs, we had become interested in German shorthairs. A friend of my father who raised and field-trialed them successfully gave us Bits as the runt of a litter. During his derby year we entered Bits in two field trials. He placed in both and beat several dogs from his original kennel, confirming that one really shouldn't look a gift horse in the mouth. Because we wanted a closer ranging dog than the field trial judges wanted that was the end of his competitive career, but he continued to prove himself every fall.

An hour into the Hole that day, the copper bell on Bits's collar (the esthetically superior if less practical means of keeping track of bird dogs prior to electronic locators) stopped tinkling. My father and I set off abreast to find him. Suddenly an explosion of wings rose from the alders ahead, and then a grouse was hurtling across a gap in my side of the brush. Assured of the shot's safety, I threw the shotgun to my shoulder, drove the muzzles in front of the speeding bird, and slapped the trigger, at which point the grouse collapsed in the most glorious puff of feathers imaginable.

While my father was both too polite and too proud to invoke the specter of luck, I sensed that something noteworthy had just occurred. As if to prove the point, several hundred yards farther into the cover we flushed a second grouse in front of Bits, and I shot again with identical results. Thus I finished my first morning of wing-shooting two for two on difficult birds in difficult cover. The consensus around the dinner table that night was that a miracle had occurred.

Indeed, it had. I've conveniently lost track of the number of shells I needed to bring down the third ruffed grouse of my career, but the statistics scarcely mattered. I was hooked. In the three remaining years prior to our departure for the West I forgot about sports, girls, and other conventional adolescent interests every October just so I could pursue the King of Game Birds. Even after decades of hunting experience in Montana, Alaska, and elsewhere around the world, I'm not sure I've ever had it better.

When I landed in eastern Montana in 1973, shotguns, dogs, and gamebirds were just as important to me as they'd been back when we hunted the Hole. The area's upland hunting, which I knew of through family friends, played a crucial role in a career decision ordinarily determined by more conventional factors such as opportunities for professional advancement and money. Armed with young legs and a limitless supply of enthusiasm I began to tackle the rich local autumn agenda, which included quarries both familiar and exotic.

I'd hunted some pheasants and Huns before in Washington State, but never in the numbers I encountered on the Montana prairie. Sharptails and sage grouse were new to me. Although I soon tired of the latter, the former became a favorite autumn staple. Throw in the staggering waterfowl numbers those wet years produced plus the area's abundant big game opportunities and it's a wonder I got anything else done from September through December. Now I'm not sure I did.

Distracted by this embarrassment of riches, it took a move to a more mountainous part of the state to make me start thinking about ruffed grouse again. Montana ruffs don't receive a lot of attention from hunters or wildlife managers, who lump them together with spruce and blues under the heading "mountain grouse" in Montana's regulations as if all three were one and the same. Few people here hunt any of the three regularly enough to matter, although I did grow to enjoy hunting blue grouse as described in the previous chapter.

The yawn with which most western upland hunters greet the East Coast's premier game bird arises from several factors, most related to the quality of the competition. Compared to sharptails and Huns, bird densities are low even in good habitat. Mountain grouse terrain is tougher than the prairie. Hunting it obligates the hunter to confront a lot more up and down. Thicker cover makes for trickier shooting, a positive or a negative depending on one's point of view. The real issues are the birds' habits and behavior, which differ so much from their eastern counterparts' that it can be hard to remember they're members of the same species.

Although classically applied to *Falcipennis canadensis*, the spruce grouse, the derivative term "fool hen" could be used to describe any of Montana's mountain grouse including, with apologies to its eastern enthusiasts, the ruffed. As a kid I hardly ever remember seeing a ruffed grouse on the ground during hunting season. They were either invisible in their excellent natural camouflage or speeding through the trees after a noisy, nerve-jangling rise. Not so for the western version. Every fall, I'd spot ruffs strutting across fallen leaves in the coulee behind our home, looking and acting like well-dressed chickens. When carrying a shotgun I always felt content to watch them until they melted back into the cover. The prohibition against shooting a bird on the ground was one of those ethical principles my father hammered into me at an early age with all the moral authority of Moses walking down off the mount.

Which is not to say that I never killed any Montana ruffed grouse. Shooting a sitting bird with my shotgun may have been anathema, but shooting one with a bow and arrow was another matter. Although I seldom targeted them deliberately, the ruffs I encountered while hunting elk or deer with my longbow always looked like fair game. On more than one occasion I spared elk camp another meal of pork and beans by killing some. Those campfire meals often included a big blue or two in the mix, often garnished with fresh shaggy mane mushrooms. Wilderness cuisine seldom tasted better.

As I became more reflective with age I began to entertain the notion of a real ruffed grouse hunt just for old times' sake. That's when I finally recognized the missing element of the equation that had subliminally dampened my enthusiasm for western ruffs as much as the birds' frequently goofy behavior. To do this right, I was going to have to hunt with the right dog.

My kennel had hardly been empty during the long interval since my arrival on the plains. Three months before I left the Montreal General Hospital for Montana I'd acquired my first Labrador retriever, a breed ideally suited to the complex job description a western gun dog faces: geese over decoys at sunrise, Huns in the grasslands in the morning, roosters in the creek bottoms that afternoon, ducks on a pothole at last shooting light. I soon had two or three Labs at all times in various stages of development and senescence. That didn't leave much room for anything else. While I never doubted that a steady flushing Lab would prove a useful companion in ruffed grouse cover, that wasn't the way I'd done it as a kid and wasn't the way I wanted to do it now.

Enter Maggie. After experiencing an epiphany while hunting Mearns quail with my old friend Mike Hedrick and his fine wirehairs, I realized that something important had been missing from my fall agenda for too many years. Maggie's emergence as a canine star by the end of her second season only added to that impression. Her appearance proved as pleasantly surprising as her talent in the field. Some wirehairs look a lot like the German shorthairs to which they are related, and Maggie matured to become one. By the time she reached early adulthood, she could have passed for Bits' sister.

Maggie holding a ruffed grouse and a mouthful of memories.

So here we are: the right day, the right dog, even the right shotgun, with the year's first dusting of snow thrown in. While the gun isn't the same 12-gauge I carried back when I was a kid, it's a spitting image clone of the Browning doubles my father loved. With no one else around today, Maggie and I set off alone together into the coulee.

I know this terrain as intimately as anyone can know a piece of ground, and why not? It would be impossible to tally the number of hours I've spent here over the last 30 years—hunting, tracking, photographing wildlife, or simply sitting and letting the weariness of the larger world evaporate as only the combination of solitude and wild places can allow. If there are grouse to be found today, they will be at the bottom of the coulee in the line of aspens and brush lining the creek bed, where no surface water has run since May.

Preparation for this hunt involved obtaining a special piece of equipment. Although I'm not a fan of technology in the field, I like to know the location of my dogs in thick cover. I eventually yielded to the practicality of a locator collar, which I find invaluable when I'm hunting Mearns quail in the oaks or ringnecks in the brambles. However, this device was not consistent with my memories of ruffed grouse hunting. When I searched for an old-fashioned belled collar I had trouble finding one. I wound up wiring a cowbell to an old leather strap. By the time we've covered a quarter mile of brush today, its musical cadence has nearly lulled me to sleep. Then it stops, leaving me to play a game of hide-and-seek with the dog. Finally I spot Maggie frozen mid-stride with an intensity that would have done old Bits proud.

Now I must ask a favor of the bird. If it waddles away in front of the dog or flutters up into a nearby tree, the whole exercise will have been in vain, but this must be my day. Wingbeats greet me as I walk in ahead of Maggie. The airborne bird cuts behind just enough brush to make the close shot challenging. A shower of golden leaves follows, but I feel oddly confident that the grouse has fallen too. Moments later, Maggie—who retrieves as capably as she points, at least on dry land—confirms this impression by delivering the bird to my outstretched hand.

Since we have done what we came to do, I declare victory and start back up the hill with Maggie at heel. The circle still lacks one element of its completion, for the generic name *Bonasa* translates roughly as "good when roasted" which is just what I have in mind. While my concept of wild game cookery has evolved since the early days, there's still no better way to prepare a ruffed grouse— plucked not skinned, as James Bond might have put it—than by roasting it simply as my mother used to do, with nothing between the bird and my palette but a dash of salt and pepper. I'll need something else to stretch the lone grouse into a dinner for two once Lori returns from work at the hospital (one of us has to do it), but with several Huns and sharptails hanging in the barn there's plenty to choose from.

And there you have it: a simple walk through the woods with none of the epic qualities that conventionally define a great day in the field. But when an hour's events can bridge a half-century's gap between the beginning of a wing-shooting career and what I hope is not quite yet its end, one point and one shot can make an epic all their own.

Partridge and Quail

13.
Dinner for Two

One of my favorite sharptail hunts begins on a rounded ridge that affords a splendid view of farmlands and prairie rolling northward toward the Missouri breaks while timbered peaks rise behind to the south. A grain field straddles the ridge and an open draw rises from its flank. A mile downhill, the draw joins a complex coulee with denser brush. That coulee eventually climbs back toward the opposite side of the grain field, allowing a nearly complete circle to the point of beginning. One could hunt this cover in any number of ways, but after countless visits over many seasons I have become a creature of habit. Sharptails favor the draw, so during September I always hunt it first, saving the heavy cover in the large coulee for pheasant season and the rare occasions when I haven't killed a limit of grouse by the time I reach it.

The field was in stubble that year, providing a vast food source for gamebirds. The cover surrounding it looked inviting. Grass still stood tall before the first hard frost. Scattered clumps of hawthorn in the open draw had already turned orange and yellow beneath an Indian summer sun as if nature had answered a challenge to paint a colorful panorama of ideal sharptail habitat. Nonetheless I felt uncertain, as preliminary reports from friends had described the year's grouse population as erratic due to variable local nesting conditions. However, I had no firsthand information, the only kind that counts.

I'd been absent from central Montana for nearly a month. Years earlier, a regular hunting partner and I swore that we'd never leave Montana in September, but I'd broken the rule that season and traveled north to join old friends in Alaska for an extended wilderness float trip. The details of that adventure properly belong to another story involving bows, arrows, fly rods, salmon, bears, and moose. I have described an earlier version of this favorite trip in the chapter on ptarmigan. As much as I love Alaska, nothing makes me appreciate my Montana home as profoundly as absence from it. I had missed Lori and the dogs the way a kid at summer camp misses his parents and I'm not ashamed to admit it. Now the promise of clear skies overhead, dry ground underfoot, and brush unlikely to contain a grizzly sow guarding her cubs offered an ideal welcome home.

What I really wanted from the cover even more than great dog work or snappy shooting was a simple brace of grouse to share with Lori. Ptarmigan had proved scarce up North that year, and subsisting for weeks on canned goods, grayling, and caribou steaks made me long for dinner from a real kitchen. After days on the river even tender caribou backstraps couldn't dispel a craving for variety. There were personal considerations as well, since Lori and I have always connected wonderfully with pots bubbling and pans sizzling. No culinary ties bind like wild game. Gone too long, I needed a few miles of bird cover and a grouse dinner with my wife to welcome me home again.

Then there were the dogs. A month is a long absence for two youngsters. Even though Lori had spent plenty of time with them while I was gone, I could already tell that Rocky was beginning his season minus some of the polish he'd shown over the summer. Kenai—Rocky's son, age six months—was still too much a puppy to know the difference between a bird hunt and a walk to the barn. Although I knew that letting them hit the cover together could lead to chaos, I couldn't bring myself to leave the puppy behind. Consequently, a duet of eager whining greeted me when I stopped beside the stubble and dropped the truck's tailgate.

Despite the sense of anticipation we took our time getting ready. This was our first upland outing of the season, and I needed a few minutes to review my mental checklist. When I opened the door on Rocky's side of the dog box, he boiled out with a forgivable lack of discipline. When I closed the back of the truck Kenai started to yip in protest at being left behind.

Rocky needed to run, and I let him. The friend who owns the property hadn't moved his cattle in yet and the grass was still thick enough to hold birds. While I'd rather hunt diffuse, open cover with a pointing dog, when I'm hunting with my Labs I let them run through it. Early in the season Huns and sharptails seldom fly far after a rise. I'd rather see birds and mark them down than walk past them undetected.

Nothing flushed from the grass. When we reached a patch of chokecherry at the head of the draw, I whistled Rocky in as per Sutton's Law: that's where the money was. Unfortunately, that morning it wasn't.

When we reached a clump of buffaloberry farther down the draw, Rocky pivoted mid-stride and charged in with his nose to the ground as I shouted a heads-up to Lori. The cackle that followed the first thunder of wingbeats identified the bird for me even before the flash of color cleared the brush. We had flushed a cock pheasant, whose season still lay two weeks away. Rocky circled back to my side as if to demand an explanation for my shotgun's silence. "Good dog!" was all I could offer, since I've never figured out a way to explain closed seasons to Labrador retrievers.

As we tacked our way along the draw the autumn scenery and the pleasant feel of the terrain beneath my boots compensated for the lack of shooting. The only other birds we flushed were two hen pheasants. I'd seen the same cover belch grouse by the dozen even when it looked less productive and could only ascribe its silence to the vagaries of the previous spring's weather. As we turned the corner at the bottom of the draw and started back up the main coulee toward the truck, I felt myself running out of philosophy. Although

I could live without an afternoon of blazing guns, Rocky still needed to taste some feathers and I wanted that gamebird dinner.

Bowhunting, of which I'd done plenty over the preceding weeks, demands a deliberate slowing of my natural pace in the field due to the need for stealth and the inherent limitations of traditional archery tackle. Not so in the pursuit of upland gamebirds, in which hunting harder offers a potential solution to most impasses. As we headed back uphill in the main coulee, the tug of the slope felt welcome against my legs. Although we sent the dog into every pocket of brush we passed, by the time we arrived back at the far edge of the stubble we had yet to hear the chuckle of flushing sharptails.

Lori was obviously growing weary of my guiding expertise. However, a tangled finger of brush extends right to the edge of the field's western edge, and I'd flushed plenty of birds there before. After I'd shouted a final word of encouragement, we took up positions on opposite sides of the brush and I urged Rocky into the thorns. To no avail as it turned out, for we reached the edge of the stubble without jumping a bird.

Max on point in typical Hun habitat. While I've taken plenty of Huns with my Labs, I now prefer to hunt them with our wirehairs.

There comes a point during every slow hunt at which you just stop hunting. As my boots hit the remains of the wheat crop, I knew I'd reached it. With the truck already in sight I was daydreaming, which is why the Huns' rise caught me off-guard. They're surprising birds even under the easiest circumstances, full of sound and fury, challenging even the keenest eye to isolate one bird from the noise and kill it. At that point in the day our eyes were no longer keen, and since the birds flushed between us without offering a safe shot we simply concentrated on marking the covey down.

The birds settled in several hundred yards away along the edge of the brush we'd just walked through. Anyone who doubts the utility of a flushing retriever in the pursuit of gray partridge should have seen what happened next. After walking down the edge of the cover with Rocky at heel, I released him from my side. Tacking into the wind, he nosed the covey into the air. I knew the steep terrain would make shooting difficult and it did, but when the birds appeared briefly—and safely—against the sky, I picked a target, slapped the trigger, and watched the bird I'd isolated tumble while the rest vanished over the lip of the rise.

I caught a glimpse of the covey again when it briefly reappeared in silhouette against the sky. Meanwhile, Rocky had been paying attention to the fall rather than the rest of the covey. By the time I had the birds marked down for the second time he was sitting at my side with the dead Hun ready for presentation. Evidently, all his polish had not been lost during my absence.

The third rise passed much as the second: a bit more trouble locating the birds; a sudden eruption of wings courtesy of the dog; the front half of a potential double followed by silence from my second barrel as the Huns disappeared into the folds of the hillside; another effortless, workmanlike retrieve. At that point, I decided it was time to declare victory, leave some brood stock behind, and retreat from the field.

Back at the truck, we let young Kenai out for a badly needed romp. When he'd settled down I introduced him to his first Hun.

That was all it took to earn his forgiveness for the indignity of being left behind. Then, with afternoon light beginning to add new intensity to the landscape's colors, we loaded up and headed for home sweet home.

I would have preferred to hang the birds a day or two, but the weather was too hot and I didn't have time, not after waiting all those long, chilly Alaska evenings for just the sort of meal I had in mind. While Lori arranged treats for the dogs, I dressed the birds and whipped up a marinade of soy sauce and sesame oil. There isn't a lot to a Hungarian partridge. I've easily torn through two of them myself after a long day in the field. We made the most of what we had, roasting them simply and serving them on a bed of wild rice with a freshly tossed green salad on the side. With both dogs snoozing beneath the table, we ate what we'd shot and talked about everything that had happened while I'd been away. By the time we cleared the dishes, I knew I'd come home at last.

We're all suckers for the Big Show, with clouds of birds and furious shooting. I've enjoyed my share of days like that myself. Writers, perhaps, bear their share of responsibility for the misconception that anything less doesn't represent hunting at its finest. As I've matured (why does that sound so much better than "grown older"?), I've learned to appreciate the experiences tucked away in the days when I had to walk a lot of miles for not many birds.

That year, the first hunt of the season provided an opportunity to enjoy something I needed even more than the sharptails that never appeared: time to appreciate my wife, my dogs, and the remarkable place I call home. I'll take a hunt like that any day.

14.

Little Fools

After my old friend Mike Hedrick retired from a distinguished career in the Fish and Wildlife Service he realized that there were better places to spend winters than Montana and Alaska, which both of our families had called home off and on for years. He eventually bought a house in southern Arizona and became a Mearns quail hunting specialist. The invitation to chase birds with him there proved irresistible.

On my first morning in Mearns country, the freshness of the desert air and the grandeur of the mountain scenery felt compromised by the litter UDAs (undocumented aliens in Border Patrol speak) had left behind on their way north. However, I wasn't there to engage in border polemics. Then and in the seasons that followed I always left a gallon jug of water on the hood of the truck in case some family's kids were dying of thirst. That wasn't politics; it was human decency.

We spent two hours hiking up the bottom of a remote canyon while Doc, Mike's wirehair, combed the oak-studded terrain on either side. When we finally crested the saddle at the end of the draw and paused to water the dog, Mike suggested that we turn around and go back down the route we'd just taken even though we hadn't flushed a bird.

"Wouldn't it make more sense to cross the ridge and hunt back downhill through some new cover?" I asked.

"Did you notice those diggings in the dirt along the bottom of the wash?" Mike replied. "That's Mearns quail sign. They roost in the grass on the sidehills and keep bankers' hours, but by now they'll be headed downhill to feed, leaving scent for the dog. I wouldn't be surprised to find several coveys on the way back to the truck."

As if to prove the point, Doc locked up tight before we were halfway back down the canyon. Mike and Lori established shooting lanes on either side of the wash while I walked in just ahead of Doc's nose. "False point," I finally declared after a circuit through the sparse ground cover. "No birds here."

"Yes there are," said Mike, who knew his dog. "Start kicking."

I shrugged my shoulders and kicked. Nothing happened. Then I kicked some more, and all hell broke loose. Covey rises by other quail species usually display some organization, with most of the birds departing in approximately the same direction. Mearns quail are more chaotic when they flush. Less a rise that a detonation, birds were suddenly everywhere—briefly. Swinging hard and fast, I decapitated a dead oak tree and could only hope that a quail had fallen somewhere amid the cloud of wood dust. Then I watched Mike drop a bird, as did Lori. Minutes later, Doc—a pointer first, a retriever a second—grudgingly presented my wife with a dark, exotically marked twin to the bird he'd just delivered to Mike. When he finally brought back a third, not even its small size could compromise my satisfaction.

Live oaks, steep terrain, and a dog on point; all essential components of a Mearns quail hunt.

Thanks to its limited range and secretive habits, the Mearns quail may be the country's most obscure game bird. The confusion surrounding its name doesn't help.

In 1914 its first scientific description came courtesy of Dr. Edgar A. Mearns, whose eponym remains attached to the species today. Coincidentally, Mearns was a military surgeon stationed in our desert Southwest as was Dr. Elliot Coues, who first described the whitetail subspecies that shares the Mearns quail's southwestern desert habitat. The proper common name Montezuma quail accurately associates the bird with Mexico, where most of its native range lies. The cock bird's clownish facial markings invoke the stereotypical *commedia dell arte* character Harlequin, an alternative common name the Mearns shares with our similarly marked sea duck and an unrelated African quail discussed in a later chapter. Yet another common name, fool quail, is a pejorative derived from the birds' willingness to rely on their camouflage and hold tight enough to let predators step over the top of them. Since it works, I'm not sure what's so foolish about that behavior.

Because of their precise habitat requirements, Mearns cover is easy to identify: steep terrain at elevations from three to five thousand feet, grassy ground cover, and a moderate to dense canopy of oak. If the hills I'm looking at don't meet those criteria, I don't hunt them.

In contrast to the Southwest's "desert" quail (Gamble's and scaled quail), Mearns depend on summer monsoons rather than winter rains for the success of the hatch—one reason why numbers of the two groups can fluctuate in different directions. While Mearns chicks, like most young game birds, eat insects, the adults' diet consists largely of oxalis and sedge tubers found below ground. Their feet are well adapted for digging, evidence of which can help locate coveys. Unlike other quail, Mearns don't form large flocks late in the season, when they remain organized in small coveys averaging six to twelve birds. They don't travel far and usually limit their home territory to 15 acres or so in the fall. Find sign, and the birds should be there somewhere.

In this book I have deliberately avoided cluttering observations and reminiscences with attempts at instruction, largely to avoid the impression of trying to pose as an expert in anything other than enjoyment of the outdoors. I make an exception here simply because the species under discussion is likely unfamiliar to so many readers.

Perhaps the best measure of the fanaticism any fish, fowl, or big game species inspires is the extent to which its enthusiasts will alter their lives to accommodate its pursuit. I would not have owned a house in coastal Alaska if it weren't for wild steelhead. I have friends who wouldn't live anywhere they couldn't hunt elk. In this spirit,

Mearns quail have inspired the acquisition of many winter homes in our Southwestern desert including, for several years, our own.

Mearns quail are strikingly beautiful birds, but it takes more than a pretty face to inspire such devotion. They have an "it" quality that can best be described as a mystique. That first hunt with Mike made me a regular in a corner of the country I'd previously visited no more than occasionally in search of javelina and Coues deer with my bow. The next addition to my kennel was a wirehair from the same bloodlines as Mike's Doc.

How to explain the fascination so many experienced upland hunters feel for this tiny gamebird? The terrain is beautiful, if physically challenging. Few upland quarries offer more exciting opportunities for pointing dogs to showcase their talents. The birds are delicious, and a good cook can easily turn a successful hunt into a celebration on the table. I think the heart of the matter lies in the Mearns quail's challenge on the wing. I don't know a tougher bird to hit anywhere in North America.

That statement can inspire endless debate, and I have no intention of insulting anyone's favorite upland quarry. However, there are a limited number of candidates for the "most challenging" title. I still remember how tough ruffed grouse and woodcock could be, but most of that difficulty arose from the density of the cover they inhabited. Out West, chukar top most lists because of the physically demanding terrain they favor, but at least they offer open shots.

Imagine the steep, rocky slopes where chukar live covered in live oaks and scrub. Next, visualize the simultaneous explosion of multiple birds from beneath the dog's nose, each whizzing off through the trees in a different direction. Now maintain your balance, isolate a target, identify a shooting lane, and slap the trigger. You get the idea.

Perhaps best of all, Mearns quail largely inhabit the public domain. As access to prime upland cover on private land declines, hunters like me have learned to look beyond pheasants to game birds that live on the wild side, from chukar to ptarmigan to mountain grouse. While some Mearns quail inhabit modest, open terrain at lower elevations, I've done my hunting up the hill on public land within Forest Service boundaries. That can mean miles of vigorous hiking in steep country, but I'd rather deal with contour lines than locked gates. If the birds next to the road have been picked over as they eventually will be, there's a simple solution to the problem: climb farther. Granted, that has become more difficult as the years have passed since that first Mearns quail encounter, but I hope I never stop trying.

As a definitive measure of the enthusiasm we developed for these birds, when Lori and I decided to trade our coastal Alaska second home for a place in the desert near the Mexican border, it wasn't to escape Montana winter cold and snow. It was so we could hunt Mearns quail.

Few hunters from Alaska and Montana can claim to be true Mearns quail experts, and I don't. However, I've hunted them long enough now to have learned a few points I wish I'd known when I started. First, it's all about the dogs. Absent a good pointing dog, you're probably not going to see Mearns quail let alone shoot any. Some dogs, even those with proven track records on other species, have trouble at first with Mearns quail for reasons I can't explain. Be patient. Because it can be a long way between coveys in convoluted terrain, a locator collar is indispensable. Beeper collars also help prevent nasty encounters between dogs and javelina, which are common in Mearns quail country. Although thorns and burrs aren't nearly the problem they are in some desert quail habitat, it's still prudent to carry a hemostat and pocket comb to remove them from dogs.

Don't forget the first rule of desert travel: Carry enough water. You may find stock tanks or springs in the bottom of some washes, but don't count on it in unfamiliar terrain. If you need a liter of water, the dog will need four. You can't carry too much.

Don't burn the dogs out by starting too early in the day, before the birds have begun to move. An experienced friend assures me that the later in the day he hunts, the more birds he finds. Eleven in the morning until three in the afternoon is about right. At that time of day, concentrate on shady areas in the bottom of the washes. While no one can predict exactly what a covey will do when it flushes, some birds are likely to fly uphill. Try to have someone covering shooting lanes in that direction before walking in on a point.

Like all game birds, Mearns quail numbers fluctuate up and down in natural cycles, in their case largely as a function of summer rainfall. I generally don't pay much attention to upland bird population forecasts because I'm going hunting no matter what they say and usually manage to find some birds somewhere. However, I've hunted Mearns quail during population peaks and valleys, and the difference is striking. If I were going to make one trip to the Southwest to hunt these birds, I'd wait for positive reports from a reliable source, preferably other experienced hunters.

As noted in the preface, the outdoor world divides into generalists and specialists. If you want to know *how* to do something, ask a specialist. I do better with *why*. Despite its potential for bruised feet, tired legs, turned ankles, banged up shotguns, and overall exhaustion, the why of Mearns quail hunting isn't difficult to define: gorgeous country, teamwork with the dogs, challenging shooting, and the most exotic looking game bird on the continent. No group of outdoor sportsmen I know defines the specialist's capacity for obsession like Mearns quail hunters.

The quarry may be fool quail, but those who devote their lives to their pursuit may be the greatest fools of all.

15.

The Best Little Partridge on the Prairie

Here in Montana, opening day for grouse and Huns arrives over a month ahead of pheasant season. Absent the allure of cackling roosters many hunters are still at home then, waiting for October. Weather sometimes counters the solitude's appeal, for relentless summer sun can leave the prairie withered and the thermometer climbing toward triple digits.

Opening day is still opening day. Despite forecasts calling for temperatures reaching the 90s, sleeping in was not an option. I addressed the predicted scorcher by loading the truck with enough water to supply a desert expedition and enough bottles and pans so I could deliver it to the dogs whenever and wherever they needed it. Since I wanted to be out of the field by late morning, the alarm clock shattered the silence at an hour more appropriate to a hunt for waterfowl than upland birds.

The summer had been long and dry, and smoke from forest fires to the west had muted the light at the edges of the day for weeks on end. By the time we arrived at the friends' ranch we planned to hunt, the sun had cleared the horizon only to appear as a fuzzy scarlet ball glowing through the haze. The atmosphere felt surreal, but the dogs plainly didn't care. They knew something was up when I stopped the truck, and the chorus from the dog box immediately established that they were ready for the season to begin.

Kenai was aging by then and I'd brought him along to do some limited hunting from heel for old times' sake. The first long coulee belonged to Maggie and the day marked the start of her second season. If her precocious performance during her first kept its promise, the birds were in for a rough morning.

"Camera or shotgun?" I asked Lori as I dropped the tailgate on the truck, released Maggie, and listened to a sustained howl of protest from the other side of the dog box.

"Camera," she replied without hesitation.

After we crossed the first fence, I loaded my shotgun and set my legs against the hill with Lori beside me and Maggie ranging ahead. Generous spring rains had been followed by months of drought and record temperatures. Nonetheless, I'd seen plenty of young Huns along the back roads, and hikes near thicker cover revealed enough sharptails to leave me cautiously optimistic about both species.

Many hunters consider Huns primarily a species of level, open terrain near grain fields. True enough, but that's not the whole story. Some of my best Hun hunting has taken place in steep coulees and foothill terrain far from ground that has ever felt a plow's bite. I've always appreciated challenging, natural habitat. Even though the hills seem to grow steeper every season now, I still enjoy opportunities to get in shape—or stay there, depending on the previous summer's agenda.

Twenty minutes up the draw, Maggie affirmed both my choice of cover and my guarded optimism about the year's hatch when she hit an invisible wall that left her frozen and quivering. When the Hun covey exploded from the grass just as I reached the edge of shotgun range I had to settle for the front half of the potential double.

The size of the covey erased whatever chagrin I might have felt about that blown second shot, for it contained at least 15 Huns. After Maggie delivered the first bird of the season, we headed in pursuit. The Huns had disappeared over the crest of the nearest rise, but intuition and experience left me optimistic that we could find them. As soon as we crossed the ridge, I set off along the contour line toward the head of the next little draw, where Maggie went on point again. This time the birds held. After staggered rises from a single and a pair I had two more birds riding in the game vest. They had even cooperated for Lori and her camera by flying silhouetted against the sky with the morning light behind us. Since that was enough from one covey, I whistled Maggie to my side and we set off to look for a new one.

Focusing on one bird is essential during a Hun covey rise.

In common with the chukar and ring-necked pheasant—and in contrast to the sharptail, sage grouse, and California quail with which it shares much of its North American range—the gray partridge doesn't really belong in the American West. (Use the technically correct term "gray partridge" anywhere in Hun country and few will know what you're taking about save for an occasional biologist.) Initial introduction attempts from the birds' home in Asia and Eastern Europe during the late 1800s failed. Our current Hun populations derives almost entirely from birds released in Alberta during the early 1900s. How they managed to get here on their own and why they thrived when earlier releases failed remain unsolved mysteries.

The biology of the Hungarian partridge has been well documented elsewhere. (For a more detailed discussion, refer to *Western Wings* by Ben Williams.) Our purpose here is not to examine the bird scientifically, but to explore the *why* of Hun hunting with a little bit of *how* included. As with Mearns quail, I offer the latter primarily for the benefit of visiting readers unfamiliar with the species.

All six prairie game birds mentioned earlier have their appeal and their admirers. With the previously described exception of the sage grouse, I hunt them all regularly. Huns remain a personal favorite despite the depth and quality of the competition.

Let's begin with the dogs. Every part of the country has species that have traditionally defined upland bird seasons for pointing dog enthusiasts: bobwhite in the Deep South, ruffed grouse in the East and upper Midwest, Mearns and desert quail in the Southwest. The situation is a bit more muddled in the High Plains and the Northwest, largely due to the number of inviting options. Save for sage grouse, all the game birds mentioned earlier offer excellent opportunities for pointing dogs. For sheer enjoyment of the complex partnership between upland hunter and gun dog, few can rival the Hungarian partridge.

Which pointing breed doesn't really matter. Williams, who knows as much about Huns as anyone, loves his Brittanies with good reason. I've hunted Huns with Brittanies myself, as well as with English setters, shorthairs, and wirehairs—not to mention my versatile Labs. What makes Hun hunting special for pointing dogs is the nature of the bird and the terrain it inhabits.

Huns ask a bit of everything from a pointer. An experienced western hunter can usually stand on a ridge overlooking a thousand acres of pheasant habitat and identify the 10% of the cover holding 90% of the birds. Given their preference for open cover, Huns are different. They can be anywhere from sagebrush to stubble fields to native grass, from flatlands to steep coulees to rocky hillsides. I have enjoyed good Hun hunting in high mountainous terrain that looked better suited to elk than gamebirds. Finding them calls for dogs that can cover a lot of ground hunting long and hard. Because I use my dogs extensively on wild pheasants I don't always want them hunting hundreds of yards away, but early season Huns provide them with an opportunity to cover ground the way field trial judges want dogs to cover ground.

Once the hunter manages to break up a Hun covey—more on this later—the game changes. Pointing dogs are at their stylish best with birds that would rather hide than run, and few hide and hold quite like Huns after the first or second covey rise. This is the time for the dogs to emphasize style over stamina, and the stauncher the dog the better. Slow down, take your time, and enjoy the show while moving into position for a close, controlled shot.

A lot of my most memorable work with pointing breeds has taken place in heavy cover while hunting species such as woodcock, ruffed grouse, and Mearns' quail. In those situations, I often feel I'm missing half the action just because I see so little of the dog. Not so in most Hun country. There's nothing better than watching a dog hit the brakes and hold that point. No prairie species offers more such opportunities than Huns even if it takes two or three covey rises before the birds cooperate.

Gamebirds differ widely in their suitability for work with young dogs still early in the learning process. Because of their enthusiasm for running and overall malicious cunning, wild pheasants make a poor choice for this purpose. Sage grouse occupy the other end of the IQ spectrum, but they can be difficult for dogs to smell, and some dogs never will point them. While sharptails are my favorite prairie birds for training purposes, Huns run a close second. If you're teaching a young dog steadiness, turn it loose on single Huns from a broken covey. The birds will likely hold longer than you will.

Huns also offer unique challenges for those who love swinging shotguns. Sage grouse are so slow and ponderous that shooting them isn't much fun once you've done it a few times. Pheasants and sharptails are faster, but the shots they offer are usually predictable. Among western gamebirds, only chukar and Mearns' quail can begin to rival Huns for challenge on the wing.

Few gamebird species can match the explosiveness of a Hun covey's initial rise. It only takes a split second for a dozen Huns to shatter the serenity of a remote western landscape. Isolating one (much less a second) target within that tightly packed airspace and following through on it can challenge the most experienced wingshooter. When a covey has broken up and left singles and pairs cooperating for the dog, the shots may be close and conveniently timed. There's still no predicting the crazy angle at which the bird might erupt from the grass, leaving the hunter tangled up and wondering how he could ever miss anything from that range. Twice.

A third consideration helps propel the Hun near the top of my list of favorite western gamebirds. Huns are delicious. I hate losing downed birds of any species, but because of their table quality I hate losing Huns more than most. Wounded Huns pose nothing like the recovery problems crippled pheasants offer, but their natural camouflage can make them surprisingly hard to find even when they're dead in short grass. This is especially true when multiple birds are down after a covey rise. The easiest solution to the problem is to hunt with a dog from a multi-purpose pointing breed. If your pointing dog isn't much use after the shot, consider backing the dog up with a retriever worked from heel.

While newcomers to Hun country can get started simply by following a good dog through likely cover, a bit of insight into Hun behavior will lead to a more productive hunt.

While Huns are frequently found in the same general area as other western game birds like sharptails and pheasants, their precise habitat choices are different. They prefer short grass that hasn't been grazed by livestock and are rarely found in thick pheasant cover unless they're pushed into it. Huns love to feed on grain and can often be found in or near stubble fields, especially early and late in the day. However, it's a mistake to assume that they *need* grain. Huns also show a consistent affinity for old, abandoned buildings, especially those surrounded by shelterbelts. If there are any in the area, they are always worth investigating.

That first explosive covey rise may well occur beyond shotgun range, especially late in the season when the cover is thinner and the birds have faced hunting pressure. I regard any bird taken on the first rise as a bonus. The important thing is to mark the covey down as accurately as possible, for it usually takes two or three rises for the birds to split up and hold.

That's easier said than done even in open country. If possible, Huns will usually put an eclipsing terrain feature between themselves and the pursuit, turning at a wide angle as soon as they're out of sight. While relocating the covey can turn into a guessing game, knowledge of Hun behavior can narrow the search. The birds will often turn uphill and fly toward the head of the next draw. If a stiff breeze is blowing, they will usually turn and glide downwind, an adaptive behavior when trying to evade predators that hunt with their noses, like foxes and coyotes. Should you lose track of the birds on the next rise, note that the third or fourth covey flush will often bring them back close to where you first encountered them.

Because of habitat preferences, much of the West's best pheasant cover lies on private farm ground. Since ringnecks are the region's glamor species, those are the first properties closed to access. In contrast, Huns' ability to thrive in habitat ranging from mountain foothills to open grasslands means there are plenty of them on public lands. I've hunted Huns in Montana for over 50 years because I live here. I've also enjoyed great Hun hunting in Oregon, Idaho, Washington, and Alberta, and this list doesn't exhaust the possibilities.

A limit of Huns rested in my game vest by the time we circled back to the truck on opening morning. Fine work on Maggie's part left me feeling satisfied and ready for a hearty breakfast back at home. But Lori was ready to trade camera for shotgun and Kenai deserved time on the ground too. After making sure that Maggie was comfortable and well hydrated, we set out on foot for a different coulee system with Kenai at heel.

That morning, we found sharptails there rather than Huns, confirming that Hun habitat frequently contains game birds other than Huns. By the time the temperature approached an uncomfortable level an hour later, cooperative early season birds had provided Lori with several grouse and allowed Kenai to make a few retrieves.

The ride home offered an ideal opportunity to compare and contrast experiences with two of my favorite western gamebirds. The sharptail shooting had been fast and furious, and watching an old pro perform on the first day of what might be his last season felt gratifying. The sight of Maggie frozen over a tightly sitting Hun and the challenge of isolating a target from a packed covey rise? Priceless.

16.

A Quail for All Seasons

There's probably no such thing as easy chukar country, and we certainly hadn't found any that morning. Even though I was still young and fit, my legs were protesting as we slid our way back down the steep, rocky Columbia River Breaks terrain after hours of climbing. To make matters worse, we weren't carrying a single chukar in our game vests.

At the bottom of the hill, we intersected a brush-lined dry wash that would eventually lead us back to our vehicle. Tired and discouraged, it took us longer than it should have to notice my friend's shorthair on point.

No cure for fatigue at the end of a tough hunt can rival the promise of birds. I felt new life in my legs as we spread out to approach the dog from opposite sides of the cover. Suddenly, the air was full of more wings than I thought one clump of brush could hold. The birds were quail, not chukar, and it was late in the season, when undisturbed California quail often gather into large groups. After the hard miles we'd just logged to no avail, I felt so eager to shoot that I didn't give the spectacle the attention it probably deserved. Instead of trying to estimate bird numbers, I concentrated on isolating one quail from the chaos and turning it into a target.

That always requires deliberate mental effort, especially when I've been away from quail for a while. Huns are the only game bird in Montana that offers true covey rises. I hunt enough of them to appreciate the importance of isolating a single target during the confusion of the initial flush. I made myself wait until I could concentrate on one bird's topknot before I put my cheek down on the stock and drove my muzzles down its flight path. Despite the bird's diminutive size, the puff of feathers that followed made up for the barren miles of rock we'd just left behind.

After my hunting partner and I both failed to complete makeable doubles, we turned our attention to the dogs. Once they had completed the retrieving chores, we followed the birds back down the wash toward our truck. Our game vests were heavier by the time we reached it. By then they contained a dozen-odd quail, dinner for friends that night, justification for the early morning alarm clock, and the hard miles we had logged.

That was not the first time California quail had saved my day.

The markings on the California quail's breast readily distinguish it from the similarly top-knotted Gambel's.

Of the five species of quail unique to the American West (this number ignores southern Arizona's rare and protected masked bobwhite), the mountain quail is probably the least known among hunters outside the region due to its limited range and habitat requirements. Even as "desert" quail attract hunters to the Southwest every winter and the reclusive Mearns enjoys its own devoted following, one hears relatively little about the final member of the quintet: *Callipepla californica*, the California quail. Odd, for a game bird whose annual harvest exceeds a million.

As its name suggests California was the epicenter of the species' historical range, which extended south through Baja and north into parts of Oregon. Locally know as valley quail to distinguish it from the mountain quail in regions where the two birds' ranges overlap, this hardy species proved easy to transplant. Successful introductions were made to western Washington as early as 1857, although the moist climate there differs considerably from the arid weather throughout its original range. Introduced populations quickly became self-sustaining throughout the Northwest as far eastward as Idaho. With a little help from their friends, the birds also made it as far away as Hawaii, New Zealand, and Patagonia.

Valley quail are vocal birds. Many residents of quail country enjoy listening to their calls, which can also provide a useful means of locating them in thick cover. They engage in communal rearing of their young, a habit that likely contributes to the large size of the coveys encountered by hunting season.

A point in favor of the species is its population stability during periods of decline for other quail. As noted earlier, Mearns quail numbers can fluctuate dramatically due to variations in summer monsoon rains in some years and for reasons that defy explanation in others. Gambel's and scaled quail numbers rise and fall for similar reasons, although they depend on rainfall during winter rather than summer and invasive plant species play a greater role in their periodic declines. In contrast, California quail numbers usually remain stable throughout most of their range allowing hunters to enjoy good-old-days shooting, often on public land.

Despite its name and status as California's state bird, I've never hunted valley quail in California. All my own experience with the species has come in Washington, where I grew up, and Idaho, where I've enjoyed hunting a variety of upland game including Huns and chukar. The species has impressed me with its ability to adapt to a wide range of habitats and offer an equally wide range of hunting experiences.

All upland birds love their security habitat, none more predictably than California quail. Along the flanks of the Cascades where vegetation is often dense, they are notorious for burrowing their way into extremely thick cover and refusing to come out. Slash piles, Russian olive, and especially blackberry tangles provide favorite sanctuaries. Few experiences in the world of upland hunting can be as frustrating as having a dog on point beside a dense patch of blackberry vines and being unable to get the birds to flush, even with help from a determined dog.

On one recent waterfowl excursion to central Washington, we decided to follow our morning duck hunt with a quail expedition. After exchanging camouflage coats for orange vests and steel #2s for lead #8s, we set off along the edge of a field lined with slash piles and blackberries. We soon heard quail calling from a blackberry tangle half the size of my house, but not even my experienced flushing Lab could penetrate it deeply enough to force a rise. We repeated that experience twice more before we located birds in a slash pile that Kenai could worm his way through and push the birds into the air. We made the most of the opportunity, but the experience still fell far short of what most of us think of as classical quail hunting.

Eastern Washington and Oregon and western Idaho include open, arid country more akin to the birds' original habitat. Whether the surrounding ground consists of dryland crops, native grass, or sagebrush, valley quail concentrate in the dry, brushy creek bottoms that interlace the high desert terrain. While hunters may have to do a bit more climbing over uneven footing than eastern bobwhite hunters are accustomed to, working the bottoms behind a good pointing dog can produce plenty of shooting.

Terrain isn't the only inconsistent variable the valley quail hunter must confront. I can't think of any upland bird in the country that has made me face a wider temperature range or more erratic weather. California quail hunts have left me sweating in shirtsleeves and shivering in snowstorms. They are the only quail I have ever hunted on snowshoes, as I did one year in Washington just south of the Canadian border. Thanks to the extended quail seasons most western states allow, hunters should expect to face more cold winter weather than most quail hunters can imagine. However, these late seasons provide welcome opportunities to keep hunting after other upland bird seasons have closed. They also represent a testimonial to the hardiness and adaptability of California quail.

My earliest memories of valley quail date back to my high school days, when our upland hunting took place on the dry eastern side of Washington's Cascades. The sagebrush we hunted was well suited to a good pointing dog and we had one. Kids love hunting that includes lots of opportunities to shoot and quail provided plenty. While my young hunting partners seemed more interested in ringnecks, chukar, and waterfowl, I always felt content to disappear up a draw with our shorthair and take advantage of the generous daily quail limit.

Fifty years later, my tastes hadn't changed much. While Montana offers a tremendous variety of upland gamebirds, it holds no quail of any kind and I miss them. This deficiency has provided the excuse for countless bird hunting road trips, to east Texas and beyond for bobwhite, west Texas for scaled quail and Gambel's, or the mountains of southern Arizona for Mearns.

While I can't pretend that I enjoy finding myself suspended in blackberry vines or feeling my feet grow numb from cold during a quail hunt, none of those venues arouses more anticipation than a drive west in search of valley quail. That's why I'm in eastern Idaho now with Lori and the dogs instead of celebrating Thanksgiving at home with family, friends, and my longbow at the conclusion of Montana's deer season.

After covering the hills for a nice mixed bag of chukar and Huns behind Maggie and our hunting partners' pointers, we've chosen to work our way back downhill toward the vehicle along a creek bottom that contains more brush than water. Even so, the cover is a far cry from some of the hellish stuff I've worked for quail in Washington. When Maggie finally locks up down in the bottom of the draw, we have no trouble locating her and reaching her side. Even so, the rise offers more noise than targets, at least for me, but not for Lori and our friends on either side of the brush. Shotguns bark and birds drop as the covey scatters and singles buzz away. Then Maggie gets to shine again as she helps the pointers sort out the retrieving duties.

Of course, she delivers the first bird to me even though I never fired a shot. If only people demonstrated as much loyalty as bird dogs. Since a season has passed since I last held a valley quail in my hand, I call a brief time out so I can examine the bird. As usual, the superficial resemblance to the southwestern Gambel's proves just that. The same jaunty topknot is there, but the valley quail is obviously darker and the neatly scaled belly is unmistakable.

We're pleasantly exhausted by the time we reach the deserted gravel road two coveys later, but the trifecta of upland game bird species resting in our vests more than compensates for the fatigue the uphill chukar country induced. While the quail may be the smallest of the lot, I prefer to measure their value by the classy dog work and snappy shooting they provided rather than their heft.

By that standard, the California quail can hold its own with any game bird in the West.

17.

The Bird that Lives Straight Up

Someday I may get to hunt terrain that turns out to be easier to cover on foot than first impressions suggest, but I haven't found it yet. From the open tundra of southwest Alaska to the Missouri River breaks, the opposite is almost always the case whenever a discrepancy between appearance and reality arises. The open hills of western Idaho quickly proved true to theory. I had been seduced by the country's initial appearance. We were hunting chukar, and the rolling terrain looked less daunting than the rocky cliffs where I'd hunted this challenging species as a kid growing up in Washington State. However, the hills proved to be neatly disguised lava outcroppings with clumps of basalt hidden in the grass underfoot just waiting for a chance to turn an ankle. I've never found good chukar hunting that didn't require climbing, sometimes at exertion levels that rivaled the pursuit of wild sheep and mountain goats.

All of which explains why I was laboring more than usual by the time we reached our friend's stylish female pointer halfway up the hillside. Just as we approached, Maggie appeared over the horizon. Although full of promise midway through her derby season, this outing represented her first opportunity to hunt with other pointing dogs, and I didn't want to risk embarrassment by having her bust Hooligan's point. But just as I tried to gather enough breath to issue the command *whoa*, she hit the skids behind the older dog. Her manners left me feeling like the proud parent of a well-behaved kid.

They also left me prepared to face the object of the point, whatever that might be. Given their preference for the brushy creek bottom habitat below us pheasants and valley quail were unlikely on the open hillside, but one never knows. Since Huns and chukar occupy similar cover in terrain like this I could only guess which species was waiting in front of the dog. Eager to revisit my youth, I hoped for the latter.

I got them. The rise left me momentarily rattled, but then I picked out a single chukar on the edge of the covey and dropped it in time to knock feathers from a straggler with my other barrel. Although I chided myself for the sloppy second shot, my questionable technique scarcely mattered when Maggie retrieved the second bird a hundred yards down the hillside.

Time for a pop quiz. Which of the following is NOT a chukar?

1. A target drone aircraft manufactured by Northrop.
2. A period in a polo match.
3. A member of the Kansas City Royals farm team based in Idaho Falls.
4. The national bird of Pakistan.

Congratulations to those who chose #2, although it's close (the correct spelling of the polo term is *chukker*). The rest are all true, although I find it simpler to define chukar as one of the most challenging upland gamebirds in the country, perhaps second only to Mearns quail.

Although chukar are plenty speedy on the wing, that challenge arises more from habit and habitat preferences than the birds' air speed. *Alectoris chukar* is native to a long swath of mountainous country stretching west across the Himalayas from Nepal through the Middle East until the red-legged partridge replaces it in southern

Europe. (Although chukar also have red legs the two birds, after decades of argument by biologists, are separate species.) The common factor throughout its native range is steep, arid terrain, a fact of life that defines both the perils and the rewards of chukar hunting here at home.

Compared to ringnecks and Huns, chukar are a relatively new arrival in North America. Idaho was the first state to sponsor an organized introduction effort, in 1933. Forty-four other states eventually followed suit although the birds established sustained populations in just a handful, all in arid portions of the Mountain West. In addition to Idaho, the best chukar hunting today can be found in Nevada, Oregon, and Washington, where the birds thrive in steep terrain that also contains abundant rattlesnakes, cheat grass (a preferred food source despite its invasive status and otherwise adverse habitat impact), and not much else.

In sparse cover chukar would rather run than fly, and they usually run straight uphill. Although I've cursed it often while laboring in pursuit of running birds or sliding precipitously downhill through loose scree, such habitat will likely be the salvation of chukar hunting. Since this terrain has little to offer development or agriculture it is likely to remain intact. Most of it lies within the public domain. Hunting pressure remains light since few hunters are willing to do what it takes to hunt it.

If you agree with Aldo Leopold that the value of the hunt reflects the effort invested in it, chukar are the upland species for you.

This Idaho chukar habitat actually isn't as steep as the Columbia River Breaks I used to hunt as a kid.

I have enjoyed a long and occasionally contentious relationship with horses. I grew up with them, and although I never really felt part of the cowboy culture I once did a lot of mountain packing in both Montana and Alaska. However, my former wife was really the heart of our equine program by then, and when she went down the road the occupants of our stable went with her.

Lori, on the other hand, enjoys the distinction of being one of the few women I know who grew up in rural Montana without a horse in the barn and a barrel racing arena alongside it. She practically hates horses, largely because her professional career as a ranch country emergency room nurse has left her convinced that horses are more dangerous than grizzly bears, perhaps even grizzly bears with rabies.

A complex web of friendships had led us to the Idaho ranch where the hunting described earlier in this chapter took place. Its owners raised horses. After two days of climbing hills to reach dogs on point our legs were tired—pleasantly so, but tired nonetheless. With Montana's mountain lion season barely three weeks away I really didn't mind, because at my age chasing hounds through the mountains on foot all winter made a good argument for all the pre-season conditioning I could get. Despite Lori's reservations, I greeted the sight of saddled horses outside the barn with relief.

The horses offered a practical means of transportation as well as evoking classical plantation quail hunting with horse-drawn wagons. Rain had fallen that morning, turning the ranch's back roads into gumbo. We weren't driving anywhere. Unless we wanted to set out on foot from ranch headquarters in the mud our choices boiled down to horses or an early cocktail hour. With Maggie and our friends' dogs ranging eagerly ahead, we climbed into our saddles and headed into the hills.

An hour later we crossed a ridge and spotted Maggie on point in front of a cluster of brush, foliage yellowed by the season, the only thick patch of cover on the grassy slope below. As we dismounted and the other two dogs honored her point, I could hear chukar calling in the brush. With their reins dropped loose upon the ground, the horses did exactly what they were supposed to do, which was nothing. We removed our shotguns from their scabbards and set off around opposite sides of the brush.

Since the patch of cover wasn't much bigger than my kitchen this flanking maneuver didn't take long, but we didn't flush a bird. When I glanced back over my shoulder I saw that all three dogs remained frozen in place. The grass underfoot didn't look thick enough to hide a sparrow. What had happened to the chukar?

Just then a single flushed, quartering away down the hillside. I made the shot look easy because it was. As I gave Maggie the command to fetch, birds began to explode in all directions from the same grass we had just walked through, politely staggering their rises so each of us could drop a bird.

After Maggie completed the retrieving duties, we regrouped at the horses only to see one of the other dogs silhouetted against the skyline on point a hundred yards away. By the time we climbed the hill, Maggie was also on point facing the opposite direction. Both singles rested in our game vests by the time we walked back to the horses.

But it ain't over until it's over. As soon as I'd climbed back into the saddle, I noticed Maggie on point again right where we'd started. Although it seemed impossible that the sparse grass could still be hiding birds, I decided to trust my dog. Rather than trying to keep track of the details, I will just say that more birds rose and more birds fell. Maggie then left me with an enduring image of the versatile gun dog as she stood with a dead bird cradled gently in her mouth while she solidly pointed one last straggler.

That certainly isn't the only limit of chukar that I've killed in my life, but it may be the only one I've taken without working up a shirt full of sweat and boots full of blisters.

18.

Quail Hat Trick

Around the winter solstice, weather begins to visit challenges upon our home. Mercury that has fallen overnight has more trouble rising than an old bird dog at the end of a long day. Engines balk and pipes freeze. The road to our country home drifts in faster than we can plow it out. Worst of all, the upland bird season that began four months earlier finally comes to an end.

After shivering my way through more long Montana winters than I care to count, escape to warmer places became a regular feature on our calendar at that time of year. While target destinations ranged from Argentina to New Zealand and Hawaii, none proved more consistently appealing than a return to my ancestral homeland in Texas. While pursuing quarry from redfish to mule deer, I quietly fell for the Lone Star State's three legal species of quail, each as unique and distinct as different vintages of wine.

Climatic considerations aside, can any bird the size of a human fist justify all those days of driving, rattlesnakes, and cactus spines? Let me walk you through an intriguing trio.

It's hard for me to set foot in Texas bobwhite country without experiencing a measure of regret. Long gone before I was born, my paternal grandfather ranched a large spread south of San Antonio prior to losing the whole place to wine, women, and song (with heavy emphasis on the first two). No matter the irresponsible reputation he left behind, he was an avid outdoorsman and I wish he'd stuck around long enough for us to go hunting together.

That all took place so long ago that my late mother couldn't remember the ranch's precise location, but our friend Arthur's place was certainly in the neighborhood. By the time we visited him there some years ago, Arthur had reached the age at which a once avid hunter can be forgiven for enjoying the social aspects of the chase more than the shooting itself. Consequently, he followed behind in the jeep explaining the intricacies of his quail management program to Lori while mutual friend Dick Negley and I set off on foot behind a brace of pointers. Everyone seemed perfectly happy with this arrangement including the dogs.

The edges of two opposing fields provided civilized walking removed from the thorn brush in the draw between us, which we were happy to leave to the pointers. We'd barely started to hike by the time the dogs' collar bells fell silent down in the cover and the air filled with the buzz of wings. Screened by brush, I could only listen as Dick's double barked twice across the little draw. Two shots, two birds: no surprise to anyone who has hunted with Dick.

The cooperative little birds were bobwhite quail, game I'd hunted occasionally across the south but never in Texas. A hundred yards farther down the draw, we enjoyed an opportunity to appreciate them at their finest. The scattered covey had gone to ground in thick cover that Arthur deliberately left standing for the benefit of wildlife, and the pointers treated us to a fine display of dog work. I killed a pair myself over staunch points (admittedly using three shells to do the job of two) and then we left the covey alone and moved on. With the cover in fine shape due to generous spring rains and sound management, it didn't take us long to find new birds.

Back at home, our pheasants, grouse, and Huns offer a definitive example of what the British rather dismissively term rough shooting. While I'm not sure I could ever acquire a taste for formal driven birds, by the end of that glorious Texas morning I knew that I'd just enjoyed a rare opportunity to hunt like a gentleman.

If only my late grandfather had been more of one himself.

For many sports fans the term Blue Devils refers to the Duke basketball team, but to me it means scaled quail, *Callipepla squamata*. Hunters expecting the dignified process those bobwhite offered us farther east should stand forewarned. West of the Pecos, another world of Texas quail hunting awaits.

Rarified desert air magnified the visual impact of the sunrise as cool light radiated from the buttes surrounding the ranch headquarters. As Lori and I crossed the courtyard to have breakfast with our old friends and hosts, I congratulated myself for packing a set of long underwear. Two hours' drive from El Paso, the high desert terrain of the Sierra Diablo is hardly the steamy south Texas quail country where we'd hunted bobs before.

A successful San Antonio businessman, outdoor enthusiast and student of the natural world, Chris Gill became a friend via one of those convoluted series of relationships that illustrate an important social principle: hunt long enough and you will eventually meet every dedicated hunter in the world. While chasing ringnecks in Montana with us earlier that fall, Chris had made an offer we couldn't refuse. Would Lori and I like to join him at his west Texas ranch for a week of quail and mule deer hunting? As our then teen-aged daughters were fond of saying… *duh!*

Chris pursues land stewardship passionately and his dedication to habitat enhancement could serve as a role model anywhere. Since acquiring the ranch, he had devoted considerable effort to giving this vast chunk of desert terrain what it needs most: relief from soil erosion caused by decades of misguided human intrusion and a holistic grazing program that addressed the needs of wildlife as well as livestock. The result was a boon to species as diverse as bighorn sheep and desert quail.

No stranger to blue quail, I'd hunted them before across the breadth of their range from Arizona to northern Mexico and found few easy birds along the way. Contradicting Muhammad Ali's famous dismissal of a hapless opponent, they can run *and* they can hide, and they do both quite well, thank you very much. Somehow, my anticipation that morning made me forget the memory of all the thorns and futile wind sprints I'd endured while chasing blues before.

After breakfast, Chris, whose commitment to a water management project prevented him from joining us in the field, offered me my choice from his splendid selection of doubles. An hour later Lori and I were hiking along a shallow draw where I'd run into birds while bowhunting mule deer the day before. In contrast to the truly nasty thorn brush habitat where we'd previously hunted blues along the Rio Grande, the high desert offered pleasant walking through stunning scenery. With Rocky at heel, we forged onward toward the rising sun. After a mile of desert eco-tourism, our hard hiking earned its reward. "Birds ahead!" sharp-eyed Lori cried. I turned in her direction just in time to see flickering motion evaporate from the desert floor like mirage water. This is the moment when the blue quail hunter must forgo any pretense of decorum and do just what the quail are doing: run.

Despite considerable experience as a flushing retriever, Rocky was having trouble following the birds in the dry desert air. Finally, the covey of 30 flushed as one at the edge of shotgun range. I held my fire and marked the birds down as they settled into the brush ahead. Without breaking stride, we hurried forward and then stopped to listen. We'd broken the covey up enough to produce a few calls, which was all we needed.

Following my ears, I charged a clump of brush, urged Rocky forward, and watched a plump little bundle of cotton-topped feathers explode from the other side. Still heaving from exertion, I had to settle myself consciously for the shot, which somehow managed to extinguish the buzz of wings. My peripheral vision detected more motion somewhere on the ground, but I suppressed the temptation to try the back half of a double. Even with a retriever along crippled blues can be difficult to collect, and I kept my line of sight riveted on the yucca that marked the fall. Unnecessarily as events proved, for Rocky quickly ran the bird down and delivered it to my waiting hand. We managed to collect another single from the scattered covey before we set off up the draw in search of new players.

By the time we arrived back at the truck mid-morning, I had a half-dozen birds resting in the back of my game jacket, admittedly at the cost of more than a half-dozen shells. Nonetheless, I felt proud of every bird simply because I'd collected them the old-fashioned way: by earning them.

I acknowledge that hiking behind a flushing retriever isn't everyone's idea of classical quail hunting. By the time Lori and I were wintering in southern Arizona a few years later as described elsewhere in this text, Maggie had turned into an excellent pointing dog. By then I wouldn't have considered hunting quail of any kind without her. Although we focused tightly on Mearns there, we made several trips into desert quail country every year and sometimes hunted habitat where Gambel's and scalies overlapped. During one visit, my father even made a mixed species double. The Gambel's held wonderfully for the dog after a covey broke up, but the scalies usually just kept running.

Like all devils, blues never give up easily.

By curious coincidence, the range of the Gambel's quail coincides almost perfectly with the boundaries of the original Apache homeland. I killed my first representatives of the species years ago in Arizona near the mountain where Geronimo made his last stand, and the final Apache battle in Texas took place near the ranch where we'd hunted the blue quail. While the Gambel's lacks the multiple official nicknames of our other desert quail species, they'll always be Apache quail to me.

As sunlight spilled over the crest of Arizona's Pinaleno Mountains, I understood why visual artists from Georgia O'Keefe to Ansel Adams came there just for the light. It seemed to have a unique optical quality that gave the empty panorama of cactus, sand, and rock a magical glow. In fact the miles of desert floor spread out before us weren't "empty" at all, except for the absence of human habitation, surface water, and no-trespassing signs. In addition to countless species of exotic flora I still hadn't learned to identify, it contained a robust population of rodents, deer, javelina, and the predators that preyed upon them as well as neo-tropical birdlife that occurred nowhere else north of the nearby Mexican border. That day it was the quail that provided us our excuse for being there.

We were targeting Gambel's that morning, and the habitat before us looked ideal. Foothills behind us offered rolling terrain, brushy dry washes provided cover, and abundant prickly pear cactus rose from the sand. Although the association is likely an epiphenomenon, I have long regarded prickly pear as an indicator of desert quail habitat. After fitting Maggie and Max with locator collars, Lori and I set off abreast down opposite sides of the nearest wash with the dogs ranging in front of us. Despite the modest distraction of their beeping, the collars served two useful purposes. While most of the terrain was open enough to allow visual contact with the dogs, thick brush along the wash could hide a dog on point. Furthermore, a close-range encounter between a bird dog and a squadron of javelina would likely end badly for the dog. Hunting into the breeze, I wanted to give any desert pigs in the area advance notice of our approach.

Walking up a point in typical desert quail habitat.

The walking in desert quail country is generally easy, in contrast to the steep, rocky Mearns habitat nearby. We scarcely noted the mile that passed underfoot before Maggie's collar began to beep steadily from a tangle of mesquite, cat's claw, and cactus ahead. Then the deeper tone from Max's collar created a crude but welcome harmony as he moved in to back her point. I had just spotted the vibrating tip of his tail in the brush when the covey flushed.

As is often the case on a Gamble's covey's initial rise, the birds rose just beyond shotgun range. They then stayed together until they strung out and settled back into the wash several hundred yards ahead. I anticipated solid dog work on scattered singles as we approached the area where I'd marked them down. The team didn't disappoint.

This time Max locked up first, and Lori practically had to kick the hidden bird into the air as she walked in ahead of the dog. The opportunity wasn't wasted on her 20-gauge. Before Max had completed the retrieve Maggie was pointing on my side of the draw. The rise provided a double as easy as doubles get.

I estimated the covey contained 15 birds, from which three seemed enough. We called timeout to admire the birds' jaunty topknots (all three were males) and provide the dogs water from the canteens in our game vests. Miles of public land beckoned like an invitation, but the comfortable morning chill had already started to yield to the sunlight rising overhead. When Lori suggested that we cut cross-country to the next wash and work it back uphill to the truck, I concurred.

I felt confident that the cover would produce another covey or two before we had to call it a morning, and the desert kept its promise.

Odd Birds

19.

Lone Star Doodles

The ambience that greeted us as I followed Monty's rig to a stop looked nothing like any terrain I'd encountered in Texas before, a testimonial to the Lone Star State's tremendous variety of habitat. To the east, dappled morning light filtered down through a barren canopy of winter hardwoods and played across the layer of oak duff carpeting the forest floor. To the west, a stand of planted, half-grown pines stood like rigid sentries above an understory of wax myrtle and briars. As a kid, I'd grown up hunting woodcock in upstate New York, but this looked nothing like the cover I remembered there.

Fortunately, the perfect foil for my own ignorance was lowering the tailgate of the pickup in front of us. Professor Emeritus Montague Whiting spent his academic career at nearby Steven F. Austin University, teaching wildlife biology and forestry to a generation of eager students. In the process, his scientific knowledge of elusive little *Scolopax minor* grew to rival his passion for hunting them. Lori and I first met Monty when he accompanied mutual friends from Texas north to hunt with us in Montana. Now, after a long wing-shooting road trip that had taken us to the Texas Gulf Coast for waterfowl by way of the Arizona desert and its quail, we were finally enjoying an opportunity to accept his longstanding invitation to join him on his home turf. I couldn't have felt more excited by the prospect.

Mike Hedricks, our old friend from Montana and Alaska who readers have met previously, had accompanied us on our marathon. As a retired wildlife professional from the USFWS, he, Monty, and Chris Comer, a young faculty member in Monty's old department, had been talking up a scientific storm from the moment of their first introduction. Despite a lifetime in the field, Mike spent his entire career in the West and had never seen a woodcock. Our canine contingent represented a similar blend of innocence and experience. Zeus and Bacchus, Monty's classically named Brittanies, had pointed countless timber doodles, as had Chris's Trampus. And then there was young Maggie, who had just finished an excellent puppy season in Montana and Arizona but had never seen a woodcock. My goals for her did not extend past obedience, good behavior, and honoring other dogs' points, assuming we found some birds somewhere in the expanse of cover surrounding us.

While the plan of attack seemed random to me, as the dogs frolicked and sniffed Monty studied the lay of the land like a chess master considering a gambit. "I think we'll head off along that thick seam of myrtle running through the hardwoods to the top of the hill," he began. I noted that a "hill" in east Texas is not the same as a hill in Montana and breathed a sigh of relief. "Then we'll hunt down the little draw on the other side, and back through the pines just across the old logging road looking for males." While the final allusion to gender went right over my head the overall strategy sounded fine, if only because it suggested that someone in our party knew what he was doing.

Then we were off through the thick cover beneath the oaks, listening to a steady chorus of beeps and bells from the dogs' collars. Although many seasons had passed since my last woodcock hunt, I knew that it was now pretty much up to all to those canine noses. They quickly justified my confidence when, a few hundred yards up the hill, the steady beep of a dog on point rose from a locator collar somewhere in the underbrush ahead.

The thick cover readily justified that concession to technology, as it still took several minutes to obtain a visual on Bacchus locked up staunchly in the brush. After ordering Maggie to whoa behind him, I carefully counted orange hats and vests: woodcock flying erratically through thick cover demand meticulous adherence to basic principles of hunter safety. By then the bird had endured all of our presence it meant to take, and a buzz of wings rose somewhere in the myrtle. Someone shot at the bird going away, but when it erupted unscathed on my side of the cover I brought my gun up, fired quickly, and watched it fold.

While the dogs worked out the retrieve, I did some quick calculations. Forty-eight seasons had passed since I'd killed my last woodcock.

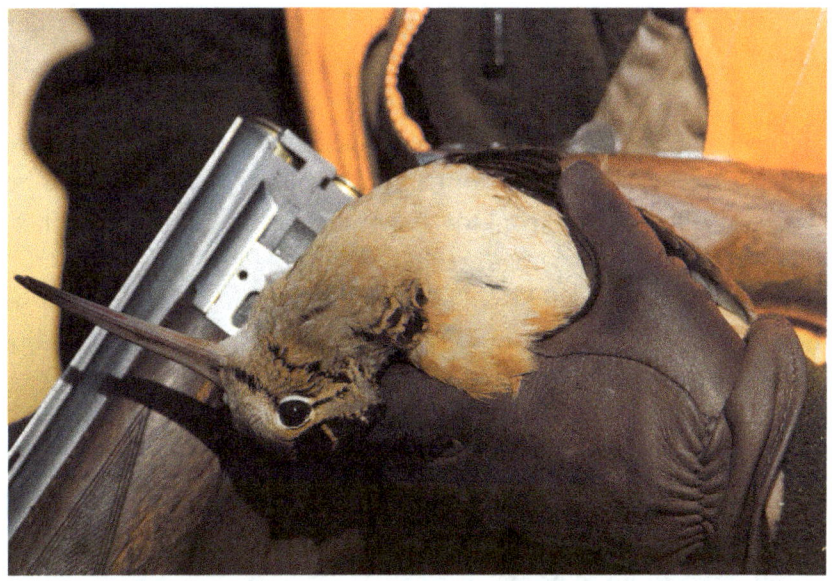

While they may be small, woodcock provide some of the most challenging wing-shooting in the country.

The name *woodcock* derives from an old English term for a foolish or silly person. In *Love's Labours Lost*, Shakespeare refers to a quartet of characters as "four woodcocks in a pan" after they violate an earlier promise not to fall in love. Granted, the woodcock's spectacular aerial spring courtship display can look foolish, as can the courtship displays of other species including our own. However, I doubt that the connection between woodcock and gullibility derived from anyone who hunted them regularly with a shotgun.

Growing up in northern New York, my father and I were limited to two upland species when we took to the field each fall: ruffed grouse and woodcock. While I cut my wing-shooting teeth on the former, I developed a particular fascination for woodcock right from the start, at least in part because of the evanescent nature of their appearance. Although I did observe plenty of those spring displays above the swamp in front of our rural home, during the fall we were hunting migrating birds and the unpredictability of their arrivals and equally abrupt disappearances leant them a particular aura of mystery.

One of our favorite grouse coverts was a nearly impenetrable alder swamp I have already introduced: the Hole. Every year sometime in late October, Bits would vanish on point only to appear as if he were pointing his own front toe when we finally located him. When no thunder of grouse wings greeted our approach, I would mentally brace myself for the first woodcock flush of the season. Often to no avail—the bird's startling rise and erratic departure through the alders proved challenging enough for guns more experienced than mine. They taught me a lot though and I eventually killed my share. When my family departed for the Pacific Northwest, the woodcock joined the black duck, native brook trout, and a ninth-grade girl I will not embarrass by naming here on a short list of things I missed about my childhood home.

To think I had to go all the way to Texas—my own parents' childhood home—to find woodcock again.

Accustomed to the feast or famine nature of woodcock hunting as I remembered it, I expected that first bird to indicate an upcoming flurry. That wasn't quite the case, but by the time we reached the top of the hill the dogs had made two more points and Mike had killed his first woodcock. Then Monty called a brief timeout for a field biology lesson.

"These birds are actually breeding here, even though they'll head north soon to nest," he explained. "I know that sounds illogical, but our field studies confirm that the females here are carrying fertilized eggs by the time they depart. Many of these birds never make it as far north as what you think of as traditional woodcock country. Based on the cover we're hunting I'm going to say these birds are all females. Let's take a look."

I'd always heard that you had to dissect the bird to determine the sex of a woodcock, but he dispelled that notion. First, he produced a dollar bill from his wallet and inserted it crossways in my bird's bill. The tip overlapped the edge slightly, indicating that it was a female. (The male's shorter bill doesn't reach the edge, as we later confirmed.) Then we examined the inner flight primaries, which are substantially wider in females. A final study of the mottling pattern on the wing feathers' trailing edge revealed that we'd taken one mature bird and one sub-adult. Thus enlightened, we continued our loop back toward the old logging road. Chris and I grew one bird shy of our limits in the process. I have to confess some inflation in this report, since the limit was three.

The shooting did not evoke quite the same eerie *déjà vu* as the birds themselves, although it proved equally challenging. My memory recalled fleeting visions of barely visible birds flittering away through dense tangles of alders. Here, the cover beneath the hardwoods was more open, and I made a couple of shots at distances that once would have been unimaginable in woodcock cover. But we still had to shoot quickly and deal with the quarry's erratic flight pattern. Every downed bird felt like a minor miracle.

The dog work proved as enjoyable as the shooting. Few game birds demand the services of a staunch but wide-ranging pointing dog like woodcock. All three Brittanies were clearly skilled veterans of the game. Without them, I doubt we would have seen a bird, much less killed any. Woodcock dogs remind me of Mearns quail dogs; they're specialists, and it takes experience for them to recognize the unusual scent signature of the quarry. As expected, young Maggie did nothing brilliant, but she obeyed her commands, backed the other dogs, and contributed a retrieve or two.

Crossing the old roadway and entering the pines for the swing back to the trucks felt like entering another world. Although the sun had nearly reached the zenith, the ambience beneath the evergreen canopy felt darker and spookier. As I calculated the hypothetical geometry of a woodcock's flight across the neat, tightly spaced rows of loblollies I began to feel sorry for the trees, which were obviously going to take some pellets if we got into birds. After pausing for a brief discourse on the unique habitat demands of the endangered red-cockaded woodpecker, we set off behind the dogs again.

Maggie's first point of the morning wasn't picture perfect, but it did produce a rise that confirmed my earlier concerns when my first shot produced a shower of pine needles. My second barrel managed to put the shot column through a gap in the trees though, and when Maggie retrieved the bird I traded my shotgun to Lori for the camera.

"Now these birds will be males," Monty announced when we regrouped a few points and several fewer birds later. An examination of their wings and bills confirmed as much by previously established criteria. The males, Monty explained, were flying the open roads at night in display, hence their proximity to the old logging track. While the males tend to remain near these roadside breeding areas, the females they attract to their displays usually retreat to thicker cover by morning, explaining why we'd found them in the thickets earlier.

By mid-afternoon we were back at our trucks carrying all the birds we were allowed (not quite the accomplishment it sounds), newly educated in my case, pleasantly tired, and ready for an evening of Texas hospitality courtesy of Monty's gracious wife, Nancy.

Mike, Lori, and I had to leave the following day to begin the long drive back to those neglected Arizona quail, but we calculated that we could still hunt until noon and stay on schedule. Chris couldn't join us that morning, but we did add a new canine member to the cast of characters: Rocky, my veteran yellow Lab, who had made the long trip from Arizona to serve in the duck blinds on our route up the Texas Gulf Coast. In deference to Maggie, I'd recently converted him from a pheasant-busting flushing dog to a no-slip retriever working from heel, so I knew he wouldn't hurt us. With all due respect to the retrieving chores as handled by Maggie and the Britts (we hadn't lost a bird the day before), some of the game had arrived in hand worn harder than I would accept from a trained Lab. I wanted to hold an unruffled woodcock in my hand and figured Rocky offered the best way to make that happen.

Monty took us to a new place he hadn't hunted all year, and I didn't blame him. When friends visit me I don't let them pound my best cover day after day. I didn't expect him to either. Guests should be willing to do their own fair share of scouting.

Our first swing through some promising hardwood habitat produced a resounding nothing. My mind had already started to wander ahead to the long drive awaiting us when we looped into another stand of planted pines, and suddenly dogs were pointing everywhere. I heard Mike and Monty shooting behind us as Lori and I moved in behind Maggie's first point of the day, and the bird tumbled as she snapped off a shot through the trees. Despite her precocious retrieving instincts Maggie was not yet steady to wing and shot. She broke immediately toward the fall but wasn't quick enough to beat Rocky, even though he was still supposed to be at heel. I forgave him his bad manners out of respect for his age.

Two hours later we were back at the trucks right on schedule with more limits of woodcock resting in our vests. After extending invitations to Monty to visit us in Arizona, Montana, Alaska, or pretty much anywhere else he wanted, we were back on the road again. Did a day and a half of hunting really justify the long side trip to east Texas?

Indeed, it did: every minute, every mile.

20.

Snipe Hunt

I was alone when the snipe hunt began. I didn't even have the dog with me, because I wasn't hunting at the time and didn't want my old Lab causing any problems with the bears along the stream. Some dogs can't resist acting tough around bears, which can be a real mistake when dealing with sows and cubs especially if your dog decides to retreat in your direction when you're armed with nothing but a fly rod. So, I left Sky behind at the duck shack when I hopped into the Cub for the short flight north to the river. After I shut the airplane down and secured it, I started to walk across the grass toward the confluence of a little clear water stream and the river's turbid glacial current. The loneliness of the place aroused the peculiar combination of excitement and trepidation only Alaska wilderness can evoke.

It was the afternoon before the opening day of duck season. The grass on the tide flats still stood high before the first hard frost, but fresh snow on the peaks to the west—Termination Dust, in local parlance—reminded me how eager the seasons were to change. I had noticed a nice smattering of puddle ducks on the potholes during the flight from the cabin, but the waterfowl were still just of passing interest. Their time would come the following day. That afternoon, I was interested in silver salmon.

I took the long way to the fishing hole, working my way upstream along the river so I could scout the water. The tracks in the mud along the bar where the two currents met confirmed that several other fishermen had beat me to the pool earlier that day, but they had all walked on four legs rather than two. At least I didn't see any cub tracks as I scanned quickly through the sign underfoot. A series of strong boils at the edge of the clear water confirmed that the salmon were where they were supposed to be, fresh from salt water and—I hoped—ready to fight. After rigging my rod and tying on a bright streamer, I worked a loop of line into the air and let it drop. Three strips later, the rod tip went down hard. The fish took to the air like a promise fulfilled.

Since this is at least nominally a hunting story, I'll spare readers a detailed description of the next hour's events. Suffice it to say that by the time I broke my rod down to head back to the airplane, I had satisfied my need for fish even though I'd released most of those I'd caught. I had kept one to cook for my friends back at the cabin that night, and one was enough. As I wrapped the salmon in a plastic bag, dropped it into my daypack with my fishing gear, and set off for the airplane, I could already imagine a good meal with friends prior to opening day.

With the important part of that mission accomplished, I decided to take a shortcut back across the flats to the airplane. Thirty yards into the grass, the sound of wings erupted practically underfoot. I was on edge anyway because of the bears but it was only a snipe. As I tracked its erratic flight with an imaginary double, I felt myself yielding to the mental transition between summer and hunting season.

The first few birds didn't really get my attention, since I ran into them occasionally on the tide flats and managed to shoot an incidental snipe dinner almost every year. But by the time I had kicked dozens of birds out of the grass on my way to the airplane I realized that I had blundered into a great wing-shooting opportunity. The snipe seemed to be asking for 8-shot as they zigzagged away at the goofiest angles imaginable. I couldn't imagine how many more I might have flushed with the dog. I didn't know where the birds had come from or how long they planned to be there, but by the time I reached the airplane I had come to a decision. My opening day of duck season would include a snipe hunt.

The following morning, dawn broke clear and still over my makeshift duck blind and for the next two hours the pace of the shooting felt as relaxed as the weather. As I shot a few teal in unhurried fashion, I reminded myself that opening days are a matter of tradition rather than body count. Sky had reached the point in his career when he hunted because he liked to and not because he had anything to prove. His workmanlike attitude suited the mood of the day perfectly. He didn't do anything brilliant, but I never had to ask him to. As I picked up the decoys and started back to the cabin, I left the field with the satisfaction of knowing that every duck I had shot at was resting in the back of my game vest. Well, almost every one. Granted, that wasn't a lot of birds, but the day felt so pleasant I didn't care.

Over breakfast, my friends and I chatted easily about the shooting and the dog work until there wasn't anything more to be said on those subjects. Once the dishes were cleaned up and put away, I dug an old box of light loads out of the chaos beneath my bunk and announced that I was going snipe hunting. I invited everyone to come along but the idea evidently sounded preposterous. As everyone else dispersed to pluck ducks and tinker with gear, I found myself walking down to the little grass airstrip next to the duck shack alone except for the dog.

There should probably be a rule against putting a muddy Lab into a carefully maintained aircraft, but that was the only kind of dog I had. Sky had logged his share of time in the air over the years and as we took off for the river he sat alertly in the back seat as if he might be called upon to navigate. The flight was so short that our trajectory resembled a softball's more than an airplane's, but I would have needed the rest of the day to cover the same ground on foot—if doing so were even possible. That's just Alaska, where the going is always easier with air beneath your wings rather than with mud beneath your boots.

This time when I landed in the sand beside the river I pulled my shotgun out of the airplane rather than my fly rod. As I remembered the tracks in the mud the previous day, its heft felt welcome in my hands even though I knew the shotgun wouldn't be much more help than the 7-weight if it came to that. As I stuffed my pockets with shells I sat Sky down for some last-minute council. "Remember, buddy!" I barked into his face with all the authority I could muster. "No bears!" He responded with one of his *Oh, please!* looks and then I dropped a pair of shells into the gun and set off into the grass.

We hadn't covered fifty yards before Sky nosed the first snipe into the air. Even though I was anticipating the rise, the bird's raspy *bronk* and the buzz of its wings caught me off guard and I snapped the stock to my shoulder awkwardly. The shooting over the decoys that morning had been kid stuff, but the snipe's erratic flight proved another matter. I missed cleanly. Chiding my incompetence, I reloaded just in time to hear another bird flush behind me. When I turned and dropped it, the time had come for Sky to do what retrievers are supposed to do and he did.

Despite the noise and surprise they generate when they flush, snipe turn out to be remarkably small birds. When Sky finally emerged from the grass bearing his prize, there wasn't much to see except an elongated bill dangling from the corner of his mouth like a toothpick. I accepted this offering gratefully and scratched his head before reloading, checking the safety, and turning back toward the cover. It seemed important to reassure him that despite their small size these were gamebirds, an unnecessary precaution as it turned out. One definition of a bird dog is the ability to distinguish gamebirds from all the rest. Sky had been at this way too long to miss an opportunity to retrieve.

Craziness ruled for nearly an hour, with snipe skittering away across the beautiful, barren flats at one wild angle after another. The shooting proved as challenging as anything I could remember in the field, but I managed to pocket the bird I needed to complete a limit just before I exhausted my supply of shells. As we made the long circle back through the grass to the airplane, salt mud sucked eagerly at my boots as a determined cloud of mosquitos whined hungrily about my face. The fatigue of the long day had finally caught up with me. A wayward teal rocketed by overhead, but I didn't even bother to raise my gun. Sometimes in the outdoors, knowing when to quit can be as important as knowing when to pull out all the stops. The snipe had brought me to just that point of closure.

My vest full of snipe aroused plenty of interest back in the cabin that night, and after another relaxed round of waterfowl over decoys the following morning I led my friends on an expedition back to the snipe fields. This time we really looked as if we meant business: two Super Cubs, three guns, three dogs, and every light load we could scrounge from the neglected corners of the cabin. As we set off across the flat, whose reaches Sky and I had barely touched the previous day, I found myself remembering early Winslow Homer sporting studies and the grand traditions of American marsh hunting for snipe, plover, and rail. Smug and impressed by my previous day's discovery, I couldn't wait to share the novel pleasures of another snipe hunt with friends.

While going on a snipe hunt may sound like an adolescent joke, the little birds can challenge the most experienced guns. They're also delicious.

The weather on the second day of duck season felt even balmier than it had on the first. Warm air lay still and lifeless above the flats and swarms of insects rose eagerly to greet us. Sweat began to build as I labored through the mud. No matter—after the experience I had enjoyed the day before, I felt certain we would soon be too busy shooting snipe to notice these distractions. Sky led the charge through the cover while I settled into the determined pace of the hunt and waited for the first noisy flush to rise beneath our feet.

This time it was not to be. Sensing a gathering of the seasons we could not appreciate in the unnaturally warm weather, the birds had all departed as suddenly and mysteriously as they had arrived. It took us two long hours to prove the point. Finally there was nothing to do but acknowledge that the birds had snookered us, proving just how hard it can be to get the last laugh on nature. "Great snipe hunt," someone observed as we slogged back to the airplanes without having fired a shot. Then we broke our guns, loaded the dogs, and set off back to the duck shack to devote ourselves to more conventional wing-shooting pursuits.

As we lifted off above the alders, I banked the Cub around for one last pass over the flats as if I needed to confirm that the scene of this humiliation was really the same place where the snipe had led us on such a glorious chase the day before. That's when I saw the bear. Standing still as a statue in a patch of brush between the flats and the river, it seemed to be waiting for the clamor of our interruption to recede so it could get on with the business of catching its next fish. While its size and the shaggy translucence of its auburn coat made it look obvious from the air, it seemed to feel well hidden in the brush. I wondered how many times I had walked right by it during the last two days. Then it slid by underneath the wing and the lonely expanse of grass and willows looked as empty as I remembered it from ground level.

Great snipe hunt! I thought to myself above the throb of the engine, echoing the disappointment expressed earlier by my hunting partners as visions of childhood pranks danced capriciously through my head. Snipe hunts were supposed to be a joke after all. True to form, this time the joke had been on me. While I knew that I would be hearing about this one from my friends for the rest of the season, I still remembered the racket the birds made as they flushed and the satisfaction I felt every time I dumped one into the grass. It *had* been a great snipe hunt, even if no one knew it but me and the dog and the bear. Those seemed to be the only opinions that truly mattered.

21.

On the Wings of a Dove

Although my roots in the area went back as far as those of anyone in the hunting party, I felt oddly lost and befuddled. Thanks to the efficiency of GPS navigation, Lori, the Labs, and I had arrived at the old ranch house ahead of everyone else. Along the way we had passed through the town where my mother was born. The site of her family's old ranch lay somewhere nearby. Due to a combination of alcoholism and craziness on the part of my maternal grandfather, who had abandoned the family long before I was born, my Mom couldn't remember the exact location of the place and I'd never been able to track it down. As we stood alone next to our friend Steve's gracefully aging stone ranch house, I had to wonder: Was this a bird hunt or a search for a past I'd never find?

The early morning air felt chilly at least by south Texas standards, but it *was* the middle of January. The trip had begun with a long drive from our Arizona winter home to hunt ducks with friends on the Texas Gulf Coast as described in a later chapter. When Steve reported lots of doves at his place a brief detour sounded justified. As we stood in his yard and waited, it quickly became apparent that the dove forecast was accurate as a mixture of mourning doves and white-wings traded back and forth overhead. I felt especially intrigued by the latter, since I'd never enjoyed an opportunity to shoot them before.

My trigger finger had started to itch by the time Steve and Dick rolled in 20 minutes behind us. "Where do you want us to set up?" I asked Steve as he climbed from his truck.

"Unless you see something wrong with those birds flying over your head, I'd suggest setting up right here," Steve replied in his laconic, Marlboro-man drawl.

"In your *yard*?"

"I reckon so."

That was good enough for me. As Dick and Steve headed around the far side of the house, Lori and I carried our shotguns to the end of a shelterbelt running beside an old outbuilding with Rosy at heel. Moments later we were locked and loaded, tracking black dots silhouetted against the winter sky.

I had been hunting doves—as had my dogs—almost as long as I had been hunting anything. Doves weren't on the wing-shooting menu during my earliest years afield with a shotgun because there was no dove season in New York. When my family moved to Washington State, that gap in my hunting education closed abruptly. Like my mother, my father had grown up in Texas. As a boy, doves were his favorite gamebird, probably because they were the only gamebird around. He missed hunting them when we lived on the East Coast and never let an opening day slip by once we arrived in dove hunting country.

The early September dove opener in eastern Washington became an important date on the calendar every year while I was in high school and later when I attended medical school in Seattle. The timing was crucial, because Washington's mourning doves departed for points south as soon as the first cold front arrived. Good shooting seldom lasted longer than a few days, but the doves taught me a lot about wing-shooting, gun dogs, and life. The first hunting piece I ever sold was an admittedly sentimental story about an opening day dove hunt with a high school friend who later died in Viet Nam. I'll always feel grateful to *Retriever Journal* editor Steve Smith for opening that door for me.

Pass-shooting doves—the only way we ever hunted them—offers a unique wing-shooting challenge. Dad used to describe them as "jet propelled robins." Appearing at altitudes, speeds, and angles that fluctuate constantly, doves always seemed to have something new to offer with every shot. No bird teaches a novice to *swing* those barrels quite like doves. In Washington the first legal light of each new season always arrived on a dove hunt. If all went well, I had most of the kinks worked out of my shooting by the time we headed back over the Cascades to Seattle.

High overhead shots are the rule on most dove hunts.

Montana didn't even have a dove season when I first arrived on the prairie after completing my medical education, a remarkable oversight in a state with such strong hunting traditions. Fortunately, this grave cultural oversight was eventually corrected. Since the season for Huns and sharptails began around the same time, the dove opener there didn't have the nearly religious significance that Washington's did. I still kept my eyes open for stock tanks with cottonwoods growing around the edges and stubble fields nearby. Whenever I found the right one, I usually enjoyed a day or two of fast shooting before the doves headed south.

Dove hunting offers retrievers an atypical job description. Doves are perhaps the only upland birds one can hunt responsibly without a trained dog. They are easy to kill, don't travel far if wounded, and often fall on open ground where they are easy to locate.

A good dog can still be useful in certain dove hunting situations, as I learned to appreciate at an early age. The reason my father loved dove hunting so much when he was a kid was that meat was hard to put on the table in Depression-era rural Texas. He always regarded an unrecovered bird as a crime against nature. If a wounded dove dropped out of the sky and fell into a tangle of briars a hundred yards away, either our shorthair was going to find it or I was going to stop shooting and go get it myself. When the birds were really flying and several guns were on their game, it was easy to put a lot of doves down in a field during a short period of time. A capable retriever could keep track of them better than we could.

In the early days we accomplished those goals with a mixture of shorthairs and Brittanies and all did fine. When Labs entered my life in Montana, they did just as well and sometimes, in the case of long falls in rough terrain that required handling, even better. However, I rapidly became aware of several caveats regarding doves and retrievers no matter what the breed.

Most of my dove hunting took place when eastern Washington and the Montana prairies were hot places. If temperatures weren't scorching, the doves had probably headed south. Although the dogs spent a lot of time sitting quietly between retrieves, they still did a lot of panting. Fortunately, a lot of the best shooting took place near surface water in the form of stock ponds. When it didn't, I made sure to pack along ample water for the dog.

The second difficulty for retrievers on typical dove hunts arises from the birds' loose feathers. It's rare for a dog to have more than a feather or two in its mouth after a waterfowl retrieve. Even grouse and partridge seldom leave enough plumage behind to bother an experienced retriever. Dove feathers, on the other hand, come loose like hair from a shedding Lab. Start with a hot, panting dog and coat the inside of its sticky mouth with a handful of feathers and you can wind up with a retriever that doesn't want to hold birds. Experience plus adequate hydration in the field will usually cure that problem, but doves can be a hard way for a young dog to start a retrieving career. Tempting as it can be to get a youngster hunting at the start of its first season, I rarely take mine dove hunting until they've had a year of other birds behind them.

The world is home to dozens of species of doves and pigeons of the family *Columbidae*. With limited exceptions, all my early experience came with the familiar mourning dove. Before I started hunting beyond Washington and Montana, those exceptions were limited to a few memorable days spent pass-shooting band-tailed pigeons near rivers that hosted summer steelhead runs. As I began to travel the world writing about the outdoors, my dove hunting horizons inevitably broadened.

While I've never felt much enthusiasm for "high-volume" South American dove hunts, whenever I was fly-fishing or bowhunting in Argentina I customarily headed out with a borrowed shotgun and a box of shells during the inevitable siesta, sat under a tree, and shot doves until I ran out of ammo or everyone else woke up. Twenty-five birds made a convenient theoretical maximum, and while I seldom felt the need for more, the absence of a dog always made the hunting feel incomplete.

During my extensive bowhunting experience in southern Africa I became acquainted with a variety of dove species along with sand grouse, francolin, and guineas. We'll visit some of those hunts in later chapters. Most of my African wing-shooting took place incidentally with a beater .410. I packed that little clunker during those trips on the assumption that if it disappeared from a baggage department somewhere I wouldn't miss it. The majority of that hunting also took place without dogs, although we did spend some memorable days with friends in northern Zimbabwe who raised and trained pointers. That came to a halt after thugs loyal to then President Robert Mugabe shot them (all the dogs and one of the friends). I didn't go back to Zim until it settled down 30 years later, a trip we'll explore in an upcoming chapter.

Throughout all this, I somehow managed to avoid opportunities to hunt our own second native dove, the white-winged, but not for lack of interest. I just never managed to get myself in the right place at the right time during an open season. I've never been a box-checker, but there aren't a lot of North American gamebirds I haven't taken over the years. How the abundant white-winged dove made it onto that short list remained a mystery. I didn't let this aberration survive that morning in South Texas.

The doves were flying high with a modest tailwind behind them, and I was already thinking about my borrowed-gun excuse when the first single approached shotgun range. To my pleasant surprise that excuse proved unnecessary. The bird tumbled into a field of knee-high grass when I shot. The ground cover made me glad I'd brought the dogs, and Rosy made short work of the retrieve. Moments later, I was holding my first white-wing, a noticeably larger bird than the familiar mourning doves with which I'd grown up.

Rosy hadn't enjoyed an opportunity to hunt doves at all in Montana that fall, but she handled the mouth full of feathers gracefully, leaving me thankful for the cool winter weather. After dropping several more birds—the ratio of white-wings to mourning doves was nearly even—I talked Lori into setting the camera down and taking the shotgun. Since we apparently weren't going to have bird recovery problems, I left Rosy with my wife (it was never hard to get a Lab to stay with whoever was doing the shooting) and walked back to the truck for young Kiska.

Kiska had turned in an ambivalent performance during her first season. I didn't expect much from her now, but she'd held plenty of birds and I didn't think dove feathers would be a problem for her given the cool temperature. As I returned, Lori made a nice shot on an incoming bird high overhead. I anchored Rosy with a whistle blast since her steadiness sometimes faltered in my absence. Kiska had seen the dove fall, and I sent her. Granted, it was a routine retrieve, but she handled it perfectly and held the bird without protest until I told her to drop it in my hand.

Action proved steady throughout the morning. By the time we broke for enchiladas in the ranch house we had nearly taken limits and didn't need any more. All but two of the many retrieves came on birds we likely could have picked up by ourselves. The first exception came from a white-wing that couldn't have come down with much more than a broken flight primary. As it hopped and fluttered along the ground for a hundred yards Rosy ran it down. The second was a bird that Dick dropped into a nasty patch of nettles that didn't faze Kiska in the least.

After cleaning the birds, we loaded up and headed for a dove dinner on the coast. Saddled with an unfamiliar oven I managed to overcook them to my shame and embarrassment, but the fresh oysters that accompanied the doves helped compensate for my lapse. Then it was time to crawl into bed and await the early morning alarm clock while dreaming of the teal that would be awaiting us at first light.

The late, great Kenai with a wigeon from the Washington coast.

II.

Waterfowl

If hit squarely a bird staggers and spins, pauses for a moment, and then sinks gracefully like a handkerchief from a lady's hand.

– Lawrence Durrell, *Justine*

My first memory of duck hunting remains vivid even after more than 60 years, a testimonial to my fascination with the experience. My father had built a crude offshore blind in Otsego Lake, a long, deep body of water surrounded by the wooded hills that inspired James Fennimore Cooper's *Leatherstocking Tales*. I remember the lake as lovely, but it contained little waterfowl habitat. By my later standards it was a ridiculous place to hunt ducks.

Reaching the blind required wading 50 yards through the dark, but no one made waders that fit a child my size. My father slung me over his shoulder like a sack of potatoes and off we went. I couldn't see anything except the black water below, but I trusted my dad so completely that I never worried about falling in. Bits, the German wirehair familiar to readers by now, was also a capable water dog. I can still remember hearing him swimming ahead of us through the darkness toward the blind.

There's little more to tell about the rest of the morning other than that I heard some ducks, saw some ducks, and my father even shot a few teal, which Bits capably retrieved. Once the sun cleared the hills my attention turned to the marvelous iridescent streak of green in the birds' coverts. Their appearance proved a portent of sorts since the first duck I ever shot myself turned out to be a green-wing. While there wasn't much to the bag that morning, the experience left me fascinated and eager to repeat it.

As much as I already loved trailing along behind my dad on grouse hunts, I recognized something qualitatively different about that duck hunt, although I was too young to know the one word I eventually used to describe it. The luminous sunrise, dark water, bobbing decoys, whistling wings overhead, the splash of the dog hitting the water... The word I was groping for was pageantry.

Incidentally, while Durrell is known as a novelist rather than an outdoor writer, his fictional account of an Egyptian duck hunt at the end of *Justine* is some of the best wing-shooting prose I've ever read.

Ducks

22.

Fowl Weather

I have previously commented on the acoustics of cold air when the thermometer descends below zero, but the effects can be sufficiently dramatic to warrant repeating. The physics are straightforward, but to the observant outdoorsman the complexity of the results defies their simple explanation. That morning, the sound of the creek babbling past the front of our makeshift blind offered an orchestral range of tone and timbre. Dry snow squeaked beneath our boots. The tinkle of frozen willow branches disturbed by a browsing whitetail sounded intimate even though the deer would have been out of range for a bow if I had one. When the first wave of mallards rose from the stubble fields a mile to the south, I could hear their contented chuckles long before I saw the birds.

I have been told by responsible adults that hunting waterfowl in such conditions is a lunatic passion and they have a point, but they don't know the local game the way I do. Lori and I live in an arid county on the cusp of the Pacific and Central Flyways. Absent abundant wetlands and a position in the middle of the great autumn flight paths, the first two months of duck season here can be unproductive, with some welcome exceptions. That's not to say I don't hunt ducks then. I just don't expect to kill a lot of them. Come December though vast flocks of mallards winter nearby, feeding in grain fields and living on whatever open water they can find. Once ice grips the rivers and reservoirs, they flock to spring-fed creeks and ponds where the hunting can be spectacular. The Catch-22? If it's warm enough to be comfortable in a blind, I'm not going to shoot any ducks.

Since the converse is true as well, Lori and I were sitting on a fallen log bundled in an assortment of low, medium, and high-tech clothing adequate to stock a sporting goods store. Canine companionship that morning came from Rocky, by then the seasoned half of our kennel's yellow Lab duo. The temperature meant nothing to him. Muzzle framed in a corona of icy whiskers, he was busy scanning the sky for birds. Once we loaded our guns we had nothing to do but wait, providing an opportunity to reflect upon the correlation between good duck hunting and miserable weather.

Even as a kid, I realized that bluebird days are anathema to waterfowling. I still remember a long hike through the sagebrush to a large Columbia Basin pothole one clear, still October morning. Sunrise revealed a huge raft of puddle ducks and divers in the middle of the glassy lake, none closer than a hundred yards from shore. The few new arrivals all bypassed our decoy spread to join the pajama party far out on the water. Down to shirtsleeves by mid-morning, my hunting partner and I finally circled the shore shouting and waving in a futile attempt to get some ducks airborne.

The value of rain, snow, wind, and other forms of climactic misery is old news to seasoned waterfowl hunters, but bad weather has its place in upland cover too. Hot, dry scenting conditions can render both pointing dogs and flushing retrievers befuddled. Weather concentrates upland game as well as waterfowl. There's nothing like a foot of fresh snow to slow down running pheasants and chukar. Here in Montana I've long been partial to the waning weeks of pheasant season despite the dearth of easy limits. I'm hunting educated survivors then, and a few cagey December roosters mean more to me than game vests full of naïve birds during the opening week. The dogs can run all day without overheating. Few other hunters pursue pheasants in such conditions and they're usually folks I'm happy to encounter in the field. Indian summer days make nice pictures, but angry winter weather often makes better bird hunting.

Today's new generation of outdoor clothing has made it easier to sit still waiting for ducks in nasty weather. I take advantage of modern synthetics and rain gear when I'm heading out into the worst of it but I'm not ready to forsake all the old ways. I *like* the smell of wet wool. Like a good whiff of pronghorn or moose, that scent can instantly evoke countless subliminal memories, most of them pleasant. The crunch of icy woolens produces a similar effect. No matter how comfortable a good arsenal of modern outdoor wear can make me during the thick of the fray, I sometimes think we should chuck it all and go back to fishnet long-johns, plaid wool shirts, and no-camo slickers just for old time's sake. Granted, that kind of sentiment usually goes best at the end of the day when you're dressed in fresh, dry clothing and sitting in front of a crackling fire with a glass of wine in hand.

No matter how you're dressed, nasty wing-shooting weather can eventually cross the line between inconvenient and miserable. On one late season goose hunt, we set out our decoys before sunrise in ideal weather conditions, with enough breeze and cold to keep the birds moving back and forth between our field and the nearby river but not enough to make waiting for them intolerable. Well-dressed for the occasion, we were still warm and comfortable in our coffin blinds when the first honkers cleared the far end of the field after sunrise. For once, we'd picked the right place on the right morning and for the next hour we were too busy shooting geese to pay attention to the weather.

Lori finally had the sense to make the necessary observation. The temperature had plummeted, the wind had backed around to due north, and 10 gusting to 15 had risen to 20 gusting to 30. No wonder it didn't feel like fun anymore. Because of the flat, open terrain, I'd parked the truck nearly a mile away to avoid spooking the educated late season geese. I volunteered to hike back into the wind and get it while everyone else went to work picking up the decoy spread. Midway through the hike, the wind became so bitter that I had to turn around and walk backwards to avoid freezing my eyelids shut. The weather had made us stop shooting a few geese shy of our limit, but geese are hard to pluck. By the time we finished cleaning the birds that night I decided that the cold had done us a favor. That was a gorgeous day too, at least once it was over.

At some point, bad weather can make the jump from misery to outright danger. It's appropriately ironic that after decades of bush flying and close-range encounters with dangerous game while armed with nothing but a longbow, one of my scariest experiences came from water.

The trip's agenda was more complicated than the usual duck hunt. Doug Borland had drawn a coveted Kodiak Island brown bear tag. Since he was going to do it with his bow or not at all, Ernie Holland and I had gone along to provide firearm backup. Between white knuckle bear hunts, Ernie and I did some sea duck shooting along the tide line. Our wall tent base camp lay on a long tidal lagoon that emptied and filled every six hours through a narrow, winding bottleneck separating the lagoon from the open bay. To save ourselves the long hike around the shoreline when we wanted to hunt the other side, we'd brought along a small inflatable boat to get us across the channel. To save weight on the flight to camp we'd left behind the reliable Avons and Zodiacs in which we'd logged countless hours under difficult conditions. The substitute was a flimsy swimming pool toy we promptly christened the Rubber Ducky. It seemed like a good idea at the time.

Several days into the hunt we'd killed no brown bears (despite several interesting encounters), but we'd banged some goldeneyes and scoters at the mouth of the lagoon. Then one morning, we rose before dawn and hiked down to the channel with the Rubber Ducky. Testing its freeboard to the limit, we climbed aboard and pushed off into the dark.

It was an unusually cold morning. We were crossing at the peak of the tidal ebb and a strong current was running down the channel to the sea. Midway across, I heard an unfamiliar tinkling sound ahead. By the time I deduced its origin, it was too late. The near zero overnight temperature had frozen the fresh water where a creek entered the head of the lagoon. When the tide started to fall sheets of ice had collapsed and were now flushing down the channel. Up in the bow, Ernie tried his best to fend off the floating pan with his paddle, but the sharp leading edge of the ice hit us and popped the Rubber Ducky as if it were a child's balloon.

"We're going down!" Ernie cried helpfully as frigid North Pacific salt water reached my chin. Since I was scheduled for rifle backup that day, I had the .375 slung across my shoulders with a daypack beneath it. We were all dressed in boots and heavy wool and the current was sweeping us relentlessly out toward the bay. Oddly enough, in retrospect I don't remember being nearly as scared as I should have been.

Three considerations saved us. First, we're all strong swimmers. Second, no one wound up underneath the floating ice pan, an event that likely would have proven fatal. Third – and we agreed later that none of us had made this decision consciously – we all turned back toward the shore we'd started from even though we were probably more than midway across the channel. Swimming to the far side would have left us with a four-mile hike back to the wall tent in conditions inviting hypothermia.

Five minutes after the Ducky went down, we all crawled out on shore. I've never been happier to see others present and accounted for. There were still a few coals left in the bottom of the little sheepherder's stove back at our wall tent which we quickly breathed back to life. Incredibly, everyone had hung onto their bows and backpacks. I'd even saved the rifle although I'd been on the verge of dumping it. We'd survived without losing a single piece of equipment, not to mention our lives.

Lori and Rosy enjoying a late season duck hunt beside a spring-fed slough.

Back down at the creek, Lori, Rocky, and I are shivering and waiting for Godot. Fully adapted to the cold and clad in the best insulation nature can provide, the dog looks happy as a pig in slop. He knows why we're here and instinctively recognizes the mission as his *raison d'etre*. Lori seems less certain. She makes no bones about the fact that she'd rather shoot one shoveler on a nice day than a limit of sub-zero greenheads, but she's too proud and stubborn to show the white feather. If anyone's going to decide we've had enough and start picking up the decoys it's going to be me.

One important technical consideration amidst all this storytelling: 10-below may be damn cold, but this isn't the kind of weather that usually gets hunters in real trouble. Frigid weather like this is almost always the result of a stable high-pressure system with little wind or moisture. Hypothermia is more likely on a wet, windy day with temperatures in the 30's than in calm, clear weather no matter what the thermometer says. Today, that's my rationalization for hanging on a little longer. I know we'll survive; I just hope my marriage does too.

Face, feet, and hands always go first. Wool ski masks have the first concern covered, although frozen condensation from my breath has turned my beard into a bib of ice. Cold fingers have long been Lori's downfall, but she's learned to stuff her pockets with chemical hand-warmers. Insulated waders and heavy socks notwithstanding, there isn't much to do when your toes start to go numb except stamp your feet and hope the birds arrive before common sense prevails.

We've just reached that stage when Rocky glances sharply back over my shoulder. He's too well trained to break, but the rules don't say anything about occasional excited whining. The noise of setting wings sounds like a jet engine spooling up for takeoff. Then mallards are circling the blocks and it's time to start mentally isolating drakes from hens.

Technically, there isn't much to the shooting during the late season, when most birds fall at ranges I could reach with a fly line. The show is all mallards and the goal is to kill five birds with green heads while leaving the ladies untouched. The epic part of the morning will belong to the dog soon enough.

"Take 'em!" I whisper on the next pass and seconds later three drakes are tumbling as the rest of the flock claws its way back into the sky. Two of the fallen birds leave neat little entrance wounds in the snowbank across the creek while the third tumbles away on the dancing current. After handing my empty gun to Lori, I line Rocky up on the troublesome retrieve and he's off in a spectacular geyser of spray.

Suddenly the cold just doesn't feel cold anymore, and it's another gorgeous day after all.

23.

Redheads and Oyster Beds

The first birds appeared at improbable distance silhouetted against a cerulean blue sky that could have graced a travel poster advertising a tropical resort. They were flying at high speed in tight formation, undulating without making any member of the flock lose its place in line. The wing beats looked fast, short, and powerful. The birds sliced through the gulls and terns working the shoreline like a line of motorcycles weaving through stalled city traffic. Then they saw the decoys and banked hard in our direction.

I'd shot waterfowl from minimalist blinds before, but this one was one of the skimpiest. Lori and I had set up on a point protruding from one of the low spoil islands scattered about the Laguna Madre between South Padre Island and the Texas mainland. All we had for cover was a berm of sand and shell fragments behind us high enough to break up our outline and a strip of netting out in front.

The flock was nearly in range by the time it turned away from the sun's glare and allowed me a positive ID. "Redheads!" I whispered to Lori. She knows her waterfowl, but we rarely get to shoot big water divers around our Montana home. I felt eager for her to appreciate her first encounter with the species as seen down the length of a ventilated rib. "Pick a drake," I advised and then it was time to shoulder my borrowed 12-gauge and pick one out myself.

With bright southern sunlight flashing from a half dozen auburn heads, identifying a target proved easy. I still had to kill the bird. Most of our waterfowling consists of shooting puddle ducks over decoys in tight places. That kind of shotgun handling demands its own skill set, but dropping a diver zipping low across the water at maximum shotgun range is another matter. In these situations I've learned to override instincts developed during years of experience by consciously driving my barrels an extra two or three body lengths ahead of the duck before I slap the trigger pulling away. When I did, the drake redhead cartwheeled across the water like a seaplane catching the tip of a float before it came to a gratifying, motionless stop. Lori's bird had done the same.

By prior agreement we both ignored our second barrels for two reasons. First, while the Texas coast offered a generous waterfowl limit there were sub-limits on several of the diver species we hoped to find that afternoon, including a daily maximum of two redheads. We didn't want to end our day in the first ten minutes of shooting. Second, due to airline logistics we were doing something ordinarily unthinkable: hunting without one of our Labs. We knew we'd have to kill cleanly and keep a second barrel in reserve in case we had a live bird down on the water.

With the drakes we'd just dropped drifting safely head-down toward the cul-de-sac of shallow oyster beds behind us, we reloaded and settled back to see what the Laguna Madre would serve us next.

Redhead decoys ready to go on the Texas Gulf Coast.

I've done most of my hunting in the places I've called home: the Pacific Northwest, Montana, Alaska. In the first of those venues, the Columbia Basin usually lies shrouded in ice fog during the last half of duck season. In our part of Montana, duck hunting doesn't get good until the thermometer drops and concentrates birds on ice resistant springs. As for Alaska, well… it's Alaska. The upshot of all this geography is that December duck hunting for me usually means various combinations of rain, wind, snow, and cold.

All of which made periodic mid-winter duck hunts with our friends on the Texas Gulf Coast feel surreal. Light sweaters, no rain gear, and sunscreen… Are you kidding? Of course, it isn't always that way. On one memorable trip a cold front whacked us so hard that we were traveling to our blinds by airboats running on top of solid ice. Usually, however, the ambience feels less like a duck hunt than a trip to a saltwater flats fly-fishing destination, as in fact it is. Winter isn't prime time to enjoy casting to redfish in South Texas, but I've done it successfully while hunting ducks over salt water there.

Most of our Texas waterfowling involves the pursuit of puddle ducks and geese—honkers, speckle-bellies, and especially snows—in brackish marshes. On that trip our friends had suggested something different: a drive down to the southern reaches of the Laguna Madre to set up for divers on the salt. The first afternoon's trip by skiff enforced the importance of local knowledge when navigating the flats beyond Inter-Coastal Waterway channel markers. As we debated which side of an oyster bed to follow, I looked over the gunwale and realized we were running in inches of water. Had we come off the step to debate our route, the grounded skiff would probably have stayed there until the next high tide.

But we didn't, and the farther we ran toward South Padre Island the more flights of divers we encountered. We stopped to observe, identified a couple of active flight routes, and split into two parties. While Lori and I slogged to shore and pitched out decoys, our friends ran around the island and set up in the skiff. We didn't hear a lot of shooting from them, and they didn't hear a lot from us, but we all heard enough. By the time they returned to pick us up, we had limits of redheads and bluebills to pluck, clean, and toss onto the grill at Dick's place in Port Mansfield that night.

While I missed my dogs that afternoon, the shallow water and a steady onshore breeze left me confident that we could hunt responsibly without them no matter how much I missed their company. I felt edgier the following morning when Lori and I set up on another little island that didn't offer us a cul-de-sac to catch floating ducks. The other team had a Lab. Lori had me. We knew we needed to make each shot count to save me from a long wade or a short swim.

Dick had dropped us off at the limit of the skiff's draft far from shore, requiring us to make a long slog to reach dry land. In contrast to the previous day we enjoyed the luxury of brush for cover once we got there. Fresh wild hog tracks in the sand aroused a mixture of curiosity and interest—the latter because of the recurve bows Lori and I had left back at Dick's, the former because I couldn't fathom how hogs could survive that far from fresh water, the nearest of which lay miles across the salt on the mainland. While Lori cobbled together a brush blind on a little point of land, I distributed a mix of puddle duck and diver decoys in its lee. Then we settled in to let the birds find us again.

An hour passed before we saw ducks in the air but the interlude hardly felt boring. When hunting waterfowl I'm usually as interested in my surroundings as the shooting. A constant stream of exotic (to us) neo-tropical birdlife kept us constantly entertained: ibises and egrets, skimmers and spoonbills. Then breeze began to develop, animating our decoy spread and coaxing ducks into the air from the channel where they'd been rafted up all morning.

The first flight of the day consisted of a dozen bluebills. The scaup weren't as intent upon our decoys as the redheads had been the day before, but when they roared by I dropped the closest drake. When I saw the bird hit the water with its head up, I chided myself for taking the shot, longed once more for one of our dogs, and set off to anchor the bird with my second barrel. Oyster shells scraped at my feet as I hustled toward the downed bird and I realized that my waders might become a casualty of my ambitious shooting. Fortunately, Dick had leant me a tightly choked 12, and the scaup allowed me to get close enough to finish it with a second shot in knee-deep water. Lesson learned.

"We aren't shooting at any bird past that last decoy," I advised Lori once I'd returned to the blind and repositioned some of the blocks.

"I wasn't planning to," she replied. "Looks like you might need some new waders," she added as she pointed out some scrapes on the sides of my boots.

The freshening breeze soon had plenty of birds moving. We could now pick and choose our shots comfortably. The next two hours reminded me how different hunting divers can be from hunting puddle ducks, especially over salt water. The space around us—both water and sky—felt vast. We enjoyed the luxury of spotting inbound flocks changing course toward our decoy spread from hundreds of yards away. Even the close shots would be long by our usual standards, although neither of us had much trouble adjusting to them. The shooting lacked the chaotic excitement of mallards flaring in front of our faces, but the stately elegance of those long lines of divers and the way they effortlessly mastered the wind provided an elegant spectacle of its own.

The wigeon and teal we thought might show up from the mainland never arrived, but by the time the skiff returned for us Lori and I again had limits of redheads and bluebills hanging from our duck straps. While I would have traded my shotgun for one of my Labs at the beginning of the day, we hadn't lost a bird.

That afternoon we packed up and headed north to hunt puddle ducks farther up the coast. I commented on the oyster beds I'd been walking along the last two days. They reminded me how as a kid I used to head to the mouth of Washington's Hood Canal to shoot brant and sea ducks, armed with an oyster knife, lemons, and a bottle of Tabasco sauce. Whether or not the birds flew on the incoming tide, I never went home hungry.

We arrived too late to hunt that night, so Lori and I headed down to the shore and caught a couple of redfish with our fly rods. As soon as we'd finished turning them into seviche, Dick appeared with a cooler full of fresh oysters. Cooked slowly over a mesquite grill, the ducks we'd shot earlier that day provided the final course in a memorable meal that was pure Texas Gulf Coast.

We shot plenty of birds the next morning—green-wings and pintails for the most part, with a few snow geese thrown into the mix. Lori and I hunted with our friend Marshall, who had his Lab. With a retriever with us at last I didn't have to worry so much about lost ducks. Even so, I vowed that the next time we visited I'd bring one of our Labs even if we had to drive all the way from Montana to Texas. And we did.

Grand as the show was in the marsh that morning, that trip's most vivid memories still derive from the two days we spent on the Laguna Madre—shooting species we seldom saw at home, soaking up sunshine, and setting our decoys out atop some of the most succulent shellfish in the world.

24.

Big Water

A good boat is an essential part of the serious diving duck hunter's equipment list. In contrast to puddle ducks, divers thrive in big water and commonly trade too far from the shoreline to reach from land-based blinds. American waterfowl hunters have been building boats unique to this purpose as long as there have been American waterfowl hunters, creating a long legacy of designs. While it's theoretically possible to hunt divers from almost any craft that floats (except for the Rubber Ducky), the best feature shallow draft, broad beams for stability, adequate freeboard to remain dry and safe in windy duck hunting weather, ample storage room for decoys, and a power plant adequate to get you to and from the ducks (which may be anything from a set of oars to a 4-stroke outboard).

While our friend Fred Slyfield's skiff meets all of those specifications, I knew we would be challenging its load capacity as we pushed away from the boat ramp on the Columbia River. In addition to Fred and me, the boat held my wife, Lori; our friend from Anchorage, Greg Svendsen; and not one retriever but three: Fred's Chessie, Whistler; Greg's well-travelled black Lab, Midnight; and our own Rosy, who had never hunted from a boat before. That seemed like a lot of large canine company in a small space, but all three dogs were well-behaved. I expected them to be easily managed despite their enthusiasm. As events unfolded that afternoon, I was glad we had them all.

As discussed in the previous chapter, hunting divers differs remarkably from hunting dabblers like mallards, pintails, and teal, in ways both obvious and intangible. I do a lot more of the latter, but only as a function of opportunity. Save for an occasional ring-neck or late season goldeneye, we don't have a lot of divers around our Montana home. I rarely get to hunt them unless I'm somewhere else. Over the years those opportunities have included everything from harlequins and scoters on the Alaska tideline to redheads and scaup on the Texas Gulf Coast as described elsewhere in this book. While that's certainly not enough experience to make me an expert on divers, it's enough to make me appreciate them—and the differences between hunting them and hunting more familiar puddle ducks.

Those differences begin with the choice of shotguns. For years I've been an outlier, arguing that many duck hunters shoot too much gun with chokes too tight. I'm still perfectly happy with an improved cylinder/modified 20-gauge and 3" shells for decoying puddle ducks at close range. Shots at divers are often longer. I believe divers are tougher, if only because they so often present a smaller target when viewed laterally as opposed to exposing their breast as a mallard does when flaring over decoys. Because they swim and dive so capably, wounded divers can be harder for even the best dogs to recover. For all these reasons I carry a modified/full 12-gauge, also chambered for 3" shells, when I'm deliberately out for diving ducks.

For me, all discussion of guns, loads, and chokes is ultimately secondary to the real essence of waterfowl hunting: the dogs. Our two great American retrieving breeds—the Lab and the Chessie—were originally developed to fetch diving ducks from big water back when canvasbacks were the cream of the market hunter's crop. Their utility for hunting puddle ducks, not to mention upland game, came later. Despite this historical aside most of our dogs are less familiar with divers and sea ducks than mallards or pintails.

While a dog may be called upon to fetch an occasional goldeneye in a way that doesn't differ much from the last dozen mallards, real diver hunts add an extra measure of challenge to a retriever's job description. Because divers prefer larger, more open water than puddle ducks, retrieves are often longer and landmarks scarcer. Divers commonly fly in large flocks, and two or three capable guns can drop a lot of birds at the same time. Dogs often won't get to touch solid ground at any point during a long retrieve. Wounded divers escaping pursuit by going underwater can give even experienced retrievers fits, especially if they have a 50-yard head start on the dog.

The ocean is the biggest big water of all. Like human observers from the Book of Psalms to John Masefield, I have always been drawn to the sea and its mysteries. Waterfowl hunting on the salt offers challenges of its own for retrievers, especially along the Alaska coast where several of my dogs received their introduction to divers. A lot of that hunting took place during the winter simply because there wasn't much else to hunt then, and the weather was invariably miserable. Wind and tide could turn a routine retrieve into a marathon. While my Labs always got the job done, I still can't think of a situation that makes a better argument for a Chesapeake. The memory of my friends' Chessies crashing around happily in the surf with scoters and harlequins hanging from their mouths remains vivid to this day.

Back when I was a kid newly arrived in the Pacific Northwest, my dad and I built a wooden punt in our garage so we could navigate the tidal channels around Puget Sound while hunting divers. That's the only time I have ever owned a boat specifically designed for duck hunting. Since then I've set out on diver hunts in everything from pirogues and canoes to commercial fishing boats, all of which presented various disadvantages. In order to enjoy hunting from a real duck boat, I have had to rely on the kindness of friends like Fred.

Dogs face new challenges when they hunt from boats. One obvious solution is to leave them behind, but no matter how quick you are with anchors, buoys, and lines that option will cost you some birds. Besides, what's the point of hunting ducks without a dog?

The outbound leg of a retrieve from a boat seldom causes problems, since with experience most retrievers will launch on command once a duck hits the water. Getting them back aboard can be more difficult. Vintage drawings from Newfoundland show Lab ancestors grasping knotted lines between their teeth so their handlers could haul them into fishing boats once their work in the water was done. That has never impressed me as good training for a soft-mouthed retriever. If I had my own designated duck boat I would outfit it with a removable dive ladder off the transom and train the dog to use it. Absent such a device, I've had to make do with a hand on the scruff of the neck and a well-timed heave, a technique that Rosy among others mastered without protest.

Set up for divers on the Columbia river.

Since I live a long way from the ocean now, most of my diver hunting takes place on the Columbia River. During the half-dozen waterfowl expeditions I make to the area with Lori and the dogs every season, I usually take at least one break from the mallards to hunt the river by boat with our friends Fred or Michael Crowder.

As we were on that crisp November afternoon described earlier in this chapter. Setting out the decoys reminded me of commercial long-line fishing for halibut back in Alaska. Despite my initial concerns about over-crowding in the boat, there seemed plenty of room for everyone as long as the three dogs continued to behave. To be on the safe side, I kept Rosy on a leash despite her usually excellent blind manners.

I might have been content to spend a relaxing half-hour with old friends catching up on family news and reviewing events of the current hunting season, but the ducks denied that opportunity. Sitting casually with my shotgun broken over the reed mat affixed to the gunwale, I had to scramble when a small flock of bluebills rounded the upstream point and headed for the blocks. Stationed on the downstream edge of the boat, I didn't even bother to raise my gun as I saw a second drake hit the water courtesy of Fred and Greg. Much to Rosy's disappointment, I kept her onboard and let the other two dogs handle the retrieving, an opportunity they deserved thanks to their handlers' accurate shooting. Two ducks and two dogs seemed an adequate invitation to chaos on the first shooting of the afternoon.

I showed no such restraint when a trio of ring-necked ducks came in low from my direction. Only one was a drake, but it tumbled when I shot. As a consequence of its high speed and flat trajectory, the dead bird skipped across the water like a hockey puck before it came to rest motionless and belly-up. Rosy exploded from the bow upon my command, completed an otherwise routine retrieve, and came back over the transom as if she'd been hunting from boats all her life.

Save for another flock of bluebills that brought us halfway to our daily sub-quota of scaup, the next hour passed slowly. We could see flocks of redheads and canvasbacks trading across the middle of the river, but there just wasn't enough wind to push them into the lee where we had set up. While the four of us drank coffee and talked, the dogs maintained an intense but well-behaved vigil.

When Rosy turned her face sharply downstream and cocked her ears forward, I took the cue and set my coffee cup down on the seat beside me. I eventually spotted a lone duck inbound a hundred yards away. At first I thought it was a goldeneye, but as it closed the distance I recognized it as a bufflehead. Because of their small size, naivety, and overall cuteness I seldom shoot butterballs, but we hadn't had any action for a while and Rosy was clearly eager for another retrieve. Besides, as the drake reached shotgun range I could tell that it was an exceptional specimen, and I hadn't taken a duck to the taxidermist all year.

After making the shot, I'd barely hauled the dog back aboard when the unmistakable sound of honkers on the wing reached us. We hadn't planned for geese and didn't have a single goose decoy in our spread, but we all had goose calls on lanyards around our necks. Whether as a result of our enthusiastic calling or serendipity, a dozen honkers soon rounded the point 20 yards above the water and headed down the outer edge of the decoys.

The dogs behaved well and we timed our rise perfectly. The lead goose shuddered when I slapped the trigger, and I elected to shoot it again with my second barrel to be sure it went down and stayed there. Meanwhile, a ripple of shotgun fire had passed down the length of the skiff like a broadside from the days when naval gunboats ran on sail power. My peripheral vision revealed more birds falling. Then it was over, and we started counting downed geese. One for each dog lay floating on the water. By the time I noticed a fourth swimming hard for a low-lying islet a quarter-mile away the cripple was already well out of shotgun range. We wound up retrieving the retrievers and motoring over to the little island, where we spent an hour running all three dogs over every inch of it to no avail. That lost bird provided the only blemish on our day as well as a necessary reminder of how tough a wounded goose can be. Those who frown upon taking retrievers on goose hunts, and I know a few, should take note.

Regulations limited us to a pair of scaup apiece. While we filled most of our remaining limits with ring-necks and goldeneyes we wanted to leave some room for a few of the cans and redheads off in the distance. We never did shoot any that day, although I have killed both on similar Columbia River expeditions. Despite the refusal of those two elite species to cooperate, we still reached the boat launch with plenty of birds including a bonus of geese we never expected.

If I was happy with our shooting, I was even happier with the dogs despite our one lost goose. A small boat is no place for ill-behaved retrievers, even one of which can soon become way too many. All three of those aboard that day were not just good working dogs. They were also good company, and in tight quarters like that, I can think of no higher compliment.

25.

The Fog of War

We arrived at our blind one December morning to find the skies above the Columbia Basin shrouded in the kind of fog that looks as if it can be cut into slices and served on a pie plate. By the time we'd set out the decoys I felt disoriented in the featureless sea of corn stalks and hayfields surrounding the little pond. My confusion hardly mattered from a practical standpoint, but I've always been the kind of outdoorsman who likes to know which way north lies even when I'm not thinking about it.

Our party was unusually large that day. In addition to Lori and my father (our designated elder statesman and voice of experience at age 88), I'd spent plenty of time in the field with Michael Crowder, but I'd never hunted before with Bunce Kinney, who had kindly extended the morning's invitation, or Will Bailey, a charter boat operator from the same corner of Alaska I used to inhabit. By the time we had finished distributing the blocks around the pond they both felt like old friends. With Cutter, Bunce's eight-year-old yellow Lab, at one end of the pit and my own Rocky at the other, we had a blind full of company.

As we settled into place Michael expressed his dislike for hunting ducks in heavy fog, which he believes keeps the birds from flying. I countered with an opposing opinion, based on nothing more than anecdotal memories of a few great hunts that took place on foggy mornings. Nonetheless, I had to admit that Michael had a point. Ducks don't fly in instrument conditions. They require visual orientation to the horizon. Fortunately there were a few breaks in the fog, and a chorus of feeding chuckles interrupted this discussion before it became too bogged down in abstract theory. The birds sounded as if they were straight overhead, but I couldn't make them out through the gloom. "See!" Michael said. "They can't spot our decoys!"

While Michael and I were debating Bunce and Will were calling, and moments later a pair of greenheads came spiraling down out of the fog. Since Michael had to leave early for a meeting, we expected him to take them, and he did. Then he was gone, leaving the five of us and the dogs to make what we could from the rest of the gray, gloomy morning.

Fog has always occupied a spooky corner of the human imagination. Carl Sandburg claimed that it comes on little cats' feet and sits on silent haunches. Bram Stoker's Dracula could turn himself into fog at will. No cinematic treatment of Sherlock Holmes or Jack the Ripper would be complete without invoking London's infamous version of the stuff. Perhaps most famously, the military theorist Carl von Clausewitz used fog as a metaphor for the confusion that reigns when armies join in battle, making discipline and strategy evaporate. He probably didn't know that the same principle applies in duck blinds, especially when multiple hunters and dogs find themselves faced with a whole lot of ducks.

As we certainly did over the course of the morning, only to be plagued by an unusual problem I'd like to have more often: an excess of sportsmanship and good manners. Arriving in flocks of 15 to 20, the mallards—all prime northern greenheads newly arrived ahead of a brewing winter storm—would circle our spread repeatedly at the edge of shotgun range without committing to land. No one wanted to be the first to stand and risk shooting prematurely, especially since the flat light made distinguishing drakes from hens more difficult than usual. Whenever a drake or two would break out of formation and settle into range, everyone politely deferred to everyone else until the birds smelled a rat and flared back into the soup. In this manner, we managed to enjoy the spectacle the first several flocks provided without firing a shot.

I soon realized that despite an excellent setup we weren't going to have dozens of birds back-peddling in our faces and suggested that the next time someone had a positive ID on a drake in range, they should call the shot and take it. Leave it to feminine common sense to show the way. The next time a lone drake peeled out of a circling flock to buzz the decoys, Lori simply stood up and crumpled it. "*Someone* had to break the ice," she explained as she reloaded, and the sigh of relief from the rest of us felt palpable.

While our host kept apologizing for what he called a slow morning, we were obviously set up in a prime location. Flying above the fog layer, the birds were traveling from the north to feed in fields farther south. Even though we heard a lot of birds we couldn't see, enough descended and circled our spread to provide steady shooting. Abundant witnesses can make even a crack shot come a cropper, but the shooting itself wasn't a problem for any of us that day. Rather, it was the decision to stand and take the shots as they arose that proved difficult, as everyone kept being so damn polite.

With Lori leading the way, we finally began to ignore the circling birds overhead and take the drakes in ones and twos as opportunities arose. Then it became time for the dogs to join the pleasantly confused comedy. One of Thomas's Laws (of which there are perhaps too many) holds that experienced dogs will always reserve their most undisciplined performances for the maximum number of witnesses, and sure enough. Although I'd never hunted with Cutter before, she was by all accounts an experienced and highly capable retriever. Nonetheless, she lost the line on the first several falls, obligating Bunce to wade out into the marsh and show us that he handled better than his dog.

Because of the dugout blind's low profile a breaking dog could easily wind up in the line of fire. Bunce had wisely fitted the dog box on each end of the blind with a permanently fixed leash to prevent a disaster. I'd kept Rocky on his leash after the first several falls, but when we finally put three greenheads down on the water at once, I sent him toward a bird on the opposite end of the pond. As Cutter churned back toward shore with the first duck in her mouth, Rocky veered offline and took the bird away from her. I'd seen him pull this obnoxious stunt before, but thought I'd broken him of the habit over the summer with the help of Kenai, a bucketful of dummies, and an e-collar. Unfortunately, the excitement and confusion that morning produced a classic case of behavioral regression. With apologies to all, I gave the bird to its rightful owner and snapped the leash back on Rocky's collar.

I'd seen versions of that scenario played out countless times before: experienced hunters and dogs in a crowded blind making rookie mistakes none of them would have made had they been hunting in less confusing circumstances. As long as no one violates principles of safety, and no one came close to this one unforgivable sin on that foggy morning, those mistakes usually wind up as nothing more than the subject of humor at the end of the day. I could only hope that they didn't all come at my expense. It's still nice to avoid them if possible, and I've had enough experience with these situations to offer a few simple suggestions.

The hunters' first responsibility should be to select a *Jägermeister* to call the shots, and then support whatever decisions he or she makes. No need to draw out the selection process like a presidential election. If the choice doesn't obviously fall to the host or the most experienced member of the party, play rock-paper-scissors and be done with it. Faced with a circling flock of mallards or an inbound line of honkers, no thoughtful sportsman wants to risk discourtesy by standing up and shooting at the wrong time—when the birds are still at marginal range or when a flock of twenty birds has set its wings to follow the single you just killed into the decoys. Unfortunately, the default position is usually a state of paralysis in which everyone defers to everyone else and no one shoots anything.

It's not necessary for the hunt master to be right every time. We've all made the kind of mistakes just mentioned. It is necessary to communicate decisions clearly and effectively. "I think they might be in range on this pass," doesn't cut it. "Take 'em!" does. That's just the kind of decisive countermeasure von Clausewitz had in mind when he lamented the paralyzing effect of chaotic military engagement over a century ago.

*Lori waits for fog to lift on the Texas Gulf Coast.
When it did, we shot limits of teal.*

The dogs may need that kind of discipline even more than we will. The potential for canine confusion varies arithmetically with the number of guns in the blind and exponentially with the number of dogs, which is why bad canine performances occur so frequently in front of witnesses. This is especially true of dogs that don't customarily share blinds with lots of company, like my own. When multiple guns start going off, birds are hitting the water, and other dogs are plunging after them to a chorus of commands from several handlers, any dog can lose its bearings no matter how levelheaded and well-trained.

Dog discipline is often the first casualty when the fog of war impacts a duck blind. The urge to compete can make any retriever break no matter how steady the dog is in the yard or in a blind with no other dogs around. While I can't pretend to offer any universal solution to the problem, basic control helps. While some might consider leashes a reflection of inadequate training I see nothing wrong with them in duck blinds when dogs are going to have lots of company. Whistles are more effective than verbal commands, and the handler should be willing to unload and concentrate on the dog instead of the shooting.

Working just one dog at a time helps, especially at the start of the day. As Rocky proved that morning by picking Cutter's pocket to my embarrassment, mischief can take place any time two dogs are out of the blind at the same time even when you think you've cured them of such bad habits.

After two more hours of slow (according to our host) but steady shooting, I'm happy to report that the figurative fog of war affecting us that morning had burned off even if the literal fog overhead had not. We were taking the shots that needed taking and killing what we shot at cleanly, not that the shooting was technically difficult. The only hen that fell was a single Lori dropped with two of us whispering "drake!" in her ears. The dogs were minding their manners and doing their job in capable if not quite stellar fashion, although Cutter did a superb job of running down one long cripple. Our only unrecovered birds were a mallard we never could account for and a green-wing I dumped into thick brush a hundred yards away. We included them both as part of our five eventual limits.

Teamwork offers the one enduring solution to confusion in a duck blind, just as it does whenever individuals must pool and coordinate resources to attain a common goal, on the battlefield, the basketball court, or anywhere else in life. I can't think of a better setting in which to face such challenges then in a duck blind, surrounded by family, friends, and retrievers.

26.

The Heron Rookery

I used to see the herons silhouetted against the sunset almost every summer evening near our Montana home: long legs extended, necks wrapped gracefully back against their bodies, stately wing beats plying the air in measured cadence. During the day, they dispersed to backwaters up and down the creek to stand motionless until striking with their dagger-like bills. I don't doubt that they accounted for plenty of small trout although I never begrudged them their share. Every night they returned to their communal rookery in the stand of dead cottonwoods, where their great, sprawling nests formed a landmark visible up and down the valley for miles. I don't know just where they spent their days, but they apparently did so in solitude. At last light single birds appeared inbound from all quadrants of the sky as if responding to a navigation beacon. I felt quietly uplifted every time I saw them in flight, for the birds had a welcome way of reminding me that even in hectic times good things endure and calm eventually prevails.

    A spring-fed backwater circled the stand of cottonwoods where the herons nested, marking an abandoned course the creek once took in its younger days. The water there stayed open long after most local ponds and marshes had frozen for the winter, and because the ducks didn't have to battle the creek's robust current they loved to land there when the mercury plummeted and left no other open water. The rancher who owned the property had been a friend for years. Access wasn't anything I leased or paid for with anything other than years of medical care for him and his family. I always felt a special, personal relationship with the place based on privilege rather than possession.

Now, I regret the need to write the last two paragraphs in the past tense.

That year I spent the first two weeks of November marking the transition from autumn to winter with my bow in hand. Then one evening the whitetail buck I'd been watching picked the wrong trail to follow in search of does and my deer season ended with a twang of the bowstring. After a week of frigid weather had concentrated ducks along the creek, the end of deer season couldn't have come at a better time, not with the Labs offering me neglected looks at every opportunity. As soon as I had the deer hanging in the barn, I walked back down to the house, cleaned up, and called my rancher friend. He confirmed that the cold had brought the ducks in and that I was welcome to hunt. He had moved livestock into one of the pastures along the creek and asked that I not shoot near them, a perfectly reasonable request from a man whose livelihood depended upon the welfare of his cattle. I tried to tell him exactly where I planned to hunt, but ranchers think in terms of fences rather than terrain features. I finally concluded that I would have to investigate for myself.

The following afternoon, I left work early and drove down to the creek. I wasn't really worried about the cows since they're usually kept away from the riparian zone at that time of year. However, as soon as I heaved the decoy bag over the fence and started toward the Promised Land, I saw large bovine hoofprints in the thin layer of snow underfoot. A hundred yards into the brush I ran into the cows that had left them. Just then, a wave of mallards came chuckling in over the treetops headed for the open water. There wasn't anything to do but watch, and for half an hour I left my gun unloaded and enjoyed the show as ducks poured in by the dozen. Rocky, then age five, plainly thought I'd lost my senses, but as the member of the team responsible for landowner relations the thought of shooting where I wasn't supposed to shoot never crossed my mind. Well; almost never.

That night I called the rancher and explained my dilemma only to have him reassure me that the cows would be gone by the end of the week. Several days later, I called again to reconfirm. That afternoon, Lori and I trudged down to the backwater through the snow and set out a dozen decoys before we settled into a makeshift blind to await what I promised would be a stellar duck shoot.

Ten minutes later, the sound of whistling wings seemed to confirm my optimism. But as the flock turned on final approach, shots rang out upstream and sent the ducks clawing their way back into the sky. None fell, which hardly came as a surprise since they had still been sixty yards up in the air when our unexpected competition on the adjoining property chose to shoot. When the next inbound set made the same approach with the same result, I realized we'd had it. I only recognized three choices: a walk upstream for a pleasant discussion about sky-busting, a walk upstream for an unpleasant discussion of the same subject, or a diplomatic retreat from the field. In a rare fit of tact, I elected the latter.

Over the years I've noticed that people who shoot at ducks out of range are seldom willing to get up early to do it. Consequently, we rose in the dark the following morning and headed back down to the same place I'd already visited twice that week without firing a shot. Despite the clear, frigid November sky overhead, the temperature felt tolerable as we loaded our gear and started off through the gloom—ominously so, for warm weather could scuttle the hunt as I carefully explained to Lori as we walked along side by side. "Enough excuses!" she finally interrupted as we reached the bank. "Let's set out some decoys and shoot some ducks."

Although the spot I'd chosen to set up contained barely two feet of water, the bottom consisted of a thick layer of tenacious mud that clung to my waders as I set out the decoys. All manners forgotten, the dog insisted on romping through the muck while I set out the decoys, ensuring that both of us were spattered with the stuff when he climbed the bank and shook off. By that time, Lori had a crude blind organized back in the brush, which she clearly felt ambivalent about sharing with two wet, muddy companions. A lovely dawn had already started to break in the eastern sky, and it was just too nice a morning to complain about anything. Huddled together in the bushes, the three of us settled in to wait.

High in the cottonwoods across the water, heron nests stood aglow in the first rays of morning light. Abandoned for the winter, they looked oddly incongruous against the barren landscape surrounding us. But suddenly the sight transported me back to another season, when caddis flies swarmed from the surface of the creek and its cool water offered respite against sweltering summer days. I suddenly recalled standing in a nearby pool working a dry fly to a rising brown while Rocky treaded water at my side. The memory proved so vivid that I might have missed the first set of birds completely if Lori hadn't given me a gentle elbow in the ribs.

A pair of mallards was circling the sky behind us without making a sound. A contemplative observer no longer, I rose as they finally set their wings and committed to land, dropping the drake in the decoys and letting the hen rocket away through the trees. After two weeks of inactivity, Rocky gave us our money's worth on the easy retrieve. He hit the water in a geyser of mud and pranced about on shore after delivering the bird as if he'd done something no dog had ever done before.

The big flocks over-flew us that morning, but their lack of cooperation scarcely mattered. Singles and pairs dropped in regularly, cupping their wings and diving for the blocks as if they could imagine no other place on earth to land. With plenty of shooting at hand, Lori and I settled into a relaxed pace, trading shotgun and camera back and forth and taking plenty of time to work the dog and give him some of the attention deer season had cost him earlier. We had nothing to prove and all the time in the world not to prove it. When we flared birds while standing outside the blind to take pictures or watch the dog work, we laughed at our lapses without regrets. It was just that kind of day.

THE HERON ROOKERY

Late season duck hunting in our part of Montana usually means nothing but mallards. Because of Central Flyway regulations, eking out a bird of any other species means a "free" duck on top of the conventional five greenhead limit, although opportunities to do so are rare. As Lori and I stood outside the blind waiting for Rocky to complete another retrieve, a lone green-wing suddenly came screaming down through the cottonwoods. When it barreled past the decoys I pulled up and dropped it. I couldn't remember the last time I'd killed a teal on the creek that late in the season, and when Rocky got around to delivering it, the little bird felt like a trophy. With that, we decided to call it a morning.

As we walked back across the snow toward the truck, we crossed a fresh set of coyote tracks headed into the tangle of brush beneath the cottonwoods. Framed in glittering sunlight, the prints reminded me of the biological complexity all good duck habitat sustains. Even with the weight of the birds dragging at the strap slung across my shoulder, I had to acknowledge that the morning had been about much more than fast shooting: crisp air and a brilliant sunrise, time alone with Lori and the dog, the appreciation of a special place and all its inhabitants.

Rosy with a mallard drake from the old heron rookery. Sadly, the herons are now gone.

That evening I could already feel the promise of summer's return and imagine the sight of herons winging their way home against a warm, crimson sky. However, this duck hunt took place a decade before I wrote this essay. The herons are no longer with us. No one seems to know where they went or what happened to them. Year by year the great bundles of sticks in which they roosted eroded and fell to earth leaving the cottonwoods that held them looking lonely and abandoned. During the winter ducks still flock to that backwater, but hunting there now leaves me with a feeling of loss even when the dogs perform well and I shoot easy limits.

I miss the herons, no matter how many little brown trout they ate.

27.

Prairie Waterfowl

Specific characteristics of their sunrises help me keep track of many favorite outdoor destinations, for a variety of reasons. Crepuscular wildlife is at its most active then. Since people, in contrast, like to sleep in, I am likely to have the location to myself at that time of day. The ancient Greeks gave the sunrise its very own goddess, Eos, and no one describes her beauty better than Homer. She is always there at the appointed hour, announcing the start of another day afield, full of hope and ambition as an artist's palette of warm, luminous colors briefly paints the eastern horizon.

Over the years I have accumulated a memory catalog of sunrises all over the world, including blood red sun creeping above the rim of the Kalahari and an amorphous orange glow spreading across the Laguna Madre as I begin a search for redfish tails. For consistency, however, I have never found sunrises more compelling than those on the eastern Montana prairie.

Consider the one developing before our eyes on this opening day of duck season. Lori and I are sitting in a blind buried in a cattail bed adjacent to a marshy spring-fed pond as the slow wait for legal shooting light begins. Nothing fancy here, just a crude structure we cobbled together from discarded barn wood and chicken wire over the summer. If we were to walk southeast toward the center of the gathering light we'd probably have to search to find a paved road before we reached North Dakota. Somewhere in the distance a lone coyote howls, only to be joined moments later by an eerie chorus from his packmates as they announce that the time to hunt for breakfast has arrived.

Visible at first only as silhouettes against the orange sky behind them, waterfowl have begun to fly. Framed that way they all appear solid black, rendering the birder's usual field marks useless for identification. To an experienced waterfowler's eye, however, silhouette and wingbeat pattern will suffice. A pintail drake, its long swan neck making it impossible to confuse with any other species. A flock of teal flying at high speed in tight formation, turning as one before they disappear into the dark sky behind us. Wigeons, identified by their distinctive calls, and a pair of shovelers, their characteristic facial profiles obvious even at distance. Finally, a flock of mallards, each as stately and plump as Buck Mulligan in the opening line of *Ulysses*.

Does this potpourri of waterfowl add anything to a five-bird limit of greenheads? In my opinion it does, not that there is anything wrong with drake mallards. As we've already seen, our best waterfowl shooting here occurs during the late season when temperatures plummet, ponds freeze, and ducks concentrate on ice-resistant creeks and spring-fed sloughs. By December, however, the ducks will all be mallards, and I do mean *all*. Shooting an occasional lost teal or visiting goldeneye can become the highlight of the day. Variety really is the spice of life, and I know no better place to enjoy this opinion than beside a prairie pothole in early October.

Given the virtual certainty that no one is around us for miles, watching the minute hand creep slowly toward the official half-hour before sunrise feels unnecessary. However, declaring personal exceptions to established law has become the first step on the road to hell for lots of people. Furthermore, the wait, agonizing as it may be, will always be an established part of the ritual, reminding me of Christmas morning as a kid when my parents would insist on a long, drawn-out breakfast before giving my siblings and me permission to attack the presents under the tree. The anticipation usually proved more exciting than the socks from Aunt Opal.

I have my eyes glued on my watch when a disembodied voice announces that it is "6:15 a.m." Lori, far more digitally inclined than I, has done something with her cell phone and Alexa—or Siri, or somebody—has given us the green light to load up. As we do so, Rosy comes to attention. Ever since I finished setting out the decoys she has been sitting beside me looking like a bored teenager, but now she turns her full attention to the sky. Is she really smart enough to know that her time has come around at last after the long summer layoff? While I can't prove it, that certainly appears to be the case.

Another duck season has begun.

Set up for an early season duck hunt on a tranquil prairie stream.

Had it not been for Lewis and Clark, our Founding Fathers might not have known that America has a prairie. National ignorance about our geographic midsection endures two centuries later.

To many of our fellow citizens, the prairie remains a wasteland to cross as quickly as possible on the way from one coast to another—days of tedious driving for those traveling by car, a vast expanse of emptiness when viewed from 30,000 feet.

Wrong, wrong, wrong. Savanah wildlife habit is the temperate world's most diverse and productive. While it's the mountains to the west that appear on postcards and find their way into visitors' photo albums, the prairie can be beautiful to those who take the time to look. Ducks and geese that hatched in the Canadian pothole country just to the north are going to fly right down our alley on the way to their wintering grounds. As much as I love hunting elk and fishing mountain trout streams, I can always drive to them when the season is right. Day to day, I prefer our current surroundings—obviously, since this is where I have chosen to live.

Here in our makeshift blind, the time has come to stop bird watching and start shooting. Action begins when Rosy pivots and focuses on something in the sky behind us. How a dog whose eyes sit lower than my waist can spot birds before I do remains a mystery, but I've experienced this phenomenon often enough to trust her judgement. The object of her attention proves to be another flock of teal that banks sharply and buzzes our decoys at the edge of shotgun range.

The celestial rheostat has turned the light level up sufficiently for me to identify them as blue-wings, one of my favorite ducks. They may be tiny little things compared to mallards, but they offer challenging shooting and have always been a personal favorite on the table. I'm not surprised by their appearance this morning, for our local marshes produce a lot of them and they often predominate in the early season bag. Therein lies the rub—first to appear, first to depart. Based on prior experience, I know that by the end of the week most of the blue-wings will be gone.

We elect to let them go on their first pass at marginal range. We don't want to begin the season with an unrecovered bird, not that Rosy would allow that to happen. I'm beginning to second guess that opinion as the birds descend and settle in across the marsh. Then, teal being teal, they rise and circle for another approach to our decoys. Lori takes the first shot, not because I am a gentleman but because she's faster on the draw than I am now. By the time I'm swinging my gun and remembering my father's advice that it is impossible to shoot too far in front of a teal, I catch a glimpse of a cartwheeling bird from the corner of my eye. I connect with my first barrel. Then we fire simultaneously and a third bird falls. Who shot it? Who cares?

The first two teal lie dead in the decoys, but the third is churning for the reeds across the pond. I direct Rosy toward the difficult fall, but despite my whistle she veers off course toward the chip shots. Continuing her uncharacteristic puppy-like behavior, she returns with both birds in her mouth, this despite a regular summer program of reinforcement training in the field beside our house. Having been through this on previous opening days, I chalk her goofiness up to early season excitement and forgive her. I know how she feels.

This leaves us with a third bird to recover. Since time is of the essence with the swimming cripple, I ignore the mallards now circling overhead and give Rosy the line. Redeeming herself in short order, she swims a Michael Phelps sprint across the pond, crashes along the edge of the reeds until she encounters scent, and vanishes into the cover. Five minutes later, she is returning with the bird.

So it goes, for three more hours that pass too quickly. As we start to pick up, I glance at the duck straps hanging from the back of the blind and realize that we have accomplished a rare waterfowl hat trick without even trying, a Central Flyway limit consisting of six different species: blue-wing, green-wing, mallard, pintail, wigeon, and gadwall. Lori has concentrated on mallards, and yes, I credited her with the teal we hit simultaneously so I could keep shooting. Selfish? *Mea culpa.*

The end of the shooting does not mean the end of the duck hunt. One must observe the ritual right to the end. The sun has risen midway between horizon and zenith. I have stripped down to shirtsleeves, an ironic situation given the sub-zero temperatures in which I'll be hunting by season's end. Lori and I have the division of labor during the breakdown process worked out so precisely that we don't even need to talk to each other while completing it. She double checks the shotguns, slides them into the waterproof case a friend gave us for Christmas, and then inspects the blind for spent shells, misplaced items, and any ducks that might have fallen from the straps. Meanwhile, I slog out to collect the decoys, wondering why I bothered to wear waders on a day this warm. As usual, Rosy insists on "helping," but accomplishes nothing but tangling a decoy line around a hind leg. Off she goes across the pond trailing a fake mallard hen and looking ridiculous.

Then it's time for the 20-minute hike back to the truck with a cumbersome decoy bag across my shoulder. Halfway there, Rosy flushes a covey of Huns right across our path, making me wonder why one of us isn't carrying a loaded gun. To anyone unfamiliar with the marsh it might look as if we could save ourselves the walk by driving the truck right to the back of the blind to load our gear. I tried that once years ago, only to break through the sun-dried crust overlying a thick layer of mud, leaving the rig resting on its frame. It would likely still be there but for a nearby farmer (fortunately an old friend), his tractor, and a very long tow cable.

Our teamwork continues after the 15-mile drive back home. I hose Rosy down to rid her of a thick coating of mud, walk her to the kennel, inspect her for cuts, scrapes, or burrs, and feed her while our other dogs yap their indignity at being left behind. Since I wait to feed her until we return from the field, Rosy is already drooling like one of Pavlov's dogs as I place a food bowl in her kennel. To restore peace and assuage bruised feelings, I do the same for her kennel mates even though they usually eat in the afternoon.

Finally, it's time to address all those ducks. I routinely hang my birds for days, but now even the shady inside of the barn is a bit too warm. Furthermore, an opening day duck dinner is an old tradition, and we have optimistically invited friends to share the bounty.

Fortunately we have a bounty to share, which is not always the case. So, it's off to the cleaning table which, after a month of Huns and sharptails, has started to look like furniture from Grendel's lair. We reserve four of Lori's mallards for the evening meal and vacuum pack the rest for the freezer.

By the time we're ready to pop the ducks in the oven that evening, Rosy has dried off enough to be allowed inside. Reluctant to offend the other dogs twice in one day, I have the whole canine crew in the house and standing by the door to welcome our friends. At the dinner table I acknowledge that this is just the way an opening day of duck season should end: mallards with crisp, roasted skins; wild rice with morels we gathered that spring; Lori's Caesar salad; a bottle of cabernet (all right; two bottles); good friends; and a trio of dogs standing by waiting for leftovers.

Just another day on the fascinating, often overlooked prairie.

28.

Who's the Fairest?

It wasn't the first duck I ever shot—a distinction that befell a green-winged teal—but it was one of the first and even after all these years I remember it just as vividly.

The event took place far from the Montana prairie, Alaska tide flats, or Columbia River Basin, where I have done most of my duck hunting. The distance could be measured in scope as well as miles. Instead of far horizons, surging tides, and vast flocks of mallards circling overhead, I was looking at a half-acre beaver pond and a jungle of alders that nearly obliterated the sky. My father and I hadn't seen a duck for over two hours.

Suddenly I heard disturbed air overhead and Bits—a capable water retriever as well as the best grouse dog I've ever known—perked up his ears and looked toward the sky. The sound was subtle, not the jet engine roar I'd heard the previous week from a flock of black ducks setting their wings over the same beaver pond. At least ducks were finally arriving.

When the trio of birds made their first wheeling pass, they vanished before either of us could react. Moments later, they were settling toward the decoys on moth-like, fluttering wings. Although I'd studied Peterson's *Field Guide* and kept a life list of birds since I was in kindergarten, I wasn't sure just what they were: bigger than teal, smaller than mallards. Then my dad told me to "take the one in front." That was all the encouragement I needed.

Although I can claim to have been precocious with a shotgun, I was still so surprised when the bird tumbled that I forgot about my second barrel. My father certainly could have run the table—a decade after his death I still remember him as the best wing-shot I've ever seen—but he never raised his shotgun. In retrospect, I realize that he was more interested in me and the dog than himself.

The bird hit the surface of the pond with a gratifying *plop*, confirming that I had done my job right and the dog would have an easy time with his. I'll never forget my first impression when Bits delivered the bird to my father's outstretched hand. The light was just starting to fade, but the sun was still far enough above the horizon to make that remarkable assortment of colors glow as if lit from within. The whole duck looked shiny, as if it were made of freshly polished metal. The crest atop its head gave it a regal appearance. I counted seven distinct colors on its head and bill. The barred flank feathers looked as if they had been made for my fly-tying bench.

Despite my initial uncertainly, I soon identified the bird as a drake wood duck. As I'd leafed through my dog-eared Peterson's, I'd repeatedly paused over its gaudy image and wished I would see or perhaps even shoot one someday. Although it doesn't often turn out that way, the real thing exceeded its advance billing.

Most hunters I know agree that the wood duck is the most beautiful waterfowl in North America. No duck can match the pintail's grace on the wing and a drake mallard's iridescent green head still excites me whenever I see one hanging over the decoys. However, considered as a still life none matches the drake woody. I do not intend to sleight to the hens. With the exception of the South Pacific paradise duck (for reasons I don't understand), female waterfowl dress in subtler hues than drakes of the same species, to protect themselves, their eggs, and their hatchlings from predators while nesting.

In North America, I think the only duck that can match the wood duck's visual impact is the harlequin, the first waterfowl I ever sent to a taxidermist. However, the harlequin's striking appearance is due to bold pattern as opposed to a wood duck's bouquet of color. A harlequin could be rendered well in black and white. Several Eurasian species could give the woody a run for the beauty title, including the mandarin duck and Baikal teal. However, they are rare visitors and I've never even seen either one despite spending lots of time on the Alaska Peninsula where most of their North American sightings are recorded. Mandarins and woodies have more in common than good looks, since they are the only two members of the genus *Aix* rather than the *Anas* family of typical North American puddle ducks.

While I always find the esthetics and biology fascinating, I also acknowledge that the time eventually comes to go hunting. The dogs seem to agree.

In most circumstances Lori and I preferentially shoot mallards, pintails, and teal, but wood ducks have a remarkable record of saving the day on mornings we might otherwise be picking up the decoys without having fired a shot.

Such was the case one winter day when we were on our way home to Montana after visiting my aging parents in Seattle. The weather was exceptionally cold by eastern Washington standards. Since our route took us less than an hour away from duck camp, Lori and I decided to break up the drive by doing some shooting. We had already prepared for the possibility by bringing along our hunting gear. Since my parents always enjoyed seeing the dogs, Rosy lay curled up on the back seat looking like a bored teenager. Had we needed to debate the decision about making the detour, I had no doubt how she would have voted.

We arrived to find all the ponds frozen and no ducks circling through the ice fog. However, I noted that the water flowing through the drainage ditches connecting the ponds was moving fast enough to remain open. Already tired of freeway driving, I decided to extend the break by gearing up and exploring the next ditch we crossed.

The ditch was lined on both sides with dense stands of Russian olive, creating a thick but narrow jungle perhaps 20 yards wide. Branches spread almost all the way across the water, making it impossible to see the surface. Although I didn't feel optimistic, I let Rosy out of the truck and sent her down into the tangle to investigate. Moments later I heard the sound of beating wings, and then a dozen wood ducks erupted from the cover. As Sherlock Holmes once said, the game was afoot.

Since hunting had not been the trip's primary purpose, we had only brought one gun and a box of shells. Since the shotgun was Lori's 20-gauge, she loaded it and set off ahead of me while I concentrated on the dog. Although they were impossible to see on the water, the little ditch was loaded with ducks, every one of which proved to be a woody. Even if we had been able to bust through the brush to the water, swinging a shotgun from inside the densely woven branches would have been impossible.

Fortunately, the dog seemed to grasp the situation. Staying even with us as Lori and I walked the open bank, Rosy bulled her way through the tangle pushing little flocks of ducks up just ahead of her. The shot opportunities were close, but that didn't mean they were easy. The birds always broke up when they flushed and flew in all directions once they cleared the brush. The experience felt like shooting a sporting clays course designed by lunatics.

Flushing birds was just half of Rosy's job description. It was difficult or impossible for us to mark birds that fell on the far side of the brush, and getting to them would have been a nightmare. In addition to battling thorns, we would have had to get wet crossing the ditch since we hadn't brought any waders. With two stellar seasons under her belt already, Rosy handled the recovery duties with aplomb. After walking half an hour we had all the ducks we wanted, and Rosy hadn't lost a bird.

Every one of them was a wood duck. Abundant open water lay nearby on the Columbia, and I surmised that all the usual puddle ducks had headed there when the ponds froze. Woodies, which prefer tight cover with lots of canopy overhead, were evidently content to remain behind in brushy habitat. Although I rarely jump-shoot ducks anymore, that day I needed some relief from the realization that my father was dying. I still thank the wood ducks for providing it.

Nesting boxes such as the one in the background played an important role in the recovery from our wood duck population's historic lows.

Fifty years ago, the scarcity of wood ducks in the western habitat I regularly hunted then was striking. Despite the experience I'd had with them as a kid, I actually mis-identified the first one I ever shot in Montana back in the early 1970s. I was hunting a vast, remote marsh on the prairie when I snapped off a shot at a teal just after sunrise, experiencing a vague sense of something unusual about the bird as it went tumbling down. Although Sky was still in his first season, he located the bird easily and delivered it to my hand, at which point I realized it wasn't a teal after all. Experiencing a sudden rush of déjà vu I noted its pale eye-ring, finally recognized the bird as a hen wood duck, and regretted shooting it. How quickly one forgets. That was the first woody I shot west of the Mississippi, and for years it was the last.

Most of us are familiar with the gratifying recovery of our continental wood duck population after its nadir in the early 1900s. Commercial hunting is widely blamed for the initial crash, although I think loss of the birds' specific habitat requirement for hollow trees to nest in was probably more significant. Construction of artificial wood duck nesting boxes certainly contributed to their recovery, although I'm sure that other complex factors also came into play. In both Montana and Washington, I've noted that areas with the greatest wood duck numbers now correlate highly with the presence of invasive Russian olive. While I can't prove a causal relationship, it's an interesting observation. During a casual discussion with waterfowl biologist Chris Nicolai he volunteered the same idea about the Russian olive. He then pointed out that Fremont cottonwoods had expanded their range into the same habitat, providing wood ducks with ideal places to nest. I'm sure this isn't the only example of invasive species benefitting an imperiled native. Nature works in strange ways.

Now that I have re-familiarized myself with the species I find them one of the easiest ducks to identify on the wing, thanks to their square-sterned silhouette and distinctive flight calls. Paradoxically, the more woodies I saw, the less inclined I became to shoot them. I did make exceptions when I had a young or inexperienced hunter along or when a dog really needed some work. The next time an exceptional, taxidermy-worthy specimen appears over the decoys, Lori has a standing green light to shoot it.

Opening day, Columbia River Basin. The air is unseasonably warm, the sky overhead crystal clear as we wait for dawn to break and chase away the last of the stars. The phrase "shirtsleeve weather" may be a cliché, but underneath my jacket I'm wearing a light T-shirt and expect to be stripped down to it by mid-morning. As pleasant as the day promises to be, conditions could hardly be less conducive to duck hunting. Since we have dogs that need work, this is no time to be picky. If it's legal, it will probably hear from us.

Within an hour of shooting light's arrival, a typical opening day mix of puddle ducks is hanging in the back of the blind: wigeon, teal, a gadwall, and a young greenhead in plumage so drab I nearly mistook it for a hen. Kenai was so eager that I couldn't deny him the opportunity to make the retrieves. While none of those recoveries was really challenging, the wigeon fell in thick brush across the pond and we didn't kill two of the teal quite as dead as we should have. Precocious from the time I tossed her first dummy in the yard, little Rosy looked ready for action. I wanted her season to begin with a chip shot bird dead right in front of the blind.

As is often the case, I heard the wood ducks coming before I saw them. "It's too early in the season for a good taxidermy specimen," I told Lori.

"What about Rosy?"

"Good point. They are likely going to turn and come in out of the sun, but if you can positively identify a drake, take him."

Then they were closing over the end of the pond, silhouetted against the glare as expected, fluttering indecisively while approaching the decoys as woodies often do. "Can you pick out a drake?" Lori asked.

"I think so, but let's wait…"

The bark or her 20-gauge interrupted this advice, but when the duck hit the water it became obvious that my wife, whose younger eyes were better than mine, had made an accurate call. She couldn't have dropped the bird in a better place for the young dog. Rosy made the retrieve easily while Kenai looked on, and she delivered the bird to my outstretched hand as if she'd been doing it for years. We unloaded and called time out to praise the dogs.

As I studied the bird resting in my hand, I suddenly imagined myself standing beside a beaver pond in a galaxy far, far away.

Geese

29.

Big Birds

The expectations of the outdoor genre suggest that I should portray a scene of hardship and struggle—laborious effort invested in digging pit blinds, bitter north winds sufficient to test the limits of human endurance—but that, in this case at least, would be a lie. The ambient temperature on the southern Alberta prairie this morning is a bit too cold for shirtsleeves, but not by much. The air is still enough for us to hear the swelling racket from geese on the reservoir two miles distant—mixed flocks of honkers, snows, and specks per last night's scouting. The lacey wisps of orange and pink cirrus heralding the sunrise could illustrate a scenic postcard advertising Wild Rose Country. Whatever our difficulties today, harsh environmental conditions will not be among them.

Not that the morning started out like a Cub Scout picnic. The alarm went off at 3 am and we've spent most of the last two hours off-loading magnum goose decoys from the trailer behind our friend Jeff Lander's truck. There are exactly 230 of these decoys according to Jeff, and he should know. The chore of distributing them about the barren stubble field started out with all the childish enthusiasm of an Easter egg hunt, but that was a 200 plastic honkers ago. No one has giggled for some time now and we've had to depend upon the dogs for what comic relief we can muster. The two Labs—our Rocky and Jeff's Trigger—have been roaring around the darkened field like puppies with ADD ever since we let them out of the truck. Fine by me—their time for disciplined behavior will come soon enough. They should burn some excess energy before they have to lie down and hold still, possibly for hours.

When honker decoy #230 finally plants its phony webbed feet in the stubble at the perimeter of the spread, Jeff sets off to deliver the truck and trailer to their hiding place in some abandoned farm buildings, leaving Lori and me to wrestle with the coffin blinds and the final details of our elaborate setup. Proper placement of the blinds is critical. The idea is to have the birds gliding by into the wind and straight overhead on final approach. To my frustration the breeze remains light and variable. Finally I make an executive decision to play for wind from the west. By the time Lori and I have the blinds dragged into position and buried in chaff left over from the August harvest, Jeff and Trigger have appeared on foot as two dark dots at the end of the field. The gabbling from the reservoir has started building to a slow crescendo.

And now, to paraphrase Descartes on his deathbed, we are off to the Great Perhaps.

Six decades of waterfowling have produced abundant opportunity for reflection on subjects as diverse as retrievers and wetlands ecology. One thing I've learned over the course of all those opening days is appreciation for the qualitative differences between hunting ducks and hunting geese.

I killed my first goose on a slough in eastern Washington almost completely by accident back when Kennedy was president. I'd set up for puddle ducks but hadn't seen one all morning. It was a bluebird day, and I could hear a lone goose calling from far away. Absent a goose call and decoys there was no reason for the lost single to head my way, but the bird seemed to have a vector straight over my head programmed into its guidance system and it never deviated. Given my unfamiliarity with geese and the buck fever that long, anxious wait generated during the bird's approach, I would have had plenty of reasons to miss. Somehow I didn't. The sight of that huge, crumpled bird cartwheeling down out of the sky affected me like walking up to my first dead mule deer buck, as I'd done just a few weeks before. That was the key association that registered immediately: hunting geese was like big game hunting. In fact, it *was* big game hunting.

I spend enough time in the field to account for an incidental goose or two most seasons, but those exercises in serendipity are the exception rather than the rule. No other form of wing-shooting demands more advance planning and attention to detail than goose hunting taken seriously. Killing those occasional geese doesn't feel much like goose hunting because it *isn't* goose hunting, at least as understood by dedicated goose hunters. I've already used the word I'm looking for to capture the essence of the real thing: pageantry, with all its implied emphasis on process as opposed to tangible results. That's what you get when you rise at 3 AM and place 230 decoys in a field, whether the geese show up or not.

Most geese are a whole lot bigger than most ducks, but it's facile to ascribe the excitement differential to the size of the birds alone. Years ago I was hunting ducks in a remote prairie marsh with an inexperienced friend who had never killed a goose before. We were sitting in blinds a couple of hundred yards apart when another lone honker wandered by over his head, and he killed it in a flurry of excitement. The bird proved to be a cackling Canada (not yet designated a species of its own) that wasn't much bigger than the mallards we shot at last light, but that didn't matter. It was his first goose, and no one needed to say anything more.

I'm not sure geese are inherently smarter than ducks, but to echo Will Rogers again they might as well be. I'm also not sure geese mate for life, nor am I sure why that should automatically be considered an admirable trait. Geese are gregarious by nature, and a successful goose hunt may mean looking at hundreds of birds overhead. Via some form of herd mentality, ducks, like people, make more bad decisions when gathered in numbers, as if every member of the flock assumes someone else must be in charge. Geese behave differently. The more birds in the air at one time the warier they become, which is why so many geese killed incidentally are singles. Luring a large flock down out of the sky and into shotgun range represents an accomplishment as opposed to luck. If you believe that the value of a hunt is directly related to its difficulty, geese are the birds for you.

This anecdotal review has focused on Canadian honkers simply because I shoot more of them than other geese, as do most of us. That doesn't mean they're the only show in town come goose season. Emperor geese and black brant represent special cases beyond the scope of this discussion. Snows and speckle-belies are another matter. The mid-continental snow goose population is exploding to unsustainable levels that threaten the fragile tundra ecosystem where they nest, as described in the following chapter. Shooting some has practically become a civic duty. I have mounted springtime expeditions to places like Colorado and North Dakota to do my share of the work. If the opportunity to shoot waterfowl legally in March when other seasons have closed isn't enough to justify these road trips, the sight of thousands of snow-white wings flashing overhead should erase any lingering doubts. Notoriously difficult to decoy, migrating snows can challenge anyone's patience.

Specks, on the other hand, can reward as easily as snows can frustrate. They decoy readily, offer more close shots, and outshine the competition on the table. We rarely see them around my home corner of the Central Flyway. Specks always make me grateful to have friends in places like Alberta and the Texas Gulf Coast. With gas at high modern prices that represents expensive travel nowadays, but it's probably best that OPEC doesn't know how much I'd pour down the tank for a good morning of speckle-belly shooting.

I'm usually glad to leave discussions of wing-shooting's technical aspects to those who are either better at it than I am or can successfully pretend to be. Geese are a special case. Every year I miss geese I should kill and watch others do the same. I like to think I learn from my misses. A goose's slow wing beat tempo creates an illusion, for the birds are always flying faster than they appear. Because of their size, they're also usually farther away. To compound these problems, a lot of geese are shot (or shot at) at ranges that make the velocity of steel shot decay rapidly, a problem for those of us who shoot a lot of lead at upland birds. Because of all these factors, it's almost impossible to shoot too far ahead of a goose. As with diving ducks, I address this problem by doing everything as usual until the final moment before I slap the trigger. Then I make myself pull an extra one to two body lengths farther ahead of the bird. As an instinctive shooter I don't like interrupting the flow of the shotgun barrel with conscious decisions, but I like missing even less.

No discussion of waterfowl hunting is complete without retrievers. Several of my Labs' "Retrieve of the Year" performances involved geese over water, but a lot of geese get shot in fields. I'm always dismayed by goose hunters who contend that dogs don't belong there. Granted, a stubble field goose spread is no place for an uncontrolled retriever. A dog that flares an inbound flock of geese after hours of waiting can alienate hunting partners and ruin friendships. But when events go as planned a few capable guns can put a lot of goose dinners on the ground at the same time, making it easy to lose track of who shot what and where it fell. A honker with a broken wing can cover an amazing amount of ground in the confusion. Since I hate losing game even more than I hate missing it, I prefer to have a seasoned dog lying quietly beside me in the stubble.

My concern for unrecovered game isn't purely altruistic. I enjoy eating geese although many other hunters don't. Overcooking—the usual suspect in cases of botched game dinners involving everything from quail to moose—deserves most of the blame for the low regard geese receive as table fare, but that isn't the birds' fault. The labor of plucking a limit of geese can be intimidating. I address this problem by starting the job in the field while I'm waiting for the next flock to appear, which explains why so many of our goose hunting photos show me with feathers in my beard.

No shirtsleeve temperatures on this hunt. Don, Lori, and two friends endured brutal weather on this late season field hunt in Montana.

In contrast to upland game hunting, shooting geese usually involves waiting patiently for events beyond the hunter's control. The Spanish verb *esperar* helpfully translates both as *to wait* and *to hope*, for without the latter there can be little of the former. This morning two hours have passed since the sun crested the horizon, and the geese have yet to lift off the distant reservoir. At least this morning's wait has been graced by pleasant company, both human and canine.

After an hour supine on the ground, we've all risen to stretch our knotted legs when the volume, pitch, and intensity of the racket from the reservoir increases suddenly, leaving us to dive for the cover of our blinds like soldiers caught outside their trenches by surprise incoming fire. Only our distance from the water saves us from extreme embarrassment. I've no sooner finished heaping duff back on top of my layout blind when the first flock of the day appears over the far edge of the field with its leaders' wings just starting to cup. As if their interest in our decoys isn't grounds enough for excitement the birds are speckle-bellies. I can almost hear a pair of them sizzling in the oven.

As their rate of descent increases we face a tactical element of the goose shooting experience I've referenced previously—the need for someone to make a decision at precisely the right time. Sit up to shoot too soon and the birds will flare out of range, delay too long and the best shot opportunities may already be at an impossible angle behind you. Nothing muddles the dynamics of group decision making like inbound flocks of geese. The result is often a lot of Hamlet-like dithering while everyone defers to everyone else until the birds have passed by. Believing that a wrong decision is better than no decision, I begin a silent three-second countdown before lurching to a sitting position while bellowing, "Take 'em!"

Let the games begin.

30.

Snowstorm

The story begins in the arctic tundra, as remote an expanse of wilderness as any that remain in North America. One can still fly this country for hours at low altitude without seeing any sign of human intrusion. Between autumnal and vernal equinoxes snow and ice encase the terrain, limiting its occupancy to a select list of hardy, cold-adapted survivors: caribou, arctic foxes, ptarmigan, snowy owls, polar bears. But the sun's inevitable return each spring magically converts this apparent wasteland into an ecological opposite as ice melts and vast, fertile wetlands form in its place, providing an undisturbed summer breeding ground for a diverse assortment of shorebirds and waterfowl.

Some hunters may not care much about curlews, plovers, and their relatives, a loss for all concerned including the hunters. I've never been able to divorce my enthusiasm for any quarry from an appreciation of the habitat it occupies and the company it keeps. Regardless of where one falls on this ideological spectrum, the arctic plain deserves respect for its reliable contributions to our annual fall flight of migrating birds. Of all the diverse waterfowl species that call the tundra their summer home, none is more numerically important than *Chen caerulescens*, the snow goose.

This habitat has experienced a dangerous embarrassment of riches over the last few decades, as the snow goose population exploded from its historic carrying capacity of a million birds to a number four times that size. While the snow goose may seem an unlikely agent of ecological destruction, nature pays a price for an excess of anything. Despite its isolation and harsh appearance, the arctic tundra is remarkably fragile. As all those geese relentlessly attacked the forbs and grasses that renew the food chain every spring they laid waste to native flora, eventually threatening not only their own survival but the future of numerous other waterbird species.

Our Fish and Wildlife Service has addressed the gathering crisis by encouraging the recreational harvest of snow geese through a variety of regulatory changes: extending seasons, eliminating bag limits, and liberalizing means of take. In the politically charged atmosphere that complicates modern wildlife management, such measures predictably aroused their share of controversy. I'll admit some ambivalence myself after years of drought and limited waterfowl production during which I voluntarily chose to limit my own take.

Finally, curiosity and an appreciation of biologic reality overcame my inhibitions. Since Montana doesn't offer many snow goose hunting opportunities and declined to exercise new federal options of spring seasons and generous limits, that meant traveling. In March 1999, I set off for the plains of eastern Colorado to learn and hunt.

Down at ground level in eastern Colorado, vast brown fields of corn stalks and wheat stubble formed a gigantic checkerboard all the way to the nearby Kansas border. Barely visible in the early light, a serpentine line of cottonwoods marked the course of the nearby Arkansas River. As I braced myself against the brisk morning air I felt preoccupied by matters more immediate than scenery. The month was March and we were hunting snow geese at a time when I should have been preparing for pre-runoff dry fly fishing and spring turkey season.

Despite having hunted the prairie for years, I approached the morning as a relative novice. Our Montana home lies on the cusp of the Central and Pacific flyways, and most migrating snows pass to either side. Back when I lived in Alaska huge flights of snow geese visited the mouth of the nearby Kenai River every spring, but almost all over-flew Cook Inlet during the fall. A good retriever could fetch every snow I ever shot there in less time than it would take the dog to eat breakfast.

Fortunately, new friends John and Jeff compensated for my own lack of experience. They live and breathe geese from late October until it's time to stop hunting, which by then didn't take place until basketball playoffs were in progress and wild turkeys had started to strut. After all those mornings spent lying in barren fields they knew that a successful snow goose hunt begins with an industrial strength decoy spread.

The object, John had explained earlier when we exited his vehicle in the dark, was to make part of the field look white. It took me a while to realize that he meant *acres* of the field. The contents of his truck could have stocked an American Museum of Snow Goose Decoys, including everything from magnum shells to fliers, silhouettes, and gunny sacks full of white rags that I was assigned to plant along the edges of the corn stalks. We were not setting out dozens of decoys but hundreds. Not until dawn broke could I fully appreciate what an immense artificial spread we had created.

"Geese!" Jeff suddenly cried as he straightened from the last of the silhouettes and raised a hand for silence. The breeze had barely risen enough to add a breath of life to the rag decoys. As I concentrated on the aural blankness of the calm sky overhead I finally heard the distant, high-pitched ululation of snows on the wing. The birds were still too far off to see, but the racket confirmed that they had lifted off the nearby reservoir and headed to the fields to feed. All we could do now was hope that the host of white artifacts scattered across the barren ground would coax them into range.

As we scrambled into our blinds I found myself overcome by doubt. Our plans for concealment seemed remarkably primitive in comparison to our elaborate decoy spread. At John's urging, I simply lay supine in a furrow at the edge of the corn stalks and pulled a white sheet over my legs. I found it hard to believe this minimalist approach to goose blinds would fool birds despite reassurances to the contrary, but they knew snow geese and I didn't.

When the first line of geese finally appeared my confidence sank as rapidly as my excitement rose. The country around us looked big enough to swallow every goose in the flyway. Nothing but the artificial sea of white we had created distinguished our lonely field from the rest. However, John still had a trick or two up his sleeve. At the first sight of birds headed in our direction, he began to play a goose-shaped kite upward into the breeze with an old fiberglass spinning rod and started to call. As we all joined in the first flock of the day veered in our direction and began to lose altitude.

Never mind the possibility of shooting to follow; the sheer spectacle of the birds' appearance justified all the effort we had invested in their attraction. After beginning to approach in a disorganized, undulating formation, the geese began to coalesce into waves. Their plumage caught the early morning light high overhead and broadcast it like a beacon. As the leading edge of the flock started to side-slip downward along an imaginary glide path, I realized that the birds were about to cross the threshold into shotgun range.

Accustomed to wary honkers back home, I remained frozen to the ground until the birds were right overhead, an unnecessary exercise in discipline as I would learn over the course of the morning. Once they committed to our spread it seemed impossible to deter them despite our unconvincing concealment. As we all rose to our knees, I concentrated on picking one bird from the flock and fired. I was shooting a borrowed 10-gauge, but the heavy gun seemed to lock onto its target naturally. As I pulled through and slapped the trigger, the bird crumbled and fell from the sky with such operatic grandeur that I forgot about the second barrel.

While watching a thousand geese approach at once can be a spectacular experience, most veteran goose hunters would prefer to have a fraction of that number set their wings overhead in staggered flights of ten to twenty, which is just what happened over the next two hours. Once the large flocks committed to other fields we were shooting stragglers, but the smaller groups of birds decoyed eagerly. While few actually put their landing gear down, some provided us with elegant overhead passing shots. We missed a few and killed more. By the time we decided to stand up and begin the task of collecting all those decoys I felt as satisfied as if I had just finished a long meal at a favorite restaurant.

Lori with a snow goose taken on a pleasant Texas Gulf Coast morning.

Early the following morning we set out for a different field with a new mission. I was along on this trip only because of an invitation from friends making bowhunting videos. My unlikely mission was to kill a goose on the wing with my recurve bow while they filmed the event. Despite years of experience with bows I felt openly skeptical. I did appreciate my companions' willingness to put their own ambitions on hold and let me shoot with a shotgun the previous day.

When the first set of snows materialized just after sunrise, I picked the lowest bird, drew on it just as I would have with a shotgun, doubled my lead, and watched my arrow sail harmlessly through the air behind my target. Four sets of geese later I hadn't cut a feather, although the stubble field in front of us sprouted white-fletched flu-flu arrows like spring daisies. As a determined advocate of traditional bows and arrows in the pursuit of big game, admitting failure did not come easily. Nonetheless, I finally had to acknowledge that I was not carrying the right tool for the job.

"Hey, Jeff!" I called as yet another line of birds appeared on the horizon. "Mind if I borrow your pump?" He didn't When a single peeled away from the next flock and floated toward our spread, I rose to one knee and dropped it. As I fed another shell into the magazine I experienced a moment of regret, for that was the closest bird I had seen all morning and would have provided my best opportunity yet with the bow. As is usually the case with geese, the range had been farther than appearances suggested. Only after I paced off the distance to the limp white form did I realize that the bird had been 35 yards away when I shot it. Since that's a challenging shot for a traditional bowhunter even when the target isn't moving as fast as a flying goose, I felt less embarrassed by my earlier string of misses.

By the time we finished for the morning, vast, noisy flocks of snows had started to descend toward a nearby reservoir from dizzying heights. These were new arrivals to the area according to John since local residents didn't fly that high when traveling to and from the fields. As surely as the next sunrise, the annual northward migration had begun. But to what would these birds return when they finally reached their destination? Just how much abuse can one species inflict upon a fragile ecosystem before things fall apart, as Yeats suggested, and the center no longer holds? Despite the obvious irony of a species as destructive as our own asking this question of one as fundamentally benign as the snow goose, I found it hard not to consider the problem even as I enjoyed the bounty it had created. In the meantime, as the geese and I readied for our own northward

SNOWSTORM

journeys, I drew some consolation from the thought with which I end every hunting season: There would always be next year.

Let's hope.

31.
Accidental Geese and The Big Show

We Montanans may be proud of our Big Sky Country, but no sky is bigger than the one that spreads across southern Alberta's farms and prairies. Since all the grain had been cut earlier there were no amber waves to rhapsodize about, but devoid of other terrain features the endless rectangles of stubble stretching horizon to horizon looked dramatic in their own way. Someone had planted and harvested all those windswept acres, converting a lot of dirt and a little water into food for hungry humans who would seldom appreciate its origins. I usually feel that waterfowl should be hunted over water (duh), but there wasn't a drop in sight. Nonetheless, I couldn't help but feel impressed by the scope of the morning's undertaking.

As readers may have surmised, Lori and I were back visiting our old friend Jeff Lander. By the time we finished setting out our truckload of decoys—an integrated mix of honkers and snows—high altitude mares' tails in the eastern sky were starting to glow as the leading edge of the sun's disc crept above the earth's rim. With nothing better to do, Lori, Jeff, and I crawled into our layout blinds to begin the essential element of field-shooting geese: waiting.

Our party contained one other member: Rocky, who we were grooming as Sonny's understudy. As acknowledged earlier, a dog that breaks wildly as a flock of geese starts to descend on set wings is an obvious liability, but I had trained Rocky to flatten and remain motionless beside me as I lay supine in my blind. With his coat a near perfect match for the yellow stubble around us, I felt confident that his presence wouldn't result in flaring geese.

We had set up a long way from the nearest highway or farming hamlet. Only one sound rose above the sigh of the freshening breeze—the faint, squeaky gabbling of geese stirring themselves back to life after spending the night sleeping on a large lake a mile away. As dawn finally broke across the prairie, invoking many wonderful Homeric similes I won't plagiarize here, the volume of goose talk rose right along with the light. After nearly an hour of slow but steady increase in the distant noise level, sudden urgency informed us that geese were finally lifting off the water.

Lines of birds began to appear over the terrain fold that hid us from the reservoir, weaving back and forth like drunks recently tossed from a bar. Being in just the spot where the game wants to be is a tremendous advantage in all forms of hunting, none more so than this one. As several flocks bypassed us to the north as if they had never seen our decoys or heard our calls, I felt rising despair. Fortunately, Lori's visual scan remained more diligent than my own. "Coming over the end of the field, right out of the sun," she whispered in her best hunting voice—unnecessarily, since we could barely hear ordinary conversational tones above the racket from the sky. "Wings set and dropping!"

After a final reminder to the dog, I dropped my call to a neutral position on the lanyard around my neck and thumbed my safety. Jeff had won the election for *Jägermeister*, to my relief. It's a thankless responsibility, with lapses in judgement leading to results previously described. We experienced no such disaster that morning. Jeff made the call at the perfect moment, and suddenly I was sitting awkwardly, trying to isolate one honker from the flock of 30 and remembering how much I hate shooting from layout blinds. A leading bird fell to a chip shot from my first barrel. The second came at such an awkward overhead angle that I couldn't determine its result. My peripheral vision registered at least one bird down from Lori's double, and Jeff took full advantage of a third round from his pump.

After comparing notes, we concluded that we had dropped a total of five birds, four of which lay dead in the decoys while the one I'd hit over my shoulder flopped toward a brush-choked ditch that bordered the field. With no other geese visible in the traffic pattern, I elected to send the dog. By the time we had recovered the dead bodies from the decoys, Rocky was on his way home carrying a goose that looked two sizes too big for his mouth.

Limits were generous that season, especially on snows. By the time we declared *no mas* two hours later, we had all the Canadas we could shoot, as many snows as we wanted to clean, and even a handful of speckle-bellies.

We had just enjoyed an example of what I call goose hunting's Big Show.

The Big Show, as played out in an Alberta stubble field.

As much as I enjoy mornings like the one just described, I don't do a lot of that kind of goose hunting. I don't mind the work, but the amount of time needed to invest in scouting, arranging blinds, and dealing with mountains of decoys invariably comes at the expense of other activities I enjoy at that time of year, from hunting upland game to plotting against the local whitetails with my longbow. October and November just don't seem to last long enough.

A Big Show goose hunt such as the one we enjoyed that morning in Alberta will supply our table with a lot of goose dinners. As noted earlier Lori and I, in contrast to many waterfowl hunters, enjoy eating wild geese. Having too many is never a problem, but most of those I shoot each season fall more or less by accident. Serious goose hunters (several of my friends fall into that category) may sneer at my amateurism, but I'm perfectly happy with a goose that makes a mistake while I'm hunting teal. A honker looks and feels bigger when it's hanging on a game strap with something other than more geese.

One such accidental goose hunt arose simply because I was paying attention. Driving down the road west of town one autumn day I noticed an ordinarily barren stock pond covered with ducks. The landowner was a friend who not only gave me permission to hunt the pond but invited me to drive across a stubble field to get there, saving me from having to carry a big bag of decoys nearly a mile.

Sunrise the following morning found me along with Lori and master bowyer Dick Robertson crouched down in the lee of an old earthen dam with nothing but skimpy brush for cover. When the first flock of ducks zoomed by over the decoys, I hesitated before my shotgun stock reached my shoulder. The ducks looked unfamiliar, and I couldn't identify them positively.

I did on their next pass. "Ringnecks!" I shouted. "Take 'em," and we did. Divers usually avoid our home county. The two I knocked down from that flock were the first ringnecks I'd ever killed there.

An hour later, we had a nice mixed bag of ringnecks and puddle ducks resting on the ground beside us when I heard a goose honk.

The bird sounded sufficiently distant to allow us to switch out to heavier loads undetected. This maneuver usually looks better on paper than it proves to be in the field, but we got away with it this time. As we flattened out and tried to make ourselves disappear into the brush, a trio of honkers flew overhead and turned into the wind toward our duck decoys.

I never was sure exactly who shot what, but by the time the wind dispersed the shotguns' sound all three geese were down on the water, two obviously dead and the third headed across the pond as fast as it could swim. Larger than most local stock reservoirs, the far shore lay over a hundred yards away. After whistling Kenai off the nearest bird I kept signaling him *back* until he spotted the crippled goose, at which point it was all over but the inevitable shower of pond water when he returned to my side.

A dog's first goose can be a challenge under any circumstances. Kenai had met his on a bitter winter day right after Lori and I finished shooting limits of greenheads on a local spring creek. We were out of the blind and on our way to start picking up decoys when I heard a *honk* somewhere in the mist overhead. Because of thick snow cover, we'd dressed head to toe in white, a trick that offers more effective camouflage than any other I know.

It certainly proved effective that day, as the pair of geese flew directly over our heads with no interruption in the rhythm of their wingbeats. We had been shooting 20-gauges at the decoying mallards, and I hesitated briefly when the birds first flew into view. Since they were only 20 yards above the deck, I decided our firepower was sufficient. That proved to be the case, and both birds fell to our first barrels. One lay stone dead in the snow, but the other took off flapping down the creek on its one intact wing. In retrospect I wished I'd shot it again as it fell, but hindsight proved no more helpful than usual.

By the time we declared our shotguns safe, the wounded goose had disappeared around a bend in the creek with Kenai in pursuit. Anticipating difficulty, I hustled downstream after the chase. When

I re-established visual contact, I saw Kenai lunging around in circles looking confused. There was no sign of the goose. The latter observation left me confused too, for the creek was no more than a fly rod's length wide and two feet deep. I could see over a hundred yards downstream to the next bend, but I couldn't see a goose.

Concluding that the bird had to be hidden somewhere within this perimeter, I kept the dog working against the far bank while I set off through the snow looking for tracks. Suddenly, Kenai pivoted in my direction and leapt into a drift overhanging the water on my side of the creek. After a minor blizzard of suspended snow crystals and a racket of flapping wings and churning water, Kenai emerged holding the goose by the neck. I had walked right by the bird, which had crawled up into the dead space between the overhang and the water. Kenai's form may have been less than perfect, but I never would have found the bird without his nose.

Accidental Geese or the Big Show? Take your pick. Each option has its downsides and rewards. The important point is simply that hunting should make you happy. Even if the geese stand you up, there are friends, dogs, and time outdoors with which to compensate.

32.

The Captains' Geese

Led by Captains Meriwether Lewis and William Clark, the Corps of Discovery reached what is now Montana's Fort Peck Indian Reservation in May 1805. I moved there 168 years later. Lewis first described the diminutive cackling Canada goose at the mouth of the Poplar River, where I spent two memorable years as a reservation medical officer. Fort Peck has changed remarkably little in the decades since I left to pursue more medical education. In fact, it hasn't changed much since Lewis and Clark showed up. Because of its remote location no one else in the Public Health Service wanted an assignment there, but I looked at all that prime bird cover (which Lewis described as "beautiful in the extreme" the same morning he saw his first cackler) and told HQ to throw me in that briar patch. Not all my decisions look smart in retrospect, but that one does.

Even though over two hundred years have passed since Lewis and Clark traveled through, it's impossible for any thoughtful western outdoorsman to escape their legacy. Their powers of observation were so astute that they were the first to describe – in written English, at least – damn near everything out here. I spend a lot of time outdoors on the high plains, but no matter what the day's objective I can almost always discover some relevant wisdom in their *Journals*. So pick a card, any card. Pick… geese.

Abundant along the eastern seaboard then as now, the Canada goose was familiar to the leaders of the Corps of Discovery before they left home. Not so the white fronted goose, *Anser albifrons* to biologists or speckle-belly to waterfowlers. Lewis gets credit for their first written description, at Fort Clatsop on the Pacific in March 1806. While I've shot my share of specks north of the border I've only killed one in Montana, so this note is largely of academic interest when I'm goose hunting near home.

Not so in the case of *Branta canadensis*, our familiar honker. Modern biologists recognize a number of subspecies that fluctuates at the whim of lumpers and splitters. To complicate matters further, the small cackling Canada was declared a separate species in 2004, and it dragged some of the "lesser Canada" subspecies along into its new pigeonhole. I'm not aware of any effort to distinguish among these geese prior to the Corps' departure for the Pacific, likely because most such sub-speciation occurs west of the Mississippi. But Meriwether Lewis was sharp enough to recognize that not all honkers are created equal, and first descriptions of both the lesser and cackling Canada appear in his notes.

A large flock of Canada geese lifts of the Missouri river.

Our friends Steve and Rhonda occupy a small homestead south of Great Falls that neatly demonstrates the superiority of quality over quantity in the choice of real estate. Their ten acres represent little more than a backyard by Montana standards, but the place is remote, close to the Missouri River, and surrounded by grain fields. The line of brush and cottonwoods running its length produces pheasant dinners on demand and Steve kills a big whitetail there almost every year with his bow. When cold weather concentrates migrating geese on the river after Thanksgiving, the steep bluff behind their house offers a fine opportunity to enjoy some of the most challenging wing-shooting I know.

On a clear day, that bluff offers a splendid view of both the river and the Rockies' Eastern Front behind it in the distance. The Corps passed through in mid-July 1805, after spending nearly a month laboriously portaging equipment and supplies around the Great Falls of the Missouri some twenty miles back downstream. They were plainly relieved to have that ordeal behind them, as Lewis notes in his journal entry that July 15: "At 10 am, we once more saw ourselves fairly underway, much to my joy and, I believe, that of every individual who compose the party."

The first time I accepted an invitation to shoot geese at Steve's place I was frankly skeptical. There was no place to set out decoys and the Missouri was too far away to pass-shoot birds trading up and down the river. But when the great, gabbling flocks finally lifted off the water mid-morning to head for the stubble fields, enough of them passed over the bluff to provide a fast limit. Only a fraction of the birds came near shotgun range, but when the denominator of the fraction includes thousands of geese that's all it takes.

The following year, Lori and I arrived one December afternoon to the best hunting conditions possible: brisk but tolerable temperatures and a 20-knot southeast winds gusting to 30. I expected the high winds to keep the birds close to the ground as they departed the river for the fields. As noted earlier I've never had any patience with sky-busting. This was just the kind of weather that allows responsible pass-shooting in style.

Atop the bluff, I'd just broken my shotgun to chamber a pair of shells when Lori urgently whispered, "Birds!" Tacking back and forth against the gusting crosswind the little flock was still several hundred yards out, but their course and altitude looked promising. Moments later, they slid by 30 yards overhead and provided a perfect opportunity for me to miss. Twice.

"What was *that* all about?" Lori asked as she fiddled with her camera. Rocky's bewildered look seemed to pose the same question.

"Dunno," I replied as I fumbled through my disorganized pockets for more shells. Since I'd been hunting ducks hard all month, I couldn't invoke rustiness as an excuse. As I finished reloading, I began to experience a queasy feeling in the pit of my stomach. Suddenly, this felt like the beginning of One of Those Days.

I started shooting shotguns at flying targets around age seven, under my father's expert eye. Do a lot of anything for seven decades and you ought to get fairly good at it. But once or twice every season I still experience a wing-shooting meltdown, almost always in the same situation: shooting waterfowl in high winds. Paradoxically, ducks and geese screaming by with a stiff breeze behind them aren't much problem. I'm naturally a swing-through snap shooter, and as long as I can keep my barrels moving fast I'm fine. But birds hanging up in a stiff headwind or sliding across a breeze from either side disrupt my rhythm, with results ranging from comical to mortifying.

Mid-afternoon is hardly prime time to shoot the bluff at Steve's place. That day someone forgot to tell the geese, which repeatedly offered shots at reasonable ranges. The problem was the crab angle they were tracking in the nearly perpendicular crosswind gale. Swinging along an imaginary line drawn from tail through extended neck left the shot column upwind of the bird by the time it arrived. I'd soon missed more birds than I had all season.

Soon after I'd worked out the nature of the problem, another pair of birds invited theory to meet fact. When they were still a hundred yards out I made my eyes reduce them from geese to pinpoint spots to counter the optical illusion of birds flying sideways. Tracking the vector rather than the bird, I rose, pulled ahead, and fired. The lead honker crumpled, allowing me a chance to complete the double.

Finally, Rocky had a chance to go to work. The setting was personally significant for him, for he'd retrieved his first goose there five seasons earlier. Like most young dogs facing greater Canadas for the first time he'd seemed a bit intimidated, but he'd enjoyed plenty of experience with geese since then. Watching Rocky chase the back half of that double, an energetic cripple, across the stubble field behind us vindicated my insistence that we bring him along.

"Thank God you finally hit something," Lori said as Rocky finished running down the crippled honker. I'm years beyond pouting if I miss, but we both recognized that I'd been getting close. When the dog returned with the second goose, we finally had an opportunity to direct our attention where it had belonged all the time—to the birds.

"Look at this," I said as I examined the pair side by side and made myself ignore more birds overhead. "One greater and one lesser from the same flock." That's not a particularly unusual event, but I always find myself thinking about the Corps of Discovery when I sit on that bluff and scan their route. The smaller bird made me imagine Lewis at Fort Clatsop, where he recorded the first written description of the lesser Canada goose as well as the speckle-belly. In the middle of all that rain and misery, he'd taken time to notice something different about some western geese. What has happened to such powers of observation today, when gadgets so insistently try to substitute for woodsmanship? Give Lewis a medal.

Although the limit of geese dragging at the game strap as we walked down off the bluff that night was too heavy to ignore, I realized that the birds weren't the most important product of the afternoon's efforts. I'd given myself lessons in shooting and history alike. I wasn't sure which mattered more.

Back in town that night we met our old friend Jeff Lander, who had driven down from Alberta to visit family over the holidays. Great Falls nightlife is hardly spectacular but there's one mandatory stop after a long day in the field: the Sip-n-Dip at the O'Haire Motor Inn, once recognized by *GQ* magazine as one of the ten best bars in the world. If you live in New York or New Orleans, it's no surprise to learn of a world-class watering hole around the corner. That's hardly the case in Montana, where after-hours crowds tend toward visiting investment bankers trying to act like cowboys and cowboys trying to get drunk. After a late dinner Lori insisted, so off we three went to shut the place down.

Several features distinguished the Sip-n-Dip back then. First came Piano Pat, a Grandma Moses look alike whose keyboard and gravelly voice both displayed apparently limitless endurance. Pat's tastes ran heavily toward Neil Diamond and Elvis in his later pills-and-rhinestones phase, but that's not nearly as unfortunate as it sounds. Then there was the mermaid.

The Sip-n-Dip employed several mermaids then, of varying talent and appeal. We arrived to one of the best. Tastefully clad in a bikini top and a mermaid bottom (the mermaids never ventured beyond a PG rating), she dived and blew bubbles and turned graceful underwater arabesques behind the Plexiglas while Pat sang and we talked over old times. Finally we walked back to our motel and poured ourselves into bed.

All this should have been good news for the geese the following morning, but in the event it hardly mattered. I felt eager to re-test my new theory of crosswind goose shooting, but there wasn't any crosswind. In fact there wasn't any wind at all, which meant that the birds were all a hundred yards up when they passed overhead. We quit early without firing a shot and headed home to prepare for our kids, who were due home from college to celebrate Christmas with family. As a diehard advocate of the pluck-don't-skin school of waterfowl cookery, I had as many geese as I wanted to process anyway.

Largely content to eat elk loins, beaver tails, and "portable soup," Lewis and Clark didn't do much waterfowl hunting on their journey. Nonetheless, I'm sure they would make great companions on a goose hunt today. No doubt I'd learn a thing or two from them even after all the years I've spent in the field. Those lessons would likely focus on what really counts: the ability to stay alert and observe, and to recognize that none of us ever has nature figured out completely.

Max and Rosy sitting quietly on their dog platform waiting for their next opportunity to retrieve.

III.

Dogs

The best shotgun load in one's boat for mallards is a fine retriever.

– Nash Buckingham, *Field and Stream*

Almost every chapter in this book includes at least some mention of hunting dogs, which play a central role in most of the hunting stories. Why should they deserve a special segment all their own? That's a fair question with a simple answer. I, like most of my hunting partners, cannot envision hunting gamebirds and waterfowl without our dogs, in most cases ones we have raised and trained ourselves.

Labrador retrievers receive a lot of attention in this book simply because they have been my go-to dogs for over 50 years. However, I have had German wirehairs in my kennel for over a decade now, and I have also hunted with Brittanies, shorthairs, Chesapeake Bay retrievers, and pointers. (Commonly referred to as "English pointers," the modifier is redundant when referring to the breed, since all "pointers" are "English pointers" even though dogs from other breeds also point.)

The choice of breeds is personal, and I have no interest in debating which one is "best." The answer to that question depends on too many variables including the kind of hunting one does, the need for versatility or lack thereof, desire for a family dog, and the handlers' experience level. Most upland hunters favor pointing breeds, which will allow them to find more birds and enjoy the excitement and style of a dog on point. Waterfowl hunters are better off with a strong-swimming, cold-tolerant retriever. Many dogs from versatile breeds meet both job descriptions credibly including Max, our current male German wirehair.

The rewards of having a dog extend well beyond practical considerations in the field. They become friends, companions, hunting partners. The bring joy to entire households. Their loss can reduce grown men to tears. As the title of the last chapter in this section suggests, hunting upland birds and waterfowl is really all about the dogs. Those who have hunted with dogs they have raised and trained themselves already know this. Those who haven't should find out what they're missing.

In this text I frequently describe dogs in terms suggesting they have human emotions and intelligence beyond what they likely possess. This tendency represents a combination of sentimentality, romanticism, and anthropomorphism. I recognize the inaccuracy of these descriptions but decline to apologize for them. This is not a scientific textbook. My focus is on the experience of wing-shooting, the wild world around us, and the way we respond to it. Dogs are an essential part of this story. I trust readers to grant me some latitude in describing the impressions of all that my dogs have done for me during many years afield.

33.

One Hundred Straight

I stopped keeping score in the outdoors a long time ago because I don't consider hunting and fishing competitive sports. Efforts to make them so—record books, fishing tournaments, big buck contests—only seem to compromise the joy I experience when I'm carrying a longbow, fly rod, or shotgun. The wing-shooting world largely remains free of attempts to introduce competition where it does not belong, which may explain why I devote more time to shotguns and dogs as I grow older. In the field, I prefer appreciating my surroundings to creating artificial records of accomplishment.

This is a personal opinion, and I didn't always hold it. I used to keep a game record every season, although not as compulsively as the great (or perhaps not so great) Lord Ripon once did. At the time of his death, Edgar Oliver Robinson, Second Marquess of Ripon, had logged a truly staggering number of entries in his game journal—556,813 to be exact, ranging from snipe to Cape buffalo. In contrast, all I had after several years of similar efforts was a tattered notebook proving that I was a decent shot and ate a lot of wild game, which I already knew. I threw the notebook in the fireplace years ago.

But in 2015 I decided to resurrect the idea—not for myself, but for my dog. A lot of people who had hunted with her told me they thought Rosy, my then three-year-old female yellow Lab, was an exceptional retriever. Much of that admiration came accompanied by expressions of interest in any puppies she might someday produce, which represents flattery of an especially genuine kind. While I agreed with that assessment of her performance, my opinion didn't count. We all think our own dogs are exceptional. Field trials and hunt tests are designed to separate the grain from the chaff and I respect them, but I wanted to measure Rosy's performance where it really mattered to me—in the field, under actual hunting conditions.

I decided to limit the season record to waterfowl, since I had a pair of wirehairs that handled most retrieving duties in upland cover then. I included all ducks shot over her, whether by me, Lori, or our hunting partners. Just as I'd recorded my misses in the records I'd kept years earlier, I planned to acknowledge any birds she lost as well as those she retrieved, since those numbers would provide a real measure of her performance. Then I waited for opening day.

#1. Slam Dunk Teal. Rosy's duck season began with a mulligan during the first week of October in the Central Flyway eastern half of Montana. Lori and I had been hunting upland birds with visiting friends for two days. Rosy had largely stood by at heel as she watched the wirehairs scoop up a medley of pheasants, sharptails, and Huns. When cold, wet rains arrived overnight we decided to celebrate the opening day of duck season on a nearby prairie stream almost big enough to justify its official designation as a river..

The extent of my waterfowl planning had consisted of tossing a dozen decoys into the back of the truck before we left our house three days previously. While Lori and our friends settled into the reeds beside the spread, I parked the rig out of sight a few hundred yards away and started back to join them with Rosy at my side. When I spotted a lone teal flying in my direction, I glanced at my watch and confirmed that the 2015 waterfowl season had been open for three minutes.

The dog and I were standing exposed in the middle of a field, but the green-wing flew straight over my head anyway. I've never been able to resist a high passing shot at a teal. Stone dead in the open, the bird offered a retrieve I could have made myself. I saw Rosy start to break—no surprise after the previous days' forced restraint—but a whistle blast reminded her of her manners. The dead teal didn't offer any challenges, but I knew those would come in due course. I was right. Back at the decoys we wound up with an odd mixed bag ranging from gadwalls to mallards, but it was the day's lone teal that marked the start of the season—and the streak.

#31. A Touch of Class. In mid-October we headed to the Columbia Basin for the first week of the Pacific Flyway season. Rosy hunted for three days without losing a bird before she received her first real test of the season.

Pintails have always been a personal favorite among puddle ducks because of their wariness as they circle a decoy spread and their elegance on the wing. We'd seen a few already that week, but they had all been hens or young drakes that had yet to don their tuxedos. I'd been politely deferring to Lori and a guest all morning when I spotted a mature drake leading a trio of sprig toward the decoys. I forgot my manners, apologized in advance, and shot the bird.

I didn't shoot it very well, which introduces a new theme to this discussion. With some exceptions due to weather and terrain, a great retrieve usually implies some degree of error on the hunter's part. The toughest challenges for the dog often come on wounded birds. A great retrieve on a long cripple is like a field goal in football—a compromise that wouldn't have been necessary had someone done the job right in the first place.

Had I centered that pintail and dropped it kicking in the decoys, the retrieve would have been routine. Instead, I sent the bird tumbling down out of sight behind the blind with a broken wing. It was a tough shot, and I was shooting a twenty instead of my usual twelve because of slow recovery from shoulder surgery, but I'm not blaming the gun. If the bird had been out of range, I shouldn't have shot in the first place. The wounded bird reflected poor shooting on my part. Now it fell to Rosy to clean up my mistake.

Because the duck fell from height behind the blind, none of us had been able to mark the fall. With Rosy at heel, I exited the blind, constructed some imaginary mental vectors, and gave her the line. Then it was the bird's turn to make a mistake by flapping briefly as it swam across a narrow lead of open water a hundred yards away. Buried in the cattails Rosy didn't see the movement, but I did. After calling her out in the open where she could see me, I anchored her with a whistle blast and cast her back. She then churned across the open water, disappeared into the brush for nearly ten minutes, and then emerged carrying the pintail cradled in her mouth.

#43. Long Distance Mallard. By the time we returned to Washington after a week of chores back in Montana Rosy had still not lost a duck among the forty shot over her in the two states, which led to a new idea. Could she retrieve a hundred ducks in a row under actual hunting conditions without losing a bird? As I've emphasized previously, collecting everything I shoot has always been an important personal goal. Avoiding lost birds reflects the values my parents raised me with, which hold that it's better to hunt all day and shoot nothing than to fill a limit but lose one duck. I was doing what I'd always done for principle, and now I was doing it for the dog.

The idea almost collapsed the day after I conceived it. A stiff wind had arisen overnight. I was having trouble with a shot that frequently bothered me even though it should be easy: mallards hanging over decoys in a strong headwind. Give me a long crossing shot on a speeding teal any day. To make matters worse, Lori and a visiting friend were there to witness my bad shooting.

When a lone mallard drake came spiraling down out of the sky our friend dropped it. When it hit the water swimming for the far shore he asked if he should shoot it again. I waved him off because the bird was already beyond the surprisingly short range within which it's possible to kill a wounded duck on the water. Besides, Rosy had a job to do.

After a long head start, the bird had vanished into a dense tangle of flooded Russian olive by the time the dog reached the far shoreline. Reeds had obstructed her vision while she was swimming, but from my elevated position in the blind I'd marked the spot where the duck had exited the water. A whistle blast and a hand signal later, Rosy vanished on its trail.

I never cease to be amazed by the amount of ground—or water, or both—a wounded duck can cover. Rosy was gone for a long time back in the jungle, almost long enough to arouse my concern. When she finally reappeared with the bird and returned to the blind, I left my gun unloaded. Working a good retriever can be more gratifying than shooting ducks—especially when you're performing poorly and the dog isn't.

#88. Bottom of the Ninth. Despite my efforts to keep an artificial goal from taking over my duck season, by late October I was feeling edgy. The sound of every shot reminded me of the crack of the bat when a pitcher has a no-hitter going late in a ballgame. At least Rosy's outcome wasn't going to depend on a scorer's arbitrary distinction between a bloop single and an error. We were either going to walk out of the marsh with the next dozen birds that fell or we weren't.

The biggest scare to the streak came appropriately on Halloween, thanks to a combination of human and canine mistakes. Lori and I were hunting a favorite blind on a clear, crisp afternoon. Distracted by her camera, great light, and decoying wood ducks we didn't want to kill, Lori didn't pick up her shotgun until the last hour of shooting light. Then a pair of mallards came in over the top of the blind and she shot the drake.

Feathers flew as the bird staggered and dropped to the water in front of us, only to rise again. Both wings were beating but it was struggling to gain altitude, like an aircraft with a partial engine failure on takeoff. I was preparing to anchor it when an unwelcome sound I hadn't heard all year distracted me. Rosy had broken from her dog platform and hit the water in a loud geyser of spray. Uncertain of the dog's precise location I couldn't risk a shot at the duck, which had barely cleared the top of the reeds. All I could do was track its flight until it fluttered down in heavy cover across the pond.

All was not lost. First, a solitary tree provided a good landmark where I'd last seen the drake. Second, experience had taught me that a wounded duck that can't climb despite intact wings will likely be lying dead wherever it goes down. Before accepting this challenge I had to regain control of my retriever.

What causes a dog to go berserk suddenly after spending a month behaving like Miss Manners? I could hear Rosy circling aimlessly through the reeds in front of the blind as she ignored my whistle. It took me several minutes to call her in, get in her face, and let her calm down. Then I gave her the line to the tree and crossed my fingers.

By this time flocks of mallards had begun to arrive ahead of the imminent sunset. Most flared as I stood in the decoys, including a number we could have shot. We declined those opportunities because I didn't want to distract the dog with gunfire and more falling birds. When Rosy returned with the bird—dead, as I'd suspected—I felt an overwhelming sense of relief.

One out, bottom of the ninth…

Rosy with the wigeon that completed her run of 100 straight.

#100: The Wigeon Rodeo. Hollywood could not have scripted a more dramatic ending. In my defense I do have witnesses, only one of them a dog.

We greeted the arrival of the season's second month beneath leaden skies. Absent decent photographic light I encouraged Lori to exchange camera for shotgun and she did. We'd hit the dead week between the departure of local breeding waterfowl and the arrival of migrating northern ducks. Absent useful intelligence about the remaining birds' location, we headed for a blind on a five-acre pond bordered by tall cattails and flooded Russian olive. When a lone wigeon circled the spread after nearly two hours of empty airspace I encouraged Lori to shoot and she did.

Down with nothing more than a broken wingtip, the bird had covered a lot of water by the time Rosy exploded from the blind. Darwin must have done something wonderful with that wigeon's genes. As the dog closed the gap, the bird dived, made a hard turn underwater, and headed for the far shore with nothing but the tip of its bill showing on the glassy surface of the pond. Rosy continued to churn toward the spot where she'd last seen the bird.

I'd already left the blind, which provided such excellent concealment that it was hard for the dog to see hand signals while I was inside it. That's when I realized that I'd forgotten to slip my whistle lanyard around my neck that morning. I'd trained Rosy to respond to whistle blasts and arm gestures, not shouting. Rosy continued to swim in circles while the duck reached the shoreline and vanished into the cover. The mistake was mine and not hers.

The duck had disappeared into the Russian olive, which forms incredibly thick, thorny tangles when flooded. Once I signaled Rosy to the scent line, she charged in undaunted. I could not have followed her had I wanted to, which I didn't. This one was hers to win or lose. Although I couldn't see her at all, the sound of the chase painted a picture as clear as any my eyes could have provided. The rhythm of measured steps in the water meant she had lost the trail. Frantic splashing and breaking branches meant she'd found it. Sudden silence indicated that the duck had gone underwater and taken its scent with it. Panting and crashing meant the chase was on again. I listened to this medley of sound until I heard what I'd been waiting to hear all along: the dog lunging straight in my direction without panting, a certain indication that she held the bird in her mouth.

She'd done it.

As readers will recognize, we've just watched a highlight reel featuring a few great plays from the first half of a long season. Selective editing always creates some distortion. This account ignores a lot of routine dog work that came between the tough stuff, even though that also had to be done perfectly. It also ignores days when we waited patiently for ducks that never arrived.

All streaks come to an end as this one did in December, with the same species that had started it. The lost green-wing was number 150-something. I'd stopped counting because it no longer mattered. The marsh we were hunting that day had frozen and thawed several times by then, and the wounded bird fell in a large swath of reeds containing sheets of ice interrupted by leads of open water. The pond wasn't deep enough to make the situation truly dangerous for the dog, but after listening to her break through the ice several times I whistled her back in. No bird justified the risk of injury on the edge of an ice pan. That night I destroyed the written record, not by tossing a notebook into the fire but by hitting the delete key on my computer. How times had changed.

The following morning, we rose in the dark and just went hunting. The counting was done, and I didn't miss it.

34.

Pointers on the Prairie

I know of no hunting venue that reinforces the sense of companionship between hunter and dog more powerfully than the Montana prairie.

During a long walk through typical prairie bird cover, I frequently remember Olson's grand opening line in *Call Me Ishmael*: "I take SPACE to be the central fact to man born in America." The prairie and the sky above it emphasize one's cosmic insignificance like an endless canopy of stars overhead on a clear winter night. Today, I'm hiking a remote section of eastern Montana public land absent all evidence of human intrusion save for an occasional wooden fencepost sufficiently old and weathered to have become part of a landscape largely unchanged since Lewis and Clark first described it.

Technically I'm alone, at least with respect to human company. There is a difference between being alone and being lonely though, especially when I'm accompanied by one of my bird dogs. Today that honor falls to Maggie, my by now middle-aged female German wirehair pointer. As the grayness of her muzzle indicates she is really even older than that, although no one has bothered to tell her. Determined not to go gentle into that good night she still hunts with all the enthusiasm of an eager puppy. It's hard for me to realize how recently she was all awkward legs, floppy ears, and half her current size. I suspect this is the subconscious reason I chose her rather than one of the younger dogs to accompany me today. I just don't know how many seasons Maggie and I have left together.

Our quarry on this warm September morning is twofold: sharp-tailed grouse and Hungarian (technically gray) partridge. Picking a favorite between these two autumn standbys would be difficult. Huns offer more explosive rises and challenging shooting and have long been a personal favorite on the table. However, they, like ring-necked pheasants, are alien imports from the Old World while the sharptails truly belong here, as first described for Western science by Captain William Clark in 1804.

The important point today is that both species are wonderful to hunt with pointing dogs. They provide an interesting contrast to pheasants, which are widely regarded as the West's most popular gamebird. Often preferring to run rather than fly, pheasants are less likely to hold for a point than grouse and partridge. Because of their habitat preferences an experienced pheasant hunter can usually look at an expanse of cover and identify the fraction of it that will hold most of the birds. Open country grouse and partridge, in contrast, can be almost anywhere in vast prairie habitat. A hard-working bird dog will always find more of them than I will on my own.

Now Maggie has disappeared behind a large clump of silver buffaloberry without emerging from the other side. Working cautiously around the brush, I find just what I hoped to find: Maggie stretched out just above the ground, as rigid as if she has been struck by a taser, nose pointed straight down into the grass in front of her, docked tail quivering at her other end. She has found the birds. The rest is now up to me.

While almost any dog with a nose and four legs can become a flushing dog, pointing is a specialized, mysterious job description. While one can teach a pointing dog to range properly, hold points, and look stylish one cannot teach a dog to point, which is purely a matter of genetically determined instinct. They either have it or they don't. Long ago European hunters began to notice this trait appearing randomly in a variety of modern pointing dogs' ancestors, and generations of selective breeding led to the refinements we enjoy today. While two of our three most popular retrieving breeds have ancestral roots here in North America, most pointing breeds trace their family tree back to Europe. From pheasants to German shorthairs, we are indeed a nation of immigrants.

Because of my enthusiasm for hunting waterfowl my kennel has been home to Labrador retrievers for nearly as long as I can remember. While Labs are widely regarded as duck fetching specialists they can be very effective as flushing dogs in upland cover, especially when pheasants are the quarry. I've shot plenty of upland birds with my Labs. If had to bet someone that I could shoot a limit of pheasants from a nasty patch of cover, I would take one of them with me.

However, there is more to successful upland wing-shooting than lots of birds to clean at the end of the day. When it comes to intangibles like spectacle and tradition, nothing can rival hunting with a dog that points—the reason why my Labs usually have to wait for duck season to come into their own every autumn. I've always been a sucker for inexplicable marvels, whether the subject is the creation of the cosmos or an old dog trying to help me secure a gamebird dinner. A point is something of a miracle that no technology can begin to reproduce.

Any relationship with a bird dog will be most satisfying when the hunter has raised and trained the dog on his or her own. No matter how technically impressive a performance by someone else's dog, it will always be just that—someone else's dog, to be admired rather than loved. A pointing dog of any breed is a major responsibility that should not be taken lightly. They all need sufficient space to run far and often. Time, knowledge, and enthusiasm are necessary components of the training process. Hunters who can't provide them should pay for a started dog or go to the pound and pick up a rescue dog as a companion. The decision to raise a gun dog is analogous to the decision to raise a child. However, dogs are cheaper to feed, don't think you owe them a college education, and rarely talk back.

Maggie pointing sharptails in buffaloberry with Rosy set to go in on command and flush the birds.

Maggie is on point in short native grass next to the brush, an intermediate habitat that could hold either sharptails or Huns (or pheasants or sage grouse, although they would be less likely). Whatever the case, Maggie's body language tells me the birds aren't sneaking away on the ground. I'm within shotgun range as soon as I round the buffaloberry. "Steady, steady," I encourage soothingly, for a pointer isn't supposed to stop pointing until permission is granted. With the barrels of my 20-gauge pointed safely toward the sky, I thumb the safety back and forth and walk in behind Maggie.

Huns it is! A sudden eruption of wings immediately announces their identity as these ten flush as one. While it's not unusual to find grouse and pheasants in groups, they almost always stagger their rises at least briefly. The trick to effective shooting on a covey rise is to focus on one bird to the exclusion of all others and maintain that concentration until the bird is either dead or gone. I try not to worry about a second shot until I'm done with my first.

As I do today, feeling gratified (and perhaps a bit lucky) to complete the double on a bird that is nearly out of range. Breaking my shotgun open to ensure safety, I glance down at Maggie, who has done exactly what she was supposed to do: nothing. A dog that runs around wildly when birds are in the air and shots are firing is both a distraction and a safety concern. Maggie learned to be steady to wing and shot many seasons ago, and I'm pleased to see that she hasn't forgotten those lessons over the long summer.

Finally, I issue the command she has been waiting for: "Fetch!" Some but by no means all pointing dogs will retrieve. To defy stereotypes further, some retrievers will point, a phenomenon with which I have had no personal experience. Maggie has always been a capable retriever as long as she stays on dry land. (Her brief career as a duck dog lasted less than one morning.) I regard hunting pheasants without a capable retriever as borderline unethical since a wounded rooster can be practically impossible to recover without a dog. While wounded Huns and sharptails aren't nearly as evasive I still enjoy giving my wirehairs an opportunity to finish what they started once the shooting is over.

After Maggie has delivered the second Hun to my hand, I find a spot in the shade, fill a collapsible bowl with water from the canteen in my game vest, and sit down to watch her lap it up. Even though she's still panting from the heat and exertion, she's soon pacing around me in circles and prodding me to resume the hunt. I finally coax her to my side and convince her to "sit a spell," as my Texas ancestors would have put it. I'm also eager to find more game, but a quiet moment with my dog seems more important.

There will always be more birds. I don't know how much more time remains for me with Maggie.

35.

All About the Dogs

Darkness is falling slowly upon a favorite duck blind after an uneventful afternoon. Lori has uncharacteristically begged off today, citing the need for some "girl time," whatever that means. My only company for the last three hours has been the dog, who seems more disappointed than me by the empty airspace above the decoy spread.

This afternoon I have come more to enjoy the sights and sounds of the marsh and escape the trivial demands of modern society than to shoot ducks. Rosy has not. Given the opportunity, she will approach a retrieving opportunity with an intensity of purpose that makes her the best retriever I have ever trained. I admit that her intensity derives from her genes and not from anything I taught her. The best way to look like a brilliant trainer is to start with a brilliant dog.

So far today that opportunity has eluded us. Suddenly, a tight little flock of green-wings appears inbound for the decoys, slipping and sliding at high speed in characteristic teal fashion. Their choreographed flight pattern reminds me of a school of baitfish at sea with every member of the collective whole turning as one, complex behavior that requires instantaneous communication by means that defy biologists. Such are the matters that occupy the mind on duck hunting days that lack ducks.

Although overdue, ducks have finally arrived. Lulled into complacency by warm October weather and the day's relaxed pace, I'm slow to react. Unable to make my gun catch up with the nearest bird, I know at once that I'm behind it. Although longer range makes my second shot harder than the first, it allows me an opportunity for redemption and I make the most of it. Sort of.

Instead of crumpling, the bird flutters down beyond the far edge of the decoy spread and hits the water swimming. A wounded duck can travel remarkably fast when propelled by its webbed feet instead of its wings. Recovering this one would pose a challenge for the dog even in broad daylight. I have plenty of confidence in Rosy after six seasons together, but with darkness falling I can't rate the odds of recovering the teal better than even.

Although her excitement indicates that she knows a bird is down, the front of the blind is high enough to have obscured her vision. She could not have marked the fall accurately. The pond in front of us is perhaps a hundred yards wide. By the time I have the gun broken open and safe, the teal is recognizable only as the leading edge of a V-shaped wake cutting through the mirrored surface of the water for the far shore. When it reaches land and disappears into the grass and brush I know its recovery will require teamwork.

I step out of the blind into calf-deep water with Rosy at heel and quivering with excitement. She always seems to assume that a report from my shotgun means a downed bird, confidence I can only wish were based upon historical fact. Once she has settled down, I give her the line and launch her like a missile. At first she's running through geysers of spray. Then she hits deeper water and begins to churn quietly ahead, glancing from side to side without deviating from the vector I provided. Twice she hesitates and looks back over her shoulder for guidance. When I raise my arm overhead and shout *Back!* she resumes course without hesitation.

I was careful to mark the spot where the teal emerged from the pond. When Rosy hits the shoreline 20 yards upwind of the spot, I anchor her with a single whistle blast, setting her down on her haunches. Assured of her attention, I cast my arm to the right, shout *Over!,* and watch her follow her nose along the shoreline. I have now done all that I can do. The rest is all about the dog.

Watching Rosy retrieve this drake mallard felt more rewarding than shooting it.

Events that afternoon nicely illustrated two principles developed during the decades I've spent with hunting dogs. The first, as noted earlier, is that a great performance by a retriever is often the result of a less than great performance by the hunter. Almost any dog can recover a lifeless mallard lying on its back in the middle of a decoy spread. Most great retrieves involve birds that are wounded rather than dead. Had I been on my game that afternoon, Rosy would have delivered a dead teal to the blind in less time than it took her to swim across the pond.

The second principle results from a statement my father made to me when I was a kid and now forms the basis for this essay. Our quarry that day had been ruffed grouse rather than ducks, the dog a German shorthair pointer rather than a Lab. I was still too young to carry my own shotgun. Dad had a limit of four grouse in his vest, always an accomplishment in upstate New York back then. Bits had pointed and retrieved all four. As we shuffled through the dry carpet of autumn foliage underfoot on our way back to the car, Dad waxed philosophical. "I wouldn't have walked across the driveway to shoot these birds if I didn't have Bits with me," he mused aloud. "Remember, Donnie. It's all about the dogs."

Oh, so true. Bits was a great versatile hunter, but I subsequently learned that the importance of dogs to the hunting experience applies to all breeds and all kinds of game. Over the years I have hunted waterfowl all over North America (and other places as well). With a couple of exceptions I've killed every upland species on the continent. In upland cover I've enjoyed the company of many dog breeds, a roster that includes pointers, setters, Brittanies, wirehairs, shorthairs, springers, and flushing retrievers. While most of my waterfowl experience has been with Labs, I've also shared duck blinds with goldens and Chessies. I've hunted rabbits with beagles and chased cougars with blueticks and treeing walkers. In almost all of these cases, the dogs were raised and trained by me or members of my family.

The purpose of this extensive list is not to flout my own experience but to remark upon the commonalities all these breeds share and the relationships I've enjoyed with them in the field. Whether the quarry was mourning doves or mountain lions, the hunt was always about the dogs whether they were pointers, retrievers, or hounds. As my father put it long ago, I wouldn't walk across the street to hunt any bird without them.

There are practical reasons for the affinity hunters feel for their dogs. Pointing dogs locate far more upland birds than one would ever find without them. A capable retriever will prevent the loss of wounded birds that would never be recovered otherwise. Important as these considerations may be, I think there is more to the story of why we feel so strongly about our hunting dogs.

A descendent of the grey wolf (*Canis lupus*), the dog was the first animal our human ancestors domesticated. Today's dog (*C. lupus familiaris*) is just one of nearly 40 subspecies of grey wolf scattered about the world. Genetic studies suggest that dog and wolf genes diverged about 50,000 years ago. The archeological record suggests that dogs became domesticated sometime between 30,000 and 12,000 years ago (that's a harder date to pin down). It's worth asking why the dog's genetics—and not those of other canids—produced man's best friend.

Here's my theory. Prevailing evidence suggests that dogs' ancestors began frequenting human encampments in central Asia thousands of years ago, likely attracted by opportunities to scavenge. People began to realize that these wild animals were useful because of their ability to warn camps of approaching predators and enemies. Then people and "wolf-dogs" began to hunt cooperatively. The most useful canines were those that got along with people. These individuals made good company, weren't a nuisance around camp, and were capable of learning commands. Our ancestors began to breed them selectively for those traits, and selective breeding defines domestication. The upshot of all this is that from that vast pool of canine genetics we have been cherry-picking those that we liked and those that liked us since the dawn of civilization.

I've felt genuine affection for almost all the dogs I've owned over the years. While I've always liked animals of (almost) any kind, my soft spot for dogs vastly exceeded any I've ever experienced with horses or, God help me, cats. I find it easy to categorize my fellow humans into "cat people" or "dog people" and have made every effort to surround myself with the latter.

While much of that attachment is universal, its strength varies with both the breed and the individual dog. Most of my lion hounds, for example, were basically life support systems for their noses. They obeyed commands reluctantly and made poor house dogs. As much as I appreciated their skills and determination, I only developed emotional attachments to a few of them.

To me at least, the retrieving breeds represent the other end of the spectrum. I focus on Labs in this discussion simply because I've spent so much time with them. Labs seem to have an innate ability to engage emotionally. During one important phase of the breed's development, Labs went to sea as working dogs in the old Newfoundland cod fishery. Had I needed to share space with a dog in a small boat for weeks I'd want the dog to be good company. I imagine that modern Labs' ancestors were selectively bred for those personality traits long ago. That's speculation, but I do know that if all the people I've met over the years had treated me as honorably as my Labs have, my life would have been simpler and sweeter.

No wonder it's all about the dogs when I go hunting.

The terrain on the far side of the pond consists of little islands of solid ground scattered throughout a vast expanse of shallow water, mud, and muck, all covered in dense vegetation ranging from tightly crowded reeds to hawthorn tangles. If I were trying to hide from a determined pursuer, this is just the place I'd try to do it. The wounded teal obviously concurs. I've kept the dog in sight as she works her way down the shoreline, but the moment her nose picks up the scent the bird left in the grass, she pivots, leaps into the brush, and disappears. Now totally on her own, she is gone, baby, gone.

As an experienced dog she can take care of herself, and there are no roads, culverts, traps, or comparable hazards in the area. Nonetheless, it's hard to suppress a twinge of anxiety once she's out of sight. The feeling reminds me of watching my son march up the steps into school on his way too first grade.

Fifteen minutes later, shooting hours are over. With my shotgun unloaded back in the blind, I'm picking up decoys and wondering just how far a teal with a broken wing can possibly travel. Then the answer appears at the far end of the pond. The light level has fallen so low that I can barely see the dog despite her pale-yellow coat.

Once she hits deep water and starts to swim, she becomes nothing more than a disturbance on the surface as she strokes toward home. She has almost reached my side before I can confirm that she has the teal in her mouth. My hand accepts it, I throw the decoy bag over my shoulder, and we set off together through the gloom.

This obviously isn't a stereotypical hunting story involving waves of mallards and furious shooting. In addition to an opportunity to enjoy the serenity of a favorite duck marsh, three hours in the blind have yielded just two shots and one retrieve. Nonetheless, I feel content as we reach dry land and start down the darkened trail toward the truck.

And why not? From the moment we arrived at the blind, it was all about the dog.

Southern Africa's helmeted guineas are much smarter than their American barnyard cousins.

IV.

The Wide World of Wing-Shooting

Traveling with me you find what never tires.
          - Walt Whitman, *Song of the Open Road*

I have written a lot about hunting in distant places. Not infrequently, I have heard complaints along the lines of, "Why do I want to read about places I'll never go? I just want good stories about hunting whitetails."

For anyone who enjoys travel as much as I do, that's a hard question to answer. Granted, the mechanics can be tedious. I don't enjoy long flights, cramped seats, airport food, or lost luggage more than anyone else. The rewards come upon arrival.

As a society, we Americans are way too insular. Most of us are terrible at foreign languages, leery of new food, uncomfortable around people who see the world in different ways, and prone to longing for the familiar rather than exploring the new. I have no ready response to that world view.

Having spent my adult life in Montana and Alaska, I never had to go far from home to enjoy the outdoors. However, I hate to imagine how many formative experiences I would have missed had I not chosen to do so. Travel has enriched my life in countless ways including forming new friendships, expanding my knowledge of wildlife, and meeting the challenge of new wing-shooting opportunities. The fact that I will never hunt tigers in India does not prevent me from enjoying—and learning from—Jim Corbett's classic *Man-Eaters of Kumaon*. I invite readers to approach the following chapters in the same spirit.

36.

Wings Over the Kalahari

As we loaded our shotguns and eased our way through the acacias, I just couldn't get the rhinoceros out of my mind.

I'd always wanted to stalk a rhino. I had decided years earlier that my longbows were inadequate for Africa's thick-skinned big game. Then I decided I didn't want to shoot a rhinoceros with anything. While white rhinos were still hanging on in many parts of Africa, black rhinos had become a critically endangered species. I still wanted to experience a rhinoceros, but not from the back of a safari vehicle. I envisioned getting to close range with my feet on the ground, as if I were stalking the animal with an imaginary bow. When I saw the white rhino cow browsing just south of Namibia's Etosha Park border earlier that morning, I grabbed my camera and set off to intercept her.

With a steady breeze masking sound and smell, I made my way carefully through three hundred yards of scrub, marveling at the ease with which a beast the size of my truck could disappear so easily. Suddenly she was in front of me, a hulking gray mass gliding through the thorns as effortlessly as a canoe crossing still water. Unaware of my presence she paused to browse, allowing me to slip into camera range undetected. Since I was not carrying a long lens, that happened to be much the same as bow range, providing an opportunity to think about longbows and rhinos. Nothing about the circumstances made me reconsider my earlier conclusions.

Tranquility prevailed until I snapped the shutter. (This took place years ago with a manual film camera before shutter-silencing technology became available.) At the sound of the click, the huge animal threw up her head and pivoted like an overweight ballerina, blowing snot and raising dust as she searched angrily for the source of the intrusion. Then the cause of her ill-humor became clear as a half-grown calf trotted into view. With the nearest climbing tree over a mile away, I enjoyed a long, anxious moment to consider my folly before she rounded up the youngster and lumbered off into the brush.

She was still out there somewhere, I reminded myself later that afternoon as I started off through the acacias in search of gamebirds.

During multiple prior bowhunting excursions to southern Africa I had experienced fine incidental shooting for doves, pigeons, and francolin. On that first trip to Namibia and the fringes of the Kalahari we enjoyed an opportunity to pursue gamebirds seldom seen elsewhere. While I knew that southern Africa contained several species of true quail (genus *Coturnix*) as well as diminutive button quail, I'd never encountered them during my earlier travels. But we were full of the enthusiasm new country always arouses, and when Mush Nichols, a PH and old friend from prior trips to Zimbabwe, suggested a quail hunt he did not have to make the offer twice.

The afternoon following the rhino encounter, we rattled down a dirt track beneath a cloudless sky looking for gamebirds. An old friend from Zimbabwe, host Mush Nichols had been called away on business, but he'd left us everything we needed to carry on including Charlie, his springer spaniel. None of us really knew where we were going in that vast, featureless terrain, making our quest feel like a search for the proverbial needle in a very large haystack. When a covey of birds suddenly crossed the track in front of us I slammed on the brakes reflexively. "They looked like quail to me,"

Lori observed, and with that we uncased our shotguns, crammed shells into our pockets, and set off in pursuit.

Despite the hard chill the southern African winter can produce every night, that afternoon felt uncomfortably hot. Charlie seemed to have difficulty with the scenting conditions, and the heat threatened to drain my own energy reserves faster than I expected. Everyone felt like walking though, and we eventually completed a broad circle through the thorn brush before stumbling back to the Land Cruiser. We'd pass-shot a few turtle doves but the quail eluded us. By the time we unloaded our guns I wondered if those we'd seen had been a mirage all along.

At that point I did what I should have done in the first place, which was to ask Johannes, our laconic Shona tracker, where we should be hunting quail. "Go that way," he replied as he pointed ahead down the road. We drove for several hot, dusty miles before he finally told us to stop beside an open field of grass, still standing tall after bountiful rains months earlier. "Quail here," he announced with authority, and he was right.

We hadn't walked a hundred yards into the cover before Charlie nosed the first covey into the air. When I encounter quail of any kind after a long absence, I have to adjust to the birds' small size and bumblebee-like flight patterns I just stood and stared as the birds buzzed off into the sky. Native Georgians prior to their transplantation to Alaska, our friends Joe and Alex had spent plenty of time in quail country. They experienced no such hesitation. The sound of their shotguns reminded me abruptly of what we had come for, and when the covey's last straggler erupted from the grass I dropped it with the 20-gauge Mush had kindly lent me.

The birds were African harlequin quail, startingly similar to the harlequin (Mearns) quail of our own desert Southwest. (See chapter 14.) The cock birds' bold facial markings explained why observers on separate continents had given the two species the same common name. Like our own harlequins, the African version felt small in the hand and flew close to the ground. With our initial ornithological impressions confirmed for the record we all agreed it was time to find more.

No difficult task this time, as events unfolded. Johannes had known right where we needed to be all along. If I hadn't needed the exercise I would have chided myself for not asking him for advice sooner. Our earlier fruitless ramble proved of no real consequence, for the rate-limiting factor in the hunt turned out to be neither time nor energy but the number of shells we'd grabbed before leaving the vehicle. The thick grass contained multiple coveys. We couldn't finish walking down the escapees from one without bumping into another. While Charlie didn't lack for enthusiasm, the heat eventually began to wear on his performance. I tried to keep him at heel to save his efforts for retrieving duties where we needed him most. A young dog working in challenging conditions with an unfamiliar handler sounds like a recipe for disaster, but he performed creditably. Our vests began to fill with quail at a rate I would not have imagined possible earlier.

With my limited shell supply nearly depleted, I turned back through the grass toward the road. Suddenly, an insect-like buzz erupted at my feet. I watched what seemed to be the world's largest grasshopper flutter off through the ground cover and alight 20 yards away. When a second one flushed, I recognized the source of my confusion: these bugs had feathers. I had stumbled upon a pair of buttonquail that proved to be the first of several.

Superficially similar to true quail, members of the genus *Turnix* lack a hind toe, a feature impossible to identify on a flying bird. As I watched the miniature quail flit away through the grass, I thought of Lord Ripon loading shells with dust and stalking dragonflies on his estate, hardly a model of sportsmanship I wanted to emulate. With my ammunition supply dwindling I couldn't justify shooting birds no bigger than my shotgun shells. Furthermore, I vaguely remembered Mush telling me that button quail were protected. That uncertainty alone would have been enough to quelch any enthusiasm about shooting one.

By the time we regrouped at the vehicle, I was running on empty. The African sun had sucked the juice out of me. Even after guzzling a canteen full of water I still felt dehydrated. I'd shot up every shell I'd brought along. Panting heavily Charlie had lost his enthusiasm, an uncommon development for his breed. Lori, Joe, and Alex agreed with my suggestion to declare victory and retire from the field, a decision that owed as much to lack of ammunition as fatigue.

Evening shadows had started to crawl down the hillsides by the time we reached camp. We tended to the dog and the guns in that order. After pouring myself a cold beer, I began to prowl the unfamiliar kitchen while Johannes organized a bird-plucking detail. Smaller than our bobwhite the dressed harlequins didn't amount to much individually, but we'd shot enough to fill two large skillets. The camp kitchen didn't contain many accoutrements, but I was cooking for the kind of appetites that don't stand on ceremony. By the time our impromptu quail dinner was over there were scarcely enough scraps left to interest a jackal.

Shooting Burchell sandgrouse mid-morning in Namibia.

One highlight of that exploratory trip to Namibia was meeting PH Allan Cilliers. During several return visits, Lori and I became close friends with Allan and his family. Among many wonderful outcomes of that relationship, I credit Allan for introducing us to what became our favorite family of African gamebirds: sandgrouse.

On one return trip, *déjà vu* evoked memories of sunset in a duck blind as light began to drain from the western sky. We were hunting a small waterhole at the end of the day and birds were our quarry, but there the duck hunting analogy ended. Surrounded by nothing but mopane, thorn brush, and sand it would have been hard to imagine less likely waterfowl habitat. The sun appeared to be accelerating in its descent toward the horizon and our shooting light would be measured in minutes. Hunting with my ears as I would for turkey or elk, I raised my hand in a polite request for silence from my companions: Lori, Allan, and a taciturn Bushman tracker named Ghao (or something like that, for my phonetic version of his name was rendered from an unwritten language). As usual during the southern Africa winter, smoke from brushfires had turned the sun's disc into an eerie red orb. Just as its edge met the darkened silhouette of the mountains to the west, I heard the birds right on time.

Considering the number of avian species known to inhabit southern Africa it's little wonder that even frequently returning visitors find the constant chorus of birdsong confusing. In the case of the double-banded sandgrouse the traditional rendering of their calls as they fly to water every evening proves so accurate that they're hard to miss: "Don't WEEP, so Charlie! Don't WEEP so, Charlie!" The time had come to chamber shells and transition from observer to hunter.

Four species of sandgrouse inhabit southern Africa, of which I have hunted all but the yellow-throated. Burchell's and Namaqua sandgrouse keep banker's hours and offer sustained shooting mid-morning. Asked to pick a favorite I'd choose the double-banded, whose punctuality produces the most intense 15 minutes of wing-shooting I've ever encountered. Knowledge that it will all be over almost as soon as it starts only heightens appreciation of the moment.

Although their biological classification remains debatable, sandgrouse are not grouse as early African colonists mistakenly assumed. After ornithologists booted them from the *Galliform* order of partridge and grouse they arrived in the *Columbiform* order of pigeons and doves, thanks to the mistaken observation that sandgrouse drink like pigeons. When that turned out to be untrue they were granted their own order *Pteroclidiformidae,* although some experts believe they are related to plovers. Interesting as the biology may be (or not), it seemed less relevant now that birds were approaching shotgun range.

Enough light had already drained from the sky to compromise our color vision. When Lori and I shouldered our guns we were shooting at dark shapes silhouetted against the glowing sunset. Circling erratically above the water, the birds made such challenging targets that I didn't feel embarrassed when I missed with my first barrel (at least not until I noticed that Lori had doubled). The next few minutes made me imagine I was at the climax of a British driven grouse shoot except that I wasn't dressed in tweeds and didn't have a ghillie handing me a reloaded gun after every shot.

As the sun's trailing edge slipped below the horizon, we lowered our guns and unloaded by unstated mutual agreement. Having shot more in ten minutes than I would during a good day of typical Montana upland hunting the time had come for a moment of silence in which to observe the final stages of the evening flight. Sandgrouse continued to pour in, landing a stone's toss from the waterline and sticking to the sand like glue for several minutes before strolling forward to drink. Ghao later told me—through the familiar chain of translation from the local Koisan dialect to Afrikaans to English—how his people hunted sandgrouse by waiting for this moment and then flinging a long rotating stick across the sand, stunning or killing multiple birds with every throw.

Allan didn't have a dog yet, despite my attempts to have him add a Lab to the assortment of Jack Russell terriers and mutts back at his base camp. Not to worry—although Lori and I dropped over a dozen birds between us and the sunset had yielded to inky tropical darkness Ghao collected them all. After taking a few minutes to ensure that we weren't leaving any dead birds or empty shells behind, we piled into the Land Cruiser and headed for camp to cook a sandgrouse dinner on the *braai*.

No matter what one's primary goals, a trip to the Namibian desert is a remarkable experience. In common with the eastern Montana prairie, the apparently barren terrain is home to wildlife in surprising abundance and variety. The friendly indigenous San people are the most skillful hunters I've met anywhere. Spectacular sunsets, unique geology, surprisingly good seafood anywhere near the coast… the list goes on.

Just don't forget to cram a few extra shells into your vest before you leave the vehicles.

37.

No Barnyard Guineas

Few bird species in Africa invite attention from a shotgun more convincingly than the helmeted guinea. Raucous and brash, guineas constantly seem to be daring wing-shooters to wipe the smiles off their faces. Since they're the size of domestic chickens and just as tasty the thought of dropping a few for the kitchen provides hunters with special incentive, especially after a week in a typical safari camp with no alternative to (admittedly delicious) venison on the table. If only it were that easy. Several days after our encounter with the quail in Namibia, we decided we were ready for a guineafowl dinner.

While large, organized drives are the customary way to shoot guineas, it never hurts to think outside the box. After spotting a large flock pecking through a stand of acacias, we held a council of war. After much discussion, Lori, our friends, and I spread out through the scrub while Mush drove ahead, parked the vehicle a quarter-mile away, and climbed out with his dog. Not long thereafter we heard the grating metallic cry of nervous guineas approaching through the brush. As the racket built to a slow crescendo, I saw spotted balls of feathers skittering toward us through the trees. Although our position looked favorable I wasn't counting my guineas yet. Prior experience with them had given me a deep appreciation of just how easily things could go wrong.

However, I'd reckoned without Charlie. As soon as Mush released him from heel, the little guy tore off after the retreating flock like a dog possessed. Despite their reluctance to fly the guineas couldn't tolerate his determined pursuit. Moments later the afternoon air filled with the sound of wings. To the African wing-shooter, few sights look as appealing as the rotund outline of a guinea straight overhead, and suddenly the sky seemed full of them. After all the strategizing invested in this moment, the last thing in the world I wanted to do was miss, which probably explains why I did. When I swallowed my chagrin and bore down with my second barrel, the sight of the bird collapsing midair and crashing to the ground filled me with the kind of satisfaction ordinarily reserved for good shooting on big game. That's how badly guineas make me want to kill one, and how good it feels when I do.

"We could use a couple more for dinner," Mush observed as we regrouped and counted the birds Charlie had retrieved. As we set off toward the vehicle and what we hoped would be another flock of guineas I felt an unusual level of confidence, largely because of the dog. His speed, nose, and enthusiasm had turned the tables on a tricky species that had made a fool of me more times than I cared to remember. The thought of another cackling swarm of guineas overhead was even enough to make me forget about the rhino. Of course, that's when we stumbled across the fresh lion tracks, but that's another story.

Only in Africa.

The end of a successful guinea drive.

In 2023, Lori and I were back in Zimbabwe following a long absence. After spending a morning hunting francolin over new friend Bryre Groenewald's 's pointers, we'd waited for the air to cool before setting off in pursuit of a different quarry. We had no trouble locating them. Guineas had started to emerge from the brush to feed along the edges of the farm's irrigated fields. The contrast between their dark bodies and the brilliant green background made them visible from long distances. After studying several small flocks, we watched a swarm of perhaps 80 birds emerge from the far side of the *vlei* in front of us. An intense but disorganized strategy session followed. Then our four guns dropped down into the cover while Bryre, PH Will Schultz's son Keegan, and I jumped into the Land Cruiser and began to drive around behind the hill above the flock.

While drives are the most effective way to shoot guineafowl, the birds are so sharp that even hunters' best laid plans often go awry.

Although the shooters may think they are well hidden, guineas demonstrate an uncanny ability to know where the danger lies and often begin to take evasive action before the drive even begins. The more drivers, the easier it is to flush birds toward the guns' position, but on this occasion there were just the three of us. Since these birds had never been hunted, I still felt optimistic.

As soon as we crested the hill the birds stopped feeding and stared suspiciously in our direction even though we were hundreds of yards away. Then they started to scurry laterally while taunting us with their shrill, metallic calls. I'm glad no one had a video camera running as the three of us zig-zagged back and forth across the hill as if we were herding cats. Finally, we reached the birds' limit of tolerance and they all flushed together in a racket of beating wings and shrill cries.

I had met Will Schultz and his family on my first trip to this once wonderful, beleaguered country 30 years prior. Then came the disastrous Mugabe era, a calamity for the country, the Schultz family farm, and my plans to return. Zimbabwean farmers are tough, determined people, and when Will contacted me after Mugabe's death, assured us the country was safe again, and asked Lori and me to come advise him as he changed the focus of his guiding business from big game to wing-shooting and fly-fishing, we couldn't say yes fast enough. That July, Lori and I were on our way to Harare with a small group of friends.

After spending two days shooting a nice variety of francolin—Swainson's, crested, and Natal—over Bryre's dogs, I wanted to chase guineas again. The first point visiting hunters need to understand is that in all respects except appearance wild guineas have little in common with the noisy, obnoxious birds inhabiting American barnyards. African guineas are as smart and wary as our wild turkeys, and shooting them requires even more strategizing than hunting late season pheasants. Shots can be challenging. Most birds are taken high overhead. Like geese, their bulk makes them appear to be flying slower than they are. After having them outwit me numerous times, I derive special satisfaction from successful drives. Seeing them drop from the sky and hearing them hit the ground with a solid *whump* leaves me gratified in a way that killing other African gamebirds does not. Furthermore, I enjoy eating them.

As a biological aside, all birds mentioned in this chapter are helmeted guineas, distinguished by the horny protuberance, or casque, on top of the head. The second African species, the crested guinea, lacks the casque, has black feathers on the crown, and inhabits a more limited range than its helmeted cousin.

Despite the fast shooting a well-organized drive can produce when all goes according to plan, guinea hunting doesn't always have to be so complicated. As Much Nichols' spaniel showed us in Namibia, dogs can be useful when available, a bonus for hunters like me who have difficulty imagining upland hunting without them. We had put Bryer's pointers to good use in an unexpected way the day before the Great Guinea Drive while hunting a brushy *vlei* next to a harvested maize field. Although the dogs found plenty of francolin the thick cover made the shooting difficult. We only had a half-dozen birds in our game vests when I heard guineas calling up ahead. They made their usual racket as they flushed out of range, but I was able to track them visually as they split up and settled into the cover ahead of us. Although good landmarks let me mark some down accurately, I never really expected to see them again.

As we continued down the draw the dogs pointed four more francolin, two crested and two red-billed. Unfortunately, brush obstructed every shot, and no birds fell. When the dogs went on point again, we assumed they had located more of the same. Fellow Montanans Glenn Elison and Robert Griffin took the lead as we walked up on the dogs, for both were eager to shoot their first crested francolin.

When it became clear that the birds were going to hold in front of the dogs, Lori and I reached for our cameras just in time to receive the surprise of the day as a pair of guineas flushed right in front of the dog. Glenn and Robert shoot too well to squander an opportunity like that, and each bird came down quickly in a cloud of feathers. A double on guineas over a point? I don't expect to see that repeated anytime soon.

Now back to our elaborately conceived guinea drive. Although I knew where the shooters were supposed to be, I couldn't tell whether they had made it all the way into position by the time guineas began to flush. Then I heard a shot and watched a bird at the head of the flock tumble. All our scheming played out in seconds as shotguns barked and four more birds dropped from the sky. While I hate to embarrass other members of our hunting party, honest reporting requires me to admit hearing more than five shots. I told you guineas could be hard to hit.

We managed another drive on a smaller flock before darkness forced us from the field carrying four more guineas. I looked forward to dinner despite my fatigue. Guineas are my favorite African gamebirds on the table and our bag would feed us nicely. However, Lori and I had no access to the kitchen, and we had to turn dinner preparations over to Keegan and his siter Tyla, who had learned to cook from their English grandmother. I had previously decided that British colonials predictably brought just three things with them as their Empire expanded across the globe: tea, brown trout, and overcooked game.

As we sat around the campfire slurping guinea stew, I had to remind myself again: This Is Africa. I felt delighted to be there.

38.

Ducks of Paradise

While the rugged peaks of New Zealand's Southern Alps contain some of the wildest, most spectacular scenery in the world, the rolling hills that lie along their eastern front suggest the pastoral ambience one might have encountered in rural England a century ago. The countryside there suggests civilization at its tranquil best, characterized less by industry and progress than the notion that a happy life stems from the ability to get along with others. High in the valley of the Waitaki—a beautiful glacial river whose cornflower blue waters support wonderful trout fishing—the air lay still and clear beneath a warm autumn sun. Fresh rainfall earlier in the week had left the pastures green and the local farmers smiling. This seemed to be a died-and-gone-to-heaven day by any reckoning unless one's plans included the pursuit of waterfowl.

"No worries," our host Doug Sheldon replied when I pointed out the apparent conflict between the balmy weather and our ambitions. Since New Zealanders don't seem to worry about much of anything, his assurance didn't carry a lot of authority. However, Lori and I had already been in the country long enough to acquire our own measure of the cheerful Kiwi conviction that things will almost always work out well as long as you let them. "Let's go shoot some ducks," Doug suggested as we turned up a quiet country road that led into the hills. I quickly felt myself surrender to his optimism.

I felt ready to shoot some ducks. I had just spent seven days trying to kill a bull tahr with my bow, an experience that left me with little but conditioned quads and an abiding respect for my quarry. Despite a number of close encounters, I hadn't been able to close within the intimate distance I needed for a certain shot. As much as I enjoy the challenge of the bow, after a certain amount of that I find myself longing for the ability to reach out and swat something, an impulse best satisfied with a good shotgun. As Doug stopped the car and I climbed out to open the gate separating us from a pasture containing what looked like every sheep in the world, I felt myself anticipating the sound of wings and the thump of a gun against my shoulder even more than usual.

When we all climbed out of the car and began to organize our gear, Jimmy and Tosh, Doug's young springers, roared around us with all the enthusiasm you'd expect of spaniels that know they're going hunting. One tends to be biased by first encounters with a breed, and none of the few springers I'd ever hunted with impressed me until I met Charlie in Namibia. I felt skeptical when I first saw this unlikely pair of water dogs, but we quickly made friends with them during the drive from Doug's farm. My old biases against springers began to feel like history. While Doug made no promises about young Tosh, he assured us Jimmy would get the job done when the time came.

Doug's plan called for us to begin by jump-shooting the pond behind a tall earthen dam in the corner of the sheep pasture. When I explained that Lori and I preferred to shoot our ducks over decoys, Doug promised that would come in time. Since we didn't have any decoys with us his strategy remained a bit of a mystery, but I had already resigned myself to trusting his word. After all, this was New Zealand, the land of no worries.

The hike across the sunny pasture felt more like the beginning of a trout fishing expedition than a duck hunt. As we approached the base of the dam I could hear the unmistakable sound of waterfowl talking on the other side. After a brief discussion, Doug motioned me into position at the far corner of the dam. "Remember!" he whispered as we parted. "We have to shoot a duck or two on the rise." Once we were in position with the dogs behind Doug, I checked the safety on my borrowed shotgun and nodded. Then we marched up toward the edge of the dam.

We were hunting paradise shelducks, or parries as they are affectionately known in their native range. During our tahr hunt, paradise ducks had become a familiar sight in the fields along the river bottoms below us. Among the largest duck species in the world, they are visually impressive waterfowl. The dark drakes display brilliantly iridescent green wing specula while the smaller but more strikingly marked hens sport solid white heads that serve as field marks from hundreds of yards away. Their unique biologic origins increased the fascination I felt for them. Like most of the vast Pacific's isolated island ecosystems, the New Zealand archipelago didn't enjoy a lot of natural biodiversity among its fauna. From red stag to brown trout, most of New Zealand's premier sporting species are alien imports. The parries were there from the beginning though, and they remain as much a part of the area's unique native biosphere as the kiwi.

Many of the islands' indigenous species fared poorly after European colonists introduced their own favorite wildlife, but not the paradise duck. While their populations have faced intermittent declines they were thriving when we visited, probably as a result of abundant food supplies in agricultural lands along fertile river bottoms. Paradise duck numbers had recently exploded throughout much of their South Island range, and the New Zealand government responded with liberal seasons and limits. That explains why we were hunting them in March well in advance of New Zealand's traditional May 1 waterfowl opener, an unofficial national holiday throughout the country.

Like all experienced jump-shooters, we paced ourselves so that we crested the dam simultaneously. Because of dry conditions before the recent rain, the pond turned out to be both smaller and farther away than I expected, but paradise ducks covered its still surface like confetti. A brief moment of silence followed the surprise of our appearance and then birds began to take to the air. Most of them flushed out of range, but when a lone drake rose from the waterline right beneath the dam I dropped him. I heard another shot from Doug's direction. Then there was nothing to do but watch as the rest of the ducks disappeared into the sky and Jimmy completed two easy retrieves.

My first good look at a paradise duck made the whole expedition worthwhile. Nearly as hefty as a snow goose, the bird's striking plumage flashed like jewelry in the afternoon sun. My drake even sported a New Zealand duck tag to add to my collection. Doug had more ambitious shooting plans in mind, as he had promised all along. While Lori and I studied and photographed the ducks, he quickly whittled a pair of forked sticks from the brush along the dam face. Then he set the pair of birds on top of the dam and propped their heads up with the sticks, converting our bag into decoys.

"The rest will be back," he assured us. Then we settled in to wait.

Since Lori's waterfowl experience at that time largely consisted of frigid midwinter hunts along our local Montana spring creeks, she found the wait enjoyable. The afternoon felt so pleasant that I couldn't help but share her relaxed mood despite doubts about our ability to shoot more birds over our minimalist decoy spread on such a balmy day. Then the unmistakable nasal cry of paradise ducks cut through the still air, and we turned about to scan the sky in a futile attempt to locate them. When a flight of six appeared right over the dam behind us gliding toward the pond with their wings set, we rose to take them.

Prior to our departure from Doug's farm, I had selected a 12-gauge Miroku over/under from his gun cabinet. While it shouldered and pointed naturally it felt heavy in my hands, which sounds like a prelude to a classical borrowed gun excuse for poor shooting. Fortunately, it never came to that. As the birds floated by overhead, I picked a hen's white head from the middle of the flock and dropped her before I drove the barrels past the next bird in line and completed the double. Since Doug had killed a duck from his corner of the dam, little Jimmy suddenly became a busy boy. Fortunately, all three ducks lay dead on the pond's glassy surface. Once Jimmy completed the final retrieve, our growing decoy spread began to look more convincing.

Doug, Lori, and Doug's springers on a South Island duck hunt.

We had barely settled back into our hiding places along the dam face when a larger flight appeared over the far end of the pond, side-slipping their way downward like oversized teal. For a moment it appeared they would all land short, but half their number glided past the dam, and we dropped two more. My fascination with the ducks' appearance and biology quickly yielded to pure enjoyment of the shooting. The shots had all been long and each of the birds had fallen to the water with a satisfying plop. Then I remembered that the handloads Doug had given me contained lead shot, which was legal in New Zealand. While none of us wishes to revisit supposedly dead controversies over steel shot I'm not ashamed to admit that I hated it back then, an aversion I have since overcome. I feel embarrassed to report how satisfying it felt to reach out and kill ducks dead as I once had in bygone years.

Fast shooting continued for over an hour. The birds gave us just enough time between sets to congratulate each other on our good shots and forget about the rest while Jimmy earned our admiration in the pond. Hats off to the little guy; we didn't lose a single bird. By the time we decided to call it a day and retire to Doug's house to sample some choice selections from New Zealand's up and coming wine producers, we had enough parries slung over our shoulders to remind me of packing big game. One important issue remained to settle.

During the course of our bow hunt, local friends had assured us that parries made great shooting but poor eating. Since I love wild game on the table, that pronouncement left me discouraged. Besides, I've heard similar verdicts rendered about waterfowl back home often enough to regard all such negative opinions with skepticism.

When I explained to Doug that we would really enjoy an opportunity to eat some of the ducks we had shot, he replied in typically accommodating Kiwi fashion. Doug's wife Hilary is an accomplished chef. After a long trip up the Waitaki the following day we sat down to a splendid meal of paradise duck prepared her favorite way: ground into elaborately seasoned duck burger. While her recipe might not be my first choice for prime mallards, it addressed the issue of the parries' reputed toughness and impressed me as a fine option for early season ducks back home. The meal proved delicious and provided a memorable farewell to a country neither Lori nor I felt like leaving. We would be back. No worries.

39.

Doves, Ducks, and Beyond

"If we go out the backdoor quietly, maybe the dogs won't follow us." Our host, a gregarious Afrikaner who looked like half a rugby team all by himself, had been extolling the virtues of his two playful Labradoodles ever since our arrival at his farmhouse, but this suggestion left me suddenly pessimistic about our long awaited first African waterfowl hunt. No one tries to evade the company of good dogs prior to heading afield. My concern increased further when I offered to carry the decoy bag only to be told that there were no decoys.

However, I could hardly complain since nothing about this trip was supposed to involve duck hunting. Working intermittently for a bowhunting safari business at the time, Lori and I had been tasked with investigating the potential of a large ranch property on South Africa's lovely Eastern Cape. When, over wine the previous evening, I casually mentioned our interest in wing-shooting, the owner of the property suggested that he might be able to arrange some. He had already considered offering wing-shooting as a bonus for visiting bowhunters, but admitted knowing nothing about it. When we offered to help advance his education, he welcomed the idea while suggesting that the shooting might be better on a neighbor's farm. My interest level climbed when he mentioned that his friend had a reservoir covered with ducks. By then Lori and I had enjoyed plenty of experience with African upland gamebirds but had never had an opportunity to hunt the region's abundant waterfowl. When a quick phone call confirmed permission to hunt the place the following day, I recognized a classic example of an offer I couldn't refuse.

Our reception the following morning typified the hospitality Lori and I customarily received in remote farmhouses all over southern Africa. We met the family and played with the kids. We inspected livestock and talked about ranching as practiced in South Africa and Montana. An overwhelming lunch appeared from the kitchen as if by magic, with entrees ranging from bushbuck stew to baked kingklip from the nearby Indian Ocean. Having visited countless ranches in Africa and Montana, this was usually the point in the socializing when I started dropping hints about getting the hunt underway, but the conversation was so interesting and our hosts so gracious that I nearly forgot about the original purpose of our visit.

When we finally set off on foot for the reservoir we immediately realized that we had not outwitted the dogs, who demonstrated a remarkable ability to ignore commands. When we poked our heads over the top of the dam at one end of the reservoir, I noted ducks scattered all around the shoreline. I felt so intrigued that I forgot about our misbehaving canine company until they started running the edge of the water, flushing clouds of birds as they went.

Having enjoyed a fascination with birdlife since my early childhood, whenever I go to an unfamiliar wildlife destination like Africa I carry the best regional bird book I can find and start identifying new species. We were in an ultimate target-rich environment (over 900 avian species inhabit Africa south of the Zambezi). My African life list already contained more entries than my North American version back at home. However, since we had spent relatively little time near fresh water it didn't include many ducks. I immediately tried to start sorting out those the dogs were pushing by overhead.

"What do you call those ducks with the yellow bills?" I asked Kruger, our host, as I pointed to a flock of what appeared to be the most abundant species.

"Those are yellow-billed ducks," he replied. Duh.

"How about the ones with the white faces?"

"White-faced ducks," he replied with no suggestion of irony. As soon as we returned to camp that night, I tore open my Newman's *Birds of Southern Africa* and confirmed that he hadn't been pulling my leg.

I will now spare readers a detailed description of the rest of my first African duck hunt. We had no decoys, the dogs ran wild, and no one fired a shot. However, that was not the end of the interesting day we spent with our new friends.

White-faced ducks settling onto a pond in Zimbabwe. With no misbehaving dogs with us, we actually managed to shoot some.

Needlessly apologetic—I kept reminding our host that he was not expected to be a hunting guide—Kruger offered what he thought might be a successful alternative to our failed waterfowl hunt. He had just harvested a millet field and had noticed large flocks of doves feeding there the previous evening. He then suggested that we swing by the ranch house and pick up more shells, since we were going to need them. This demonstration of confidence was enough to make me forget about the dogs, who had already jumped into the back of the truck with Lori.

As we parked the vehicle and began to approach on foot, I heard familiar Cape turtle dove calls (work *HARD*er! work *HARD*er!) rising from the treetops along the edge of the field. Describing the reservoir as covered in ducks may have been hyperbole, but reporting the airspace over the cut field as full of doves was not. Lori and I picked out two bushes 20 yards apart, tucked in against them, and began to shoot selectively. Every variety of dove in southern Africa seemed well represented. It was easy to recognize the small Namaqua and laughing doves by size and silhouette. We ignored them in favor of the plump turtle doves and red-eyes, so similar that I couldn't tell them apart until I had them in my hand (whenever the dogs hadn't eaten them first).

Despite abundant opportunities, we spent the rest of the afternoon doing more observing than shooting. Friends' descriptions of "high-volume" dove hunts in Argentina always left me feeling queasy despite the alleged benefit of all that shooting to farmers and the local poor who received the donated meat. This is a personal observation, and I am not being judgmental about other hunters who have reached different conclusions. During the incidental dove shooting I did while traveling in Argentina, I felt content to limit myself to one box of shells, as Lori and I did that afternoon on the Eastern Cape. Our goal was to experience the shooting and enjoy a dove dinner in camp that might, washed down with a bottle (or two) of Stellenbosch wine, and we achieved it.

A successful African duck hunt would have to wait for another decade and another country.

40.

Probably Not

Before our last trip to Zimbabwe prior to the total meltdown the country experienced during the Mugabe years, our old friend Will Schultz told us that he had organized a duck hunt. Knowing him as I did, I felt confident that we would finally get to shoot African waterfowl in a productive, relaxed (no crazy dogs!) setting. Eager to sample a variety of exotic waterfowl, I studied my bird book carefully. At least I already knew how to identify yellow-billed and white-faced ducks.

After meeting at the airport, we set about addressing what had become my highest priority whenever I land in Zim: getting out of Harare as soon as possible. As we reached the open road to the north, we began to review our plans. Bushbuck and bushpig had long been my favorite African bowhunting quarries and Will had arranged for us to stay at a farm where these two difficult animals were abundant. His cousin Kerryn, who raised and trained pointers, planned to accompany us with his dogs during several days of francolin hunting. But when I asked about the ducks, Will appeared uncharacteristically gloomy.

He had returned to that ranch earlier in the week only to find it occupied by well-armed Mugabe "war veterans." I can tolerate grizzly bears and elephants when I'm hunting, but angry men carrying AK-47s were above my pay grade. I didn't even think about asking Will to reconsider. We had a great trip anyway. I managed some success with my bow, Lori stayed busy with her camera, and we enjoyed some fabulous bird hunting over Kerryn's pointers. I also made the executive decision that no matter how much I loved Zimbabwe I wasn't going back until Robert Mugabe died and the country was safe again.

That didn't happen for almost 20 years, but Lori and I finally landed in Harare again accompanied by four good friends. After two weeks of bad roads, francolin, guineafowl, tigerfish, bass and bream, wildlife photography, vehicle breakdowns, and charging elephants, we wound up in a remote wilderness camp on a vast concession containing several reservoirs. As we drove in, multiple flocks of ducks rose from the lake behind the cooking tent. Finally, it appeared that my long-delayed African waterfowl hunt was going to happen.

We rose early the following morning, distributed ourselves around the shoreline, and waited for birds to start flying. I picked the wrong spot and wound up shooting nothing but a few doves. Others did better, with the highlight coming from Glenn Elison's brace of Egyptian geese. Roughly the size of our snow geese, these birds' flashing wings and complex facial markings make them one of the world's most beautiful waterfowl.

We spent that afternoon and the following morning hunting francolin over Bryre Groenewald's pointers. There were plenty of birds representing several species, but the brush was the thickest we'd encountered yet, and the shots proved challenging. By mid-afternoon, we were hot, sweaty, and tired. Several of us bore deep scratches and puncture wounds courtesy of the thorns through which we'd been walking. Our game vests held just a half-dozen francolin and a pair of guineas. While we had enjoyed the upland hunting, an evening spent leisurely pass-shooting waterfowl sounded too attractive to ignore.

Having educated the birds on the reservoir next to our camp, we set off for an alternative about which Will seemed especially confident. After another long, dusty drive, we arrived at a lake with a smaller shoreline than the one we'd hunted earlier, which impressed me as a tactical advantage. Waterfowl of multiple varieties covered every corner of the lake, including several flocks of huge, dark geese I could not identify.

"They're spur-winged geese," Keegan explained. I had heard stories about shooting them over grain fields in South Africa, but I'd never been in the right place at the right time to see any, much less shoot one. At least I would be able to check another box on my life list of African birds. "Stick some of these in your pocket," Keegan advised as he passed me a handful of heavy loads. "Those geese are big and tough. You'll need to hit one hard to bring it down."

After another strategy session that probably went on longer than needed, we split up into pairs, decided where each should be, and hiked back into the thorn brush so we could simultaneously approach the waterline undetected. Lori and I found an old dead log on the shore that looked as if it would provide some cover without obstructing a shotgun's swing. After some last-minute trimming to establish clear shooting lanes, Lori fiddled with her camera settings while I sat back to wait.

In situations like this, I never want to be the one who shoots first. Most of the action will take place quickly after the first shot is fired. Any member of the party who hasn't established a good position by then may miss out completely. Since I value the respect of my hunting partners more than shooting a few extra ducks, I felt content to observe. As we waited for everyone to get in place, I tried to identify some of the waterfowl I'd never seen before. By this time the white-faced ducks looked like old friends, but several others left me befuddled.

Once I had spotted all the other members of the party and confirmed that they were in safe positions, I had just decided to open the season when Glenn, standing near the brush line a hundred yards away, beat me to it. As the sound of his shotgun shattered the quiet air, I saw two ducks of indeterminate species fall to the shore.

Then vortices of waterfowl took to the air as guns barked around the perimeter of the lake. Granted, this wasn't classical duck shooting over decoys. This was Africa.

Bryre had brought along an ancient Lab in addition to his two pointers. With all due respect to my new friend, I'd seen enough of the old dog in action on francolin and guineas to leave me skeptical of his ability as a retriever. As the circling ducks gained altitude the shots became progressively longer and harder. Glenn and I tried to limit ourselves to opportunities that would leave downed birds on dry land, where our excellent Native trackers would have no trouble locating them. After 10 minutes of furious shooting I had a medley of unfamiliar ducks stretched out on the log behind me.

"Geese!" Lori announced suddenly. I looked up to see what looked like two black dragons headed straight at us from the far side of the lake. I ordinarily don't waste time changing loads in a duck blind, but the birds' size convinced me to take Keegan's advice to heart. For reasons I couldn't articulate, I wanted to shoot a spur-winged goose more than I had wanted to shoot any bird for a long time.

When the lead goose reached the zenith overhead, I drove my barrels forward, extended my lead, and fired. The bird shuddered and started to fall into the brush behind me, where I heard it hit the ground with a crash so loud and abrupt that I thought the fall would have killed it even if the heavy shot hadn't. By this time the second bird was flaring at marginal range, but I felt the spirit move me and fired again. The shot felt good in an intangible way familiar to all experienced wing-shooters, but instead of crumpling, the bird established a long glide path across the reservoir in front of me. The good news was that as soon as it hit the water its head went down, convincing me it was dead. The bad news was that it was still in the middle of the lake.

Understanding subsequent events requires a brief biological digression. I have hunted and fished the Zambezi drainage from its headwaters in Namibia to the Mozambique border, encountering crocodiles all along the way. Crocs are surprisingly mobile and will travel long distances overland to populate ranch reservoirs. On this trip, we had frequently enjoyed fly-fishing these ponds for big largemouth bass, an alien species introduced from our own South decades earlier. Before wading in, I always asked our local host if there were any crocodiles in the pond. The inevitable answer was, "Probably not." Now I had a goose floating in a lake that probably didn't contain any crocodiles.

African duck hunting involves dealing with some unpleasant company.

Inexplicably, we failed to locate the goose I'd heard drop behind me. I can't explain why I was so obsessed with putting my hands on a spurwing but I was, which now meant recovering the bird in the lake. I would never ask a friend to send his dog on that retrieve, which didn't matter since we didn't have a dog capable of doing it. The shooting was over by this time, and my only option seemed to be walking the shoreline as close to the goose as possible, stripping down, and going for a swim.

I don't know whether to ascribe his decision to a professional hunter's code of honor or youthful disregard for common sense, but Keegan wasn't going to let me do that. Perhaps he just inherited mental toughness from his father, who had once been a star international rugby player. Before I was halfway to the spot where our friends had gathered, Keegan had shucked off his hunting clothes and jumped in. Obviously a strong swimmer he made it to the goose in half the time it would have taken me, but his return leg illustrated just how heavy a spurwing goose can be. Unable to carry or drag it, he had to push it forward with his nose like a water polo player racing down a pool with the ball.

Spurwings are the largest geese in the world. When I slung that one over my shoulder to lug it back to the truck, I felt as if I were carrying a large spring gobbler. We didn't have a scale, but 15 pounds would be a reasonable guess. In parts of Africa farther north, spurwings sometimes feed on a beetle larva that makes their flesh toxic. Fortunately, I was not aware of this interesting factoid until we had devoured the bird back at camp the following night.

My thanks to Keegan felt woefully inadequate for the occasion. With light draining quickly from the western sky, we were settling in around the vehicles to enjoy the great safari tradition of sundowners when I remembered one last piece of unfinished business. "I need you to help me identify a duck I shot," I told Will. "It's a small duck, about the size of our teal, with a bright red bill."

"It's a red-billed teal," Will replied, as I later confirmed with my Newman's.

Wouldn't you know it.

About the Author

After growing up in the Pacific Northwest, Don Thomas completed his higher education in California, Montreal, and Washington, winding up as a board-certified internist. He spent his 40-year medical career in rural Montana and Alaska, where he was also a pilot, commercial fisherman, and bear hunting guide.

He began writing professionally in the early 1980s. Following old advice to write about topics he both knew and cared about, he turned naturally to the outdoors for subject matter. He has written over 1700 features and columns for a wide variety of magazines including *Traditional Bowhunter, Bowhunter, Gray's Sporting Journal, Big Sky Journal, Alaska, Retriever Journal, Pointing Dog Journal, Just Labs, American Flyfishing, Sports Afield, Outdoor Life, Field and Stream, Fish Alaska, Ducks Unlimited, Pheasants Forever, Quail Forever, Western Hunting Journal, Fly Rod and Reel, Outside Bozeman, Saltwater Flyfishing, Strung, and Tail*. He has held numerous masthead positions and is currently a principal at *Strung*. His writing has won numerous awards including the Traver Award for Flyfishing Fiction (twice), the Ted Trueblood Award from Backcountry Hunters and Anglers, and the Tom Shupenis and Glenn St. Charles awards from the Professional Bowhunters Society. He was also the Co-Editor of *Traditional Bowhunter* for nearly 20 years.

Don has written over 20 books on subjects including bowhunting, flyfishing, wing-shooting, gun dogs, conservation, and natural history. His work has appeared in numerus anthologies. Working together, he and his wife Lori have also contributed numerous photo essays to the same magazines.

Don and Lori now live in rural Montana. Their four kids are grown and gone, but they still have their Labrador retrievers, German wirehair pointers, and one Jack Russell terrier.

Don has always written under the byline "E.Donnall Thomas Jr." in honor of his father, who won the 1990 Noble Prize in Medicine and was one of the most capable and ethical outdoorsmen Don ever met. He omits the "M.D." to which he is entitled because he has never met a gamebird or animal that cared.

About the Photographer

A fifth-generation Montanan who grew up in a hunting ranch family, Lori Thomas had no experience with bows, shotguns, or fly rods prior to her marriage to Don. She proved a fast learner and now engages in these activities as enthusiastically and capably as her husband.

Although she had limited experience behind a camera at the time of their marriage, Don was still doing a lot of outdoor photography then, and Lori learned rapidly. While blessed with a keen eye and meticulous attention to technique, her enthusiasm and perseverance are the keys to her success. If she must stand in the rain for hours to get the shot, she'll be there long after most photographers would have gone home to dry out. Although their photo credits go to both of them, Don's aging eyes now make it hard for him to manage the controls on a digital camera. While he still offers suggestions about shots and took some of those in this book, Lori does most of the actual shooting.

Lori graduated from high school in the same rural Montana community where she and Don now live. After obtaining her nursing degree from Montana State University, she enjoyed a challenging career as a nurse which continued after her marriage. The decision to retire from medicine was hard for both of them.

Wife and mother, skilled clinical nurse, all-around outdoorswoman, and capable photographer… Don considers himself a lucky man, because he is.

www.ingramcontent.com/pod-product-compliance
Lightning Source LLC
LaVergne TN
LVHW021956060526
838201LV00048B/1586